Floating Down The Country
By
Matthew Mohlke

11-T9-01

TO Jack

MERRY CHRISTMAS

Published by Lone Oak Press, Ltd.
Red Wing, Minnesota

Printed in the United States of America

First Edition
Second Printing June, 2001
ISBN 1-883477-49-2
Library of Congress CIP: 99-068861

Headwaters

Contents

PROLOGUE

Thirty seconds... twenty seconds... ten seconds... five seconds... a singular note invaded my ears and filled my entire existence. This was the last time I'd be a prisoner to that noxious noise. Sounds of shuffling feet and papers filled the air, joining the excited shrieks of happy children. A convoy of movement carried me away to my left toward the glowing exit sign. After the doors were upon me, the sunlight blinded my eyes for a few moments, yet the procession carried me forward.

I was no longer myself, but had become a tiny leg on a gigantic centipede. The sureness of those around me gave me confidence in my situation. This was how it had always been done, and was the moment I'd been waiting for all those years.

By the time my eyes adjusted to the brightness, the massive flow of young bodies formed a single file line. The giant jungle gym rose up ahead, overshadowing a majestic spring day. All eyes fixed enviously on the shiny steel beast as we waited our turns.

Everyone was having such a good time, and some of the older kids had learned to do tricks on it I couldn't even believe. The thing was enormous. I didn't know how long it would take me to master all of the different parts, and I wasn't sure if I'd ever be good enough to do so. There were several others in line before me, but this was the opportunity I'd been waiting my whole life for. Someday I would be the one doing those tricks in front of the newcomers, but the school had taught me patience, and I waited in line for my turn.

While I was waiting, I looked around. An empty field stretched out in all directions, but there seemed to be something going on way off on the far horizon. I wondered if maybe there were other jungle gyms that were better than this one. Maybe they didn't even have lines. I yearned to go over and take a look, but whatever it was, it was so far away, and would have taken me forever to get there. I asked several of the other kids around me what it was I could see in the distance, but they said it was just a mirage, and besides, the place to be was right in front of me. For my whole life I had heard about the great jungle gym, and I could actually see it. If I left, I'd lose my place in line, and have to start all over again. What if I went all the way over there, and it was not another jungle gym I found, but something bad? Again, I tried asking the others if they knew what was out there, but they looked at me like I was crazy. I'd waited so long to be so close to the front of the line, and to think of giving up my spot would've been insane.

Instead, I waited. The eager faces of the other kids around me convinced me I was doing the right thing. Time went by, and although it seemed like the day would never arrive, I found myself at the front of the line. My numb fingers trembled when they grasped the cold iron, but a strong hand reached out and helped me up. It was difficult at first, but with time the experts gave me some pointers. Soon I was becoming one of them. This was the place I'd always waited to be.

Rarely did I think about what might be happening out on the horizon, instead, I was on my way to becoming a hero of the big toy. Sometimes I made mistakes or wondered what else might be out there, but every time I became weak one of the stronger members of the big toy stepped in and guided me along. Occasionally, I looked down at the kids who were still down on the ground waiting, and I tried to remember what it felt like. The big toy had become my home, and I pitied them. Someday their time would come to be where I was at, but until then they would have to wait. Sometimes the tricks were hard to learn and I started getting frustrated, but the experts told me I was making progress, and one day I would become one of them.

"Remember, incorporate those little yeses, utilize your four corner sell sheets, and most importantly, I'm looking for FAB statements: features, attributes, benefits." He said those last three words with so much emphasis, they continued to ring in my ears several moments after he stopped talking.

My national sales trainer had flown in the previous night for my big evaluation. He had the beaten look of a man who'd spent too many years regurgitating corporate policy to young wannabes like myself. Considered to be one of the most important days of my career, I had pulled out my most expensive suit, and even bought new shoes.

Caged in traffic on 696 north of Detroit, watching the sun battle the fog on the horizon, I was having one of those frustrating moments. I was thinking of other places. How did I get to that place? Was there anything else, or was it a mirage like everyone said? Staring at the sunrise as we crawled in traffic, I imagined fishing topwater bass. It would have been the perfect morning, had I not sold that boat to pay for the suit.

I was a corporate man, on my way to making more money than I knew what to do with. I was on the inside track, a golden boy, part of the top two percent, climbing the corporate ladder, lavish expense accounts, fancy golf outings, exclusive cocktail banquets--stuck in traffic, staring at the sun, and dreaming of faraway places.

Meanwhile, I'd spent twenty-four years to get to that place. I'd worked my ass off to acquire two college degrees, graduate Summa Cum Laude, and create the perfect resume. I had gone through seven grueling interviews to get a higher paying job than my classmates and meet everyone else's expectations for me. The corporate world provided the carrot at the end of the stick, the gold at the end of the rainbow, the cheese at the end of the maze, and I was getting there, learning how to say just the right things to close the big sale. I was becoming a master of the monkey bars.

> *I am a hamster on a treadmill.*
> *My animal instincts are gone.*
> *Safe and secure it holds me,*
> *Afraid to escape.*
> *How could I return to my instinctual self?*
> *Now that I salivate to a bell*
> *COMPLACENT, they control me.*
> *COMPLIANT, I sit here and obey.*
> *Everything is provided for me,*
> *Oh, How happy am I?*

No one seemed to be paying much attention to me at the time, so I made a break for the big spiral slide at the end of the big toy. Around and around I went. It didn't feel like my feet were ever going to hit the ground. I just kept going around and around and my head was spinning. The ground met me hard and my legs buckled below me. My feet were like rubber. I hadn't used my legs since the day my turn in line had come, and they nearly collapsed underneath me. I was sure someone was going to blow a whistle or appear out of nowhere to tackle me, but it never happened.

Running was awkward, but I staggered as fast I could away from the jungle gym. It didn't seem to matter which way I ran, because the endless field looked the same in all directions. My feet were moving in slow motion, as if I was running through fresh concrete. I was sure that someone was chasing me, and I was afraid to look back at the big toy. I ran until I could run no more. Finally, I had the courage to look behind me. The big jungle gym was going about its business as usual, and no one had even noticed I was gone. I was free, but where in the hell was I? The field was empty with the exception of the jungle gym. What in the hell was I doing out there?

Maybe I could've crept back to where I was, and no one would've noticed I'd left. I couldn't have been gone very long. No, I'd left and had to keep going. The only way back to where I was would've been to get back in that long line. There had seemed to be something going on way off in the distance earlier, but I couldn't see anything. It must have been a mirage after all. Aiming for the place I'd seen earlier, I set off in a straight line away from everything I'd ever known. I was alone, but at least I was in charge.

* * *

My alarm clock woke me up at 6:00; my head was killing me. My friends had thrown me a wild bash for a going away party, and I was pretty hungover. After strapping the canoe to the top of my dad's 1989 Topaz, I checked my list three times to make sure I hadn't forgotten anything. We were ready to head toward Lake Itasca. It was all so surreal. I'd dreamt of paddling the entire Mississippi my whole life.

My dad drives slowly, so even though I didn't have much sleep the previous night, I insisted on driving the whole way to Lake Itasca, and man did I ever push it. The quicker we got up there, the more miles I could make that night, and the faster I could get to New Orleans. He warned me several times about speeding, and we fought about which way to go through Minneapolis. It ended up being a tense ride.

I'd talked about the trip for years, but that was what a trip like this was for, to talk about. Everyone talks about shit like this. Old men sit in nursing homes and talk about what they should have done and what they could have done. I couldn't believe it was really happening. I was cutting loose. I was severing. There was no stopping me. We grabbed a few burgers, and I felt like I was invincible. Didn't those people realize I was about to paddle the length of the Mississippi River in a canoe? I felt like I was having my last meal in civilization. My heart beat so fast, and my car couldn't drive fast enough. The trip seemed to take forever. Every mile was one mile closer to my exit from all of the bullshit. The moment I got into that canoe, everything would change forever. I couldn't even eat.

It was starting to rain, but that didn't matter. Bring rain, bring snow, and bring whatever you've got. I was going to paddle down that river, and there was nothing in the world that was going to stop me.

Day One

Chapter 1: Lake Itasca

May 15th, 1999 Day 1

I was dreaming, but knew I was dreaming. There were no consequences for my actions, were there? Maybe I'd reached the epitome of morality. I could take what I wanted whenever I wanted, or bask in eternal goodness. It was a tough decision.

At the headwaters, people looked at me with such disbelief that it made me feel like a little kid with a plastic shovel who had decided to dig his way to China. One look at that little crick they tried to call the Mississippi, and my invincibility left me completely. I'd waded through bigger trout streams. It wasn't much more than a trickle, and I spent the first few hundred yards doing more walking then paddling.

My dad gave me a look as if to ask, "Are you sure you want to do this?" but to quit at the headwaters would have been to die. It was a look of pity for me, and I was scared to look at him again. It told me how stupid and impossible it was to try to do what I was doing, but he knew I would try and try and keep trying, even if it would kill me.

I wanted to get away from all those people and the look on my father's face. I knew I would be alone for the next three months, but it couldn't happen quickly enough.

I didn't just quit my job one-day and head straight down the river. I'd spent the last few months doing a different kind of drifting. I was searching for something. Every once and awhile I caught a glimpse, but it was too big for me to comprehend. I had left everything safe to become a seeker, but ended up spending the majority of my time lost. Sometimes I found something that made me feel happy, but then I would go down the wrong path again, and end up going in circles.

> *I am falling.*
> *Although I see many ledges,*
> *I could easily grab,*
> *I prefer falling,*
> *And love to look down.*

The first two miles were an obstacle course of sticks, logs, and unmanageable corners. Downed trees and beaver dams completely blocked the river, and I spent more time dragging the canoe over snags than I did inside. I had already cut my hand, broken my watch, scratched my shiny green canoe all up, and torn my nice Winona State sweatshirt. My back hurt, the mosquitoes were eating me alive, and my arms were sore.

Deflated, I pulled out my maps to take a break and reevaluate things. I had sixty-three miles straight north to Bemidji, 400 miles to St. Cloud, and 650 to the Iowa border. There were thirteen long portages before St. Cloud. I had covered two miles, and already felt defeated. Sure, I was a canoeist. Once, when I was seventeen, I'd paddled ten miles.

Sure, I had planned things out: from drifting down the river without a care in the world, people cheering me on as I go, to triumphantly floating into New Orleans, and all of my friends welcoming me home. I had used the daydream as an escape every time I felt trapped in life. Now it was real, and not exactly as I envisioned.

I'd spent the last few years running. Not sure if I was chasing or being chased, I hadn't found a place that felt right. I knew there was a home for me somewhere and I was put here for a purpose. When I got there I thought I'd know. Jobs and relationships tried to define me, but they were never right. Sometimes I got sick of trying, and was ready to settle on the best thing going, but that was a sellout, and I knew it. Although at times I felt like I had no fucking clue who I was, at least I knew who I wasn't. Somehow, I thought three months alone on the river would show me the way.

I didn't really know why I was there, but I was. I decided to forget everything I had ever learned, and start again. This trip was life, and I was just being born. By Bemidji, maybe I could learn how to crawl. By New Orleans I'd have all the answers.

While spending most of the day dragging my canoe through the mud, getting sticks in the face, and getting lost in a maze of swamps, I caught myself singing along to the radio. At first I sang with restraint, like when you're singing in your car and pull up to a stoplight. I was completely alone, and could sing as loudly and badly as I wanted.

There is a house in New Orleans,
They call the rising son.
And it's been the ruin
of many a young poor boy,
And God, I know I'm one. (Animals).

I was deflated a good part of the day, but the elation that filled in the gaps more than made up for the low points. I was free, living my dream, and had an unlimited amount of time to spend on the river. Although it was already very dark, I kept paddling through the swamps for CoffeePot Landing, and was very excited to finally reach it.

As I pulled up to the landing in the dark, I heard what sounded like a festival of voices, and saw several people sitting around a fire. I was surprised to discover I was no longer alone. It reminded me of a dream I had long ago, but I couldn't remember the specifics. After being alone all day, it was nice to finally hear other people, and if I was lucky, maybe I had stumbled into a party or something. No one noticed me as I pulled up my canoe, but all voices stopped as I started up the landing.

A family of Indians who were enjoying the campsite seemed slightly shocked as I abruptly hobbled up the bank. The women and young children quietly disappeared into their tents as a large man approached me in the dark. Was I a demon to them? Although I felt very obtrusive, it was the only dry land for miles.

"Excuse me sir," My voice quivered slightly as I spoke. "I don't mean to disturb you, but I was wondering if you would mind if I put my tent up in the corner."

"It's a free country," he said as he waved me toward the spot. It was very dark, and I couldn't see his face. Using my flashlight to put up my tent, I looked over and saw that the only people left around the fire were the large man and three teenage boys. I decided it might be a good idea to walk over and break the ice.

"My name is Matt," I began. "Thanks for letting me stay."

"We're the Shonga Clan, and my name is Earl. Sit down and have some potatoes." I wasn't hungry, but was glad to sit down with them. "These are my three oldest sons." They all looked up shyly from the fire and nodded respectfully.

"So, where do you guys go to school?" The oldest looked up as if he were about to answer, but his father stepped in.

I watched the fire dance off Earl's face as he answered, "They're home schooled." I saw his features for the first time. He was strong and tough looking, but his face glowed peacefully and serene. His left eye was completely white, probably blinded in some life or death struggle, years ago. He reminded me of a lion hiding in the weeds. He was a wise man whose soul had seen many things.

I thanked Earl again and returned to my tent. I wanted to stay up and learn from him, but didn't want to further interrupt his time with the boys. Lying there in the darkness, I could just barely hear Earl out by the fire telling stories to his sons. Those boys were lucky. They didn't have to deal with all the bullshit of trying to be popular at school and fitting in with the crowd. They were learning to rely on their senses and stay in touch with nature.

Soon, the pitter-patter of rain covered the voices. Looking forward to the coming day, I peacefully drifted off to sleep.

DAY 2

I was up by 8:00, but when I went outside, Earl and his family were gone. The damp ground was still matted where their tents had squished the grass, and a thin column of smoke was spiraling up from the previous night's fire. The river was quite swift in front of CoffeePot Landing, and a thick layer of fog hung over the top of it.

After slicing through the fog of a narrow valley, the trees that were tunneling me on either side opened up into an endless swamp. The current had died completely, and I had no idea which way to go. Everything looked the same for as far as I could see.

I wasn't sure which way to go, so I paddled straight across toward the other side of the swamp. Sometimes it resembled an old channel, but then I'd come to a dead-end, and have to backtrack or pull my canoe through the weeds to the other side. I spent a good part of the day standing up in the canoe, looking for wherever the most water was, and trying not to get caught in any more false outlets.

The clear water below me revealed the grass to be bending slightly in a certain direction, indicating the way I needed to go. I scanned the horizon for a low point in the trees where the swamp drained into another valley, and pointed the nose of the canoe half way between the low point and the direction of the bending grass.

Gradually, the trees on the far horizon started to get taller, and luckily I saw a gap in them that marked the outflow from the swamp. All of the water in the stagnant swamp rushed to get out and race through the valley at the outflow with speed and fury. The river had grown impatient from being trapped in the bog for so long, like a kenneled dog that couldn't wait to get out and run.

For three miles, I was constantly jabbed with sticks from trees that protected the river, and several times I was forced to jump out into the raging, waist-deep water and lift the canoe up and over fallen logs. I was beginning to improve at navigating through the valley, when it opened up into another seemingly infinite swamp.

I traveled mile after mile in the boggy marsh, constantly losing myself to daydreams. Hours passed, but the scenery was still identical. Where was LaSalle Creek? Where was mile marker 1,324? Where was Stumpgh's Rapids? The area looked nothing like the map sitting in front of me. I was lost, but I didn't care. I'd been lost for as long as I could remember. I decided to put down my map and enjoy the aimless wandering.

I trusted providence to show me the way. I was tired of thinking, tired of trying to figure everything out. As I meditated only on what I was seeing and hearing, all thoughts of seeking were quickly disregarded. I forgot what day it was and where I was going.

The air was alive with the constant hum of nature, and turning every corner startled a different animal. The belching sounds of frogs rose above the others and laughed at me, reminding me I was lost and clueless. I shut them out and paddled forward aimlessly. As the day passed, it became impossible for me to discern between my daydreams and the real world unfolding before me.

Out of my daydream I broke. As the swamp began to take the shape of a river and the current began to move in a uniform direction, I followed the bending grass to an outlet in the maze of rice and entered another valley. Although I'd decided to put the map down, I broke my promise and gave it another look.

The river had become wider and the current steadier. My goal was to cover forty miles on the day, but pain was shooting from my shoulders down my back, and I felt fatigued. I stopped at the Iron Bridge Campsite, ate a snack, and considered stopping for the day. Slim Jims and Granola Bars can only do so much to boost a guy, but they seemed to help, and I decided to try to make it to the Silver Maple Campsite.

Thunder crashed. Lightning flashed. I wasn't more than three miles downstream when a big thunderstorm rolled in. The rain missed me to the north, but half an hour later another wave passed through, and this one nailed me. I paddled the next ten miles in the pouring rain as darkness closed in. I wanted to stop, but my things were already wet, and most of the shoreline was flooded anyway. I was already soaked, so I kept going.

Although I was being pelted with sideways rain and freezing my ass off, I couldn't remember feeling better in a long time. There was no bullshit around. I may not have known exactly who I was, but I knew what I had to do, and nothing else mattered.

By the time the deluge stopped, I was nearing the campsite. The river carried me through an area where the forest had been flooded. The current was hard to follow and there were always two or three options as to which way to go, so I made it a rule of thumb to always follow the heaviest flow of water. The river made a big turn and I tried cutting through the middle of some trees to save time, but after smashing into several logs, I decided to stay on the main part of the river.

The forest was flooded and the corners were very tight. Several big trees blocked the river completely. The river moved quickly, and I thought I could squeeze between an overhanging tree and a fallen log, but I crashed nose first into the log and came to a dead standstill. My canoe was taking a beating. I held my breath and listened to the pitch of limbs scratching the bottom of my boat, wondering how badly I was abusing it. I was colliding with everything in sight, and every time I did, I was sure I'd tear a big hole in the side of my vessel.

It was starting to get dark, and I still hadn't found the campsite. I was worried that I'd already passed it. At a fork in the river, I followed the wrong chute and the current became smaller and smaller until I was in a flooded field of rice with absolutely no flow. It was really getting dark fast, and I knew that I should turn back, but it had been a long time since I was sure I was even on the river. I aimed toward my right, where I had last seen any signs of moving water, but the water became too shallow to paddle through. I was completely grounded.

I was getting frantic and knew that I should turn around, but I didn't like to turn around. Instead, I dragged the canoe toward the trees on my right. I was pretty sure the river was on the other side of them, and after pulling my canoe three hundred yards and using all of the strength I could muster, I arrived at the trees, but there was still no river. I had nowhere to go. There was no way I was going to drag that canoe back again. It was too muddy and wet to stop for the night, and I had no idea where to camp. I was cold, stuck in mud up to my ankles, and it was dark. I wanted to just quit, collapse on the floor of my canoe, and sleep right there, but I had to keep going.

Continuing on my straight line, I dragged the canoe to the right, gaining only inches with each pull. Losing my grip on the bow, I fell into the water face first. It took everything I had, but after another two hundred yards, the water was deep enough for me to get back in. It was pitch dark, but light shining from the moon guided where I was going, and I used my paddle as a pole to push the canoe in the same direction. I broke through a patch of bushes like a running back into the endzone and was back on the river.

A few blind bends, and several sticks in the face later, I found the sign for the Silver Maple Campsite on my left. At the campsite, my flashlight discovered a tent, but it had collapsed from the wind, and was obviously unoccupied. I was cold, tired, and wet, and all of my things were soaked, so I crawled right in and dropped. Maybe some local kids had planned a camping trip, but the rain had scared them back into town. It was already well after dark, and although I thought about someone coming back, I was too exhausted to worry much about it. I had covered forty-three brutal miles that day, and my tired body didn't care where it crashed. After a few seconds of paranoia, I was sleeping like a log.

DAY 3

My body was in pain and I wasn't as eager to paddle, but I wanted to take off before the owners of the tent returned. Entering Bemidji, the river widened and accelerated as I watched my shadow move along with me on the sandy bottom below. I pulled up to a park where several elementary aged kids were boarding a bus.

"Andrew, get back in line. Andrew, quit chasing those grasshoppers and get back in line. Andrew, all of the other kids are in line, and if you don't join them you will get a timeout." His stern teacher said the last word as if it was the gas chamber or something, but it must have been enough to scare little Andrew, because when he heard the word timeout, he was back in line in a flash.

The kids filed into the yellow bus, and I couldn't help but notice all the little boys had the same haircut, same shoes, and similar advertising slogans on their little tee shirts. They were probably on their way back to school for some group work. No one could step forward with an idea unless the group agreed. Everywhere I'd gone I'd found committees, subcommittees, and groups. It was great to be off those monkey bars.

As I watched Andrew's little yellow school bus slowly disappear, a white van drove by, the driver made eye contact with me, did a U-turn, and came back.

"You goin' the whole way?"

"Yea, how did you know?"

"You've got that look to you," he explained. The man was about forty, had long brown hair in a ponytail, was slim, healthy looking, and had an air of knowledge and self-sufficiency. I had the feeling by the knowing look in his eye that he too had left the line at some point. He introduced himself as Lee, told me about his own experiences as a canoe racer, and gave me advice on the next few hundred miles.

"Take the south shore around Lake Bemidji. Whatever you do, don't cut across. It may look calm now, but the thing can change in a second." Looking out at the placid lake, it was hard for me to believe him. It looked so peaceful. I figured I could scoot across that lake in twenty minutes. Instead of disagreeing with him, I nodded my head affirmatively, and let him go on talking about the dangers of Lake Winniebigoshish and Cass Lake.

"Your shoulders sore?"

"Sore as hell."

"That'll go away after a week. How's your head?" He looked at me as if studying my mental health, waiting for an answer, yet relying on my facial expression to pantomime the truth.

"Great, great," I lied and changed the subject. "Where is the outlet?" He pointed me to the right of a big water tower, and explained that he had to get going.

Just like that, the cautious stranger was back in the van and gone. The school told me to wait in line, the experts taught me tricks on the big toy, and he told me not to shoot across the glassy lake. None of them made any sense to me.

I cut across the middle of Lake Bemidji, pondering all the time I was saving. First, it got a little choppy. Next, it became downright treacherous. I was moving toward the shore I was aiming at, but with no control over which way the canoe was pointing. I prayed that I wouldn't tip as three-foot waves hammered the side of the canoe, bringing me up and down and splashing me with water. Where did that wind come from? What the hell was I thinking? Why did I always think I was so damn smart?

I sat there for a few minutes, rising and falling with the waves, and going in no particular direction. I tried paddling, but the wind would not allow me to go straight, and I had no control over my back end. I wasn't sure if I was making any ground or not, and several times I leaned just a hair to one side and was within millimeters of tipping. I was stranded in the middle of Lake Bemidji, barely afloat, and scared shitless. Every time I moved it felt like the canoe was about to capsize. I gripped the sides until my knuckles turned white, and tried to keep it balanced. Luckily, there was a western wind, and it was slowly blowing me across the lake. It was a long process, and every time I lifted the paddle, it felt as if the bobbing craft would turn upside down. I picked out boats and houses on the shore and tried to gauge if I was making any progress. After over an hour of zero control, the bridge was getting closer, and I finally drifted into the shore.

I crossed under the bridge, elated to be back on the river again. It felt like I had just spent a weekend of hedonistic partying, had lost my focus in life, done a million things I'd regret, suffered through a terrible hangover, and it was Monday evening, and I was starting to feel like myself again.

Heading out of Bemidji, I felt as if I had hit my first major milestone. Even though I had made a terrible decision, it would prove to be a valuable lesson as I approached other larger lakes that would make it look like a little pond.

I needed a change of pace. After paddling a few miles past the bridge, I pulled out a little bucktail spinner and decided to drift awhile and make a few casts. A chunky northern pike ripped into my spinner on the first cast. It felt great, and reminded me of the reason why I wanted to do the trip as a kid in the first place. I had been hurrying so much in the last few days I hadn't even taken a break to fish.

The rest of the afternoon was spent casually drifting and throwing my bucktail. I tried casting a spinnerbait and a spoon, but the only thing they would really hit on was my bucktail. The fishing was fabulous. On Stump Lake, the river's northernmost point, I floated over a patch of reeds, and had my best luck yet. In four casts I nailed four northern, the last one being over thirty-six inches long. What a moment! I had caught one of my biggest pike ever, and after seventy miles of paddling straight north, I was finally turning south. The monstrous fish had completely engulfed my bucktail. The only thing sticking out of its big toothy mouth was the last few inches of my steel leader. It was the only bucktail I'd brought on the trip, and I didn't want to lose it, but I didn't want to kill the huge fish either. I snipped the line above the leader and hoped that nature would dissolve the obstruction.

After losing my bucktail, the fishing wasn't the same anymore, but I was still in a great mood. I caught two more small northern, and kept them for a meal. The trip was beginning to feel more like a vacation and less like a mission.

The river changed drastically after I portaged the Otter Dam. Eagles and Hawks glided above steep canyon walls as I shot through a narrow valley. I imagined they were messengers from a faraway place that had been sent to watch over me and keep me safe.

At 5:00, I drifted past a campsite that was too beautiful to pass up. Known as High Banks, it was on top of a steep, sandy cliff with an amazing view of Wolf Lake. The last three days had blended together, and everything was so surreal. Exploring the sandy cliffs, I felt like a little boy again, discovering things for the first time. After roaming the rugged hill for an hour, I built a small fire and enjoyed watching the river make a perfect S in front of me before joining the Cass Lake Chain. It was all so beautiful, and I wanted to just sit there forever and soak it all in. I had found my own little paradise, and was sad to realize I'd be spending only one night there. I felt like I was twelve years old again. When had I lost that feeling? What was so bad about life that it caused me to stop seeing all the magic out there?

> I swallowed a star.
> Although it glowed in my belly,
> I forgot it was there,
> Until the darkness came to blow it out,
> And it pricked my tongue as it flew away.

I was only three days into my trip, but the future in front of me was limitless, there was beauty all around me, and I was starting to get that feeling back again.

CHAPTER 2: LAKE WINNIBIGOSHISH

DAY 4

It was a chilly forty-two degrees as I shoved off toward Cass Lake. After my experience on Lake Bemidji, I would take no chances. Although Cass looked small on the map, it seemed endless, especially since I had to stay so tight to the north shore that I was forced to paddle twenty miles to go ten. I kept paddling and paddling, and every time I saw a point I thought it would be the last one before the dam. I'd get all excited to finally make it around, only to be greeted with another giant bay to tackle.

Taking a break to eat some cold chili, I realized how sore I was. My legs and face were sunburned to a crisp, puss dripped from the blisters on my hands, and my shoulders hurt so badly that getting the spoon to my mouth was an effort.

The Knutson Dam could not have appeared on the horizon any sooner. It represented my second major milestone, and after a quick portage, I was able to let the river do the bulk of the work again. The river had gained a lot of water since entering the Cass Lake Chain, and was finally starting to gain some momentum. I was entering an area known as Mississippi Meadows, where I was able to drift and read for the first time. Red-winged blackbirds were everywhere, and although a constant chirping interrupted every line, I didn't care. It was great to be able to move forward without exerting myself.

Near sunset, the steady flow through the birdy meadow began to slow, and the channel through the grasses widened. After turning a corner near a lively resort where several boats were docking for the evening, the river ahead of me opened up into a large lake on which the far horizon was invisible. I was entering the dreaded Lake Winnibigoshish. I felt like I was seeing the ocean for the first time. As one of the largest lakes in Minnesota, it was said to be one of the most difficult obstacles on my trip. It was nearly fifteen miles straight across, and to follow every nook and cranny along the southern shore would double that number. It didn't take much wind to create deadly waves on Winnie, and people were warned about traveling it in small boats. Although several of my friends had recommended I portage around the monster, I wanted to do the trip without skipping anything. My plan was to camp on the point where the Mississippi entered Winnie. I wanted to get an early start the following morning, taking the southern shoreline around Tamarack Point, and to the dam on the other side of the lake.

"Hey, dipshit, where do think you're going in that canoe?" The point at the left of the mouth was filled with a bunch of young Indian guys who were fishing, but judging from the beer cans scattered at their feet, they were doing more drinking than fishing.

"Do you guys know any good places to camp around here?"

"Nope, there are none, you better turn around."

"Paddle faster."

"C'mon, canoe boy."

"Hey, you're going the wrong way."

"Row row row your boat gently down the stream." It was no longer one guy talking, but the whole drunken crew of them. It didn't look like there was anywhere good to camp on the right side of the mouth, so although I'd have to paddle back that way, I decided to head toward a public campsite to my left marked on the map. I paddled right in front of the guys who were heckling me with my eyes fixed on the front of my canoe. They hurled insults at me as I made them disappear as quickly as possible. It was as much as I could handle not to swear back at them or give them the finger or something, but I was a stranger in a strange land, and figured it would be better not to provoke them.

Finally, they were behind me. I followed the left shoreline looking for the campsite, weaving my way around big, round, wire nets spaced along every twenty yards or so. I zigzagged around them like I was skiing a slalom course. It was getting dark fast, and I was relieved when the thick shoreline on my left opened up into a small clearing. Landing on the beach in front of the clearing, I was greeted by the serious faces of four tough looking Chippewa Indians leaning against an old pickup truck at the very spot I wished to camp. They sat there silently with their arms folded and stared at me, until the biggest of the four young men spoke.

"This is Chippewa Indian land," he explained with a stern face, rigid posture, and unswerving eyes, "and you're scaring the fish away from our nets." I was exhausted, but a rush of adrenaline made me feel strong and wiry. Maintaining steady eye contact with all four, I apologized, explained my trip down the river, and asked permission to stay there in order to get a good start on the big lake at first light.

The four seemed amused at the prospects of me trying to get across Winnie by canoe, and soon stern faces turned into welcome smiles as they began asking questions about my trip. Within three minutes, Trail Pemberton lit a fire, while his buddies were busy gathering wood for the night as I put up my tent.

After expressing their accord with my goal and wishing me luck, my new friends departed, and I enjoyed a can of Dinty Moore Stew over the fire. It was a serene setting; the lake was like glass. Winnie didn't seem like it was as bad as people made it out to be.

DAY 5

I awoke in the middle of the night to a nightmare of going over a roaring waterfall in my canoe. I was awake, but could still hear the roaring. It was coming from outside my tent, but I was still delirious from sleep and had no idea what it might be. Unzipping my tent and peaking outside, I suddenly discovered what all those people were talking about. Gigantic waves crashed against the shoreline with ferociousness. The sleeping giant had awakened.

By morning, the roaring was as strong as ever as the southeast wind pounded my western shore. I was stranded. Although the wind was only fifteen miles per hour, it didn't take much to get the lake chopping, and there was absolutely no way to keep a canoe afloat in the rough water. Looking to the right with my binoculars, I saw that the southern edge was a bit choppy, but it did provide some shelter from the wind. If only I would have paddled to my right along the southern edge the previous night instead of going north for a quarter mile. If I could have gotten to the southern shore I might have been able to make some miles. Although it was only half a mile to safety, the water between there and me was far too rough to take the chance.

There was nothing to do except wait. In order to keep my load light and make my portages easier, I was living off of the bare essentials, which meant I only had one water canteen. By noon it was empty. There was a campground on the map less than a mile away, so I followed the old trail the pickup truck had driven down, and tried to find a road to take me there. It was a long, round about way, but after walking for over half an hour, I found the place.

The campground was nearly empty, but I found a water pump and became engaged in conversation with an older gentleman who sat alone outside his camper while his wife was out walking. Gene was old and gray, and probably about eighty. His wife and he had made the campground their summer home, and spent the winters down in Florida. He told me the story about the last canoe that had tried to make the trip I was on. The father and son duo had made it as far as Winnie, but an unexpected storm had ended both their trip and their lives. Gene was very concerned about my safety and begged me to be cautious, to stay on the shoreline, and to always wear my life jacket. I had the feeling he was trying to pack eighty years of life experience into five minutes. The worried look on his face depressed me, so I cut our conversation short and started back.

Rather than take the road I had walked in on, I tried to take a shortcut through the woods. It was much thicker than I anticipated, but after tromping through for a quarter mile or so without finding a trail, I kept going through the thick brush anyway, sure that a big black bear would jump out and maul me. I was covered in scratches and feeling anxious and stupid by the time I stumbled upon my little red tent.

Back at my lonely campsite on the shores of the angry water, all of the waiting was driving me crazy. I'd been making excellent time, and my miles per day average had been shot. If I could have made it to the south shore, I'd have been safe for several miles.

For two hours I sat there watching the lake. I watched the waves hit the shore, imagining the wind was dying down, but then it picked back up stronger than ever. At 2:00, I cooked some hot tamales over the fire, and as I ate them, I was sure the wind had died down. It was still a little breezy, but the waves were no longer crashing with the ferocity they had been earlier.

I gobbled down the tamales, put out my small fire, and tore down the tent. I was nearly running at full speed, trying to pack all of my things into the canoe and tie them down before the wind picked up again. I was acting in such great haste that everything was going wrong. I ripped the bag that held the tent, dropped my toothbrush into the canteen, and buttoned my lifejacket wrong. I tried to shove the canoe off, but it was pounded back into shore.

A wave of fear crept over me, and suddenly everything felt wrong. I remembered the timid words of Gene. It was only a short paddle to get to some calmer water, but it didn't feel right. Instead, I pulled my canoe back on shore, retied everything, set the tent back up, and decided to make the site my little Walden until the wind died.

With the realization that it might be home for awhile, I crawled back into the tent and took a nap. The sound of waves crashing against the shore put me right to sleep. At 5:00 I awoke, and the roaring had stopped. Looking out at the giant, I found it sleeping again; it was time to move. I quickly broke camp again, but this time I was able to successfully launch the canoe. There was still enough wind to make the water rough, but I paddled successfully past the mouth of the river where I had been heckled, and to the southern shoreline, where I hoped it would be calmer.

The wind had shifted from the southeast to the east, and although it was nothing like before, I was forced to paddle directly against it. I was happy to be moving, and paddled as hard as I could along the southern shore, but every time I turned around I could still see the place where I started. It didn't seem like I was getting anywhere. I picked out a place ahead of me in the distance and tried to get there, but it didn't seem to get any closer. It was easier when I kept my head down and paddled, and tried not to think about it. I created a symmetrical counting cycle in order to take my mind off of my progress, and counted softly out loud to every stroke.

One.

One, one two, one, one.

One, one two one, one two three two one, one two one, one.

.... The number ten no longer exists.

Now I will destroy the number nine.

It took two hours to complete my counting cycle, and after murdering all of the digits from ten to one, I had successfully forgotten any pain or self-limiting thoughts and arrived in the town of Bena. I attempted to start a conversation with several people, but no one I encountered was overly friendly, and they all had about the same thing to say.

"You got a long ways to go."

"I'd be mighty careful out there on that lake in that."

"This is no place for a canoe."

"Didn't you hear about those two fellers who died last year?"

"Big storm coming in tonight."

"Why ya' wanna do that fer' anyway?" After finding out where I was headed, the comments were pretty similar from everyone. They all looked at me like I was crazy, so I kept paddling. I had another hour or so of light left, but it was getting calmer, and I was prepared to paddle as far as possible before it stormed, even with the light of the moon if I had to. I had been sitting still for too long, and wanted to take as big of a chunk out of the lake as possible.

By 9:00, I was about half way through another counting cycle when a loud clap of thunder startled me. In the next twenty minutes, the sky to the southwest changed drastically. Sharp sounds of thunder pierced the sky, and lightning flashed majestically at regular intervals. It was dead calm for the first time all day, but ominous, dark clouds were joining the sunset, making it a strange blend of orange, yellow, red, and gray.

Four drunken women were leaving their dock to get away from the storm as I paddled past. Big, poofy hair and ripped blue jeans revealed they'd grown up in the eighties. "Hey, you in the canoe are you off your tree?" A lady in a black Motley Crue shirt with a twelve pack under one arm was clearing everything off from the picnic table as her three guests smoked cigarettes and waited for the little party to move inside. I lingered awhile, trying to get invited over, but they were in too much of a hurry to notice. Before I could think of anything clever to say they were running to the cabin as the rain began falling.

The approaching storm looked like a real doozy, and although it was raining, I thought I could make it a little farther before the deadly part of it ripped into me. I paddled harder and harder. The eminence of the storm added to the adrenaline building inside me. The lightning moved closer, the thunder became louder, and I could no longer distinguish the falling raindrops from the sweat dripping off my forehead. Every time I saw a place to camp I planned on stopping, only to pass it up as the storm enveloped me. I'd hit the next one. I could make it another quarter mile. I was covering miles like I had never done before, and every inch I paddled on the bitch of a lake was one less I'd have to traverse the next morning.

The storm was on me. I paddled until I couldn't feel my arms under my rain-soaked sweatshirt. It was time to seek shelter. Covered with sweat in the ever-faster falling rain, I was aided by flashes of lightning as I fought the gusting winds to put my tent up on the first spot I found in the dark. The tent was up in seconds and I jumped into the shelter as the hail came. The pounding of the rain mingled with the pelting of the frozen pellets on the roof of my tent until I was sure it would collapse. The wind made a howling noise as one side of the tent was sucked in against my shivering body. Ear shattering blasts of thunder occasionally covered up the crashing of the waves against the shore. There was so much lightning I could've read a book in the dark if my hands were not shaking so badly. I prayed to God my tent would stay together, a tornado wouldn't wipe me out, and I wouldn't be struck by lightning. If it was adventure I was seeking, I had found it. Never had I felt so alive.

DAY 6

Dreaming of a nice slow drift, I awoke at 4:30 a.m. to find the giant sleeping again. It was dead calm, but looked overcast; I decided to try to get up that beanstalk while I had the chance. I covered five more miles of Winnie before the sun came up. It looked like rain, and I wanted to make it to the dam before another storm stopped me.

One thing I loved about canoeing was setting a point on the horizon and later passing it. I'd been staring at Tamarack point forever, and was finally reaching it. By 7:00 I was around it, and the dam was in sight. It stood for freedom. That dam represented successfully getting past the hardest part of my trip. I knew if I could make it past Cass and Winnie, I could get through any obstacle the trip had to offer.

It started sprinkling within a mile of the dam. By 8:00, I was only a quarter mile away, but the sprinkle turned into a downpour. I sought shelter at Logan's Resort, and luckily ran into a fisherman in a yellow rainsuit who invited me into his cabin to get out of the rain. Five other grizzled fishermen were curious about the tired but excited young man was who was dripping all over their floor. They gave me a little crap about being crazy enough to be out on Winnie in a canoe in the rain, but it ended up that I lived just miles from their hometown of Stewartville, Minnesota, and one guy even had my dad as a high school teacher. That made me okay, and they proceeded to fill my canteen and load me up on cookies from their various wives. They didn't seem to believe I was really on my way to New Orleans, but they had a good laugh anyway. After an hour with my new buddies, the rain let up, and I was headed toward the dam.

I was really feeling the exertion of paddling around Winnie, and it took me three long trips to portage the dam. Soon I was drifting in the light current, on top of the world and having acquired a new respect for nature. Feeling like I deserved a break, I spent the rest of the day paddling the canoe backwards with a line trolling behind me. Fishing was great. Despite losing several lures, I caught over a dozen northern, and several walleye.

After passing the confluence with the Leech Lake River, the current quickened considerably, and it became too fast to troll effectively. I was making great time on the day, but out of nowhere, another storm developed, and I was forced to stop a few hours early at Gambler's Point Campsite. It was one of those quick movers that produced hail, wind, and lightning, and I barely made it in the tent before the hail bombarded me. The sun was out half an hour later.

Rather then keep paddling, I spent the rest of the afternoon drying my things on a clothesline. I craved fish for dinner, and caught a few more dandies by trolling a Rapala along the weedline in front of the site. Starting a fire was very difficult, but I got one going long enough to cook dinner, and was sleeping soundly by 9:00.

CHAPTER 3:GRAND RAPIDS

MAY 21, 1999 DAY 7

I awoke early to a cold, drizzly, breezy morning. Although I was tired, sore, and lacking ambition, it was Friday, and I wanted to make it to Grand Rapids and find a place to have a few beers. After a quick breakfast of hot tamales, I was paddling by 7:30.

There was already a stiff south wind, and within minutes, my cold hands were so numb I couldn't even feel them. The river meandered back and forth lazily. It looked like the swamps near the headwaters, only a bit wider. The banks were undefined, and it was very challenging to stay on the channel without getting lost.

I was looking forward to added flow from the Vermillion River and making some phone calls at Schoolcraft State Park. I'd been on the river for a week, and couldn't wait to take a few minutes to check out the park, get water, and talk to some people, any people. I hadn't had a conversation with anyone since the previous morning.

The river was very high and spilled over the banks taking alternate routes through a series of meanders and oxbow lakes. Somehow, I went past the State Park, and didn't even notice when the Vermillion River came in. Lack of water was starting to make me feel like a camel, and I was frustrated about having missed an opportunity for socialization. Although I was out of water, more than anything, I was just using the need for water as an excuse to find someone to talk to.

Just before Cohasset, I watched an old Oldsmobile pull up to a house on my left, and a nice looking blond lady in a pink waitress outfit got out, slammed the door, and walked toward a house nearby. I yelled over from my canoe, and she walked out to the dock to talk to me. Sue had just gotten off work in Grand Rapids. She was about forty and pretty, but looked like she was sick and tired of being a waitress. After she went in, filled my canteen, and brought me out some homemade cookies, I tied up to her dock and we got into a good conversation, mostly consisting of her complaining about her boss. Her husband came home as we sat innocently talking; he was a big, tough looking Harley guy who looked like he could tear me in half.

I pushed hard to make Grand Rapids while it was still light enough for me to look around. After passing a big power plant I'd been staring at all day and fighting the wind over a series of lakes, the town was finally opening up in front of me. I'd made excellent time on the day, so when I paddled past a bar sign on my left, I figured I'd earned the right to have the first beer of my trip.

I was drained from a day of hard work, but it was kind of an adrenaline rush to know it was Saturday night, and I was looking for a good time in a strange town. The bar was quiet and dark, and besides the barmaid and a few old farmers, the only other people inside were three guys shooting pool. My first beer went down quick, my second even quicker. My original plan was to go the whole way to New Orleans without diluting my body with any chemicals. I had gone a week, but there was something about that bar sign peeking out of the trees that seemed to beckon me over for a cold brew. After finding out about my trip, the bartender gave me my first beer. The second and third were picked up by the quiet farmers at the end of the bar.

After finishing my fourth beer and getting another, I got up to use the restroom and made a few calls on the phone. Calling my dad, I discovered my cousin was staying at a cabin just a few miles away. I called the number he was at, and Mitch made plans to meet me by the river in an hour and take me out walleye fishing.

After hanging up the phone and retrieving my empty beer glass from the top, one of the guys who had been playing pool walked over to me. He was a big, serious looking guy, and wore army pants and a black, sleeveless shirt. He had several wicked tattoos on his muscular arms, and a thick Go-T made his tough face look even meaner.

"You shoot stick?"

"Yea, but I'm not the greatest."

"Good, we need a fourth, and you can be my partner." Donnie was about thirty-five, and although he looked like some kind of street fighter, he seemed to know everything about just about everything, and loved to tell me his views on the world. He was very opinionated, and everything he talked about seemed to always come back to Y2K, and an impending disaster our nation was about to face.

"I tell ya, airplanes are gonna be falling out of the sky. People are fucking weak man; they don't have any clue what it takes to survive. See these two guys here, they're killers man, they've got what it takes. You, you're a killer too, I can tell by the look in your eye, but these other people man, they're fucking weak. They don't have a chance."

Neither guy we were playing against looked older than twenty, but they both had the same intense look Donnie had. They listened to everything he said as if he was the next great prophet. Donnie hated everything and everyone, and was convinced that every law the government had ever passed was nothing but a big conspiracy. I didn't agree with everything he said, but some of it did make sense. The fact I was out on such a long trip and was eager to listen to his ideas really got him going, and since I was catching a buzz and having a good time, I could start to feel some camaraderie developing.

Donnie was a sharp pool player, and he kept my beer from going past the halfway point by refilling it with his pitcher nearly every time I took a drink. Despite his rough appearance, he was a smooth talker, and I found myself agreeing with a lot of his crazy views. The more I seemed to concur, the more radical his ideas became. At one point, the two younger looking guys were out of earshot, and he looked at me real serious and stared intensely into my eyes.

"Man, I wouldn't say this to a stranger, but I have a good feeling about you for some reason. We have some plans. We're going to be ready. I have a list of guys like you and me that we can depend on. Nothing too crazy, but when that Y2K shit starts hitting and everybody goes nuts, we'll be ready man. We'll have our own little country while this one dies."

It was his turn to shoot, so he stopped talking, but what he said really made me think, and I wanted to hear more. Donnie had just sunk the eight ball when a scrawny, goofy looking guy that was about my age busted through the door and ran up to him. He wore a permanent grin on his face and had messed up eyes.

"Donnie, we need your truck, man, Shane got his car stuck down by the river."

"That dumbfuck, I ain't pulling his ass out again unless he's got some money."

"He ain't got no money, but he's got plenty of smoke." That seemed to be good enough for Donnie. After nodding to the two young guys, slamming down the rest of his beer and grabbing his leather jacket, they were on their way out. My hour was almost up before I had to meet Mitch, so I figured I'd walk down and help them.

The car was only a hundred yards from my canoe. The front wheels on the old rusty blue Camaro were completely buried in the sand, and when we got there, he was spinning his tires, making things even worse. Shane had long bushy red sideburns, and they made his thin face look really funny. He was also about my age, and had a really stupid look on his face like he did that kind of stuff all the time. There were four of us to help, so Donnie suggested we all push from the front instead of hooking up his truck. The thing was buried pretty badly, and we couldn't budge it the first time. I ran and got my canoe paddle to use as a shovel, and after digging a little path, we got it rocking, and finally popped it up and over the little sandy hill.

We were all pretty tired from the exertion, and leaned up against the freed Camaro to rest while Shane sat inside and packed up a big bowl. It was his way of saying thanks. It was something I definitely intended to stay away from on the trip, and I felt a little tinge of uneasiness as they passed it around in a circle nonchalantly.

Shane seemed to be the scapegoat of the group, and they all started telling stories about him and giving him shit. They referred to him as Red, and the bitter look on his face revealed that he hated the nickname. I let it go by me without partaking on the first round and nobody said a word, but they offered it up with inquisitive looks on their faces every time around, as if I might have changed my mind or something. It had been a long time for me and definitely stoked my curiosity. I was out to find some crazy experiences, and already had a safe place to stay for the night and no more paddling ahead of me.

No association
No hidden description
All things have come untied.
Society's rules blasted apart,
Here, deduction has died.
Tangled webs of this means that,
Thousands of fences to ride.
Today all things stand alone,
Breathe In, deduction has died.
Prejudice defeated,
Our instincts take over,
Senses our only guide.
Barriers shredded,

Pretense expires,
Exhale, deduction has died.

The car was out, the bowl was cashed, and it was time to go back into the bar. They had no more than pulled out and left me all alone to wander in my thoughts when Mitch's El Camino showed up pulling his boat. After securing the canoe and hopping in, we were on our way to the lake for a night of walleye fishing.

It was strange being off the river and flying down blacktop roads in the car. The effects were just starting to creep up on me, and everything was starting to slow down and separate. I felt like the wheels were lifting off the ground at every hill, and we were doing 200 miles per hour. In minutes, we were sipping cold Budweiser and lowering the boat into the water. The sun was just setting, and it was already colder than a witch's tit. I was numb all over, and felt like I was moving in slow motion through a daydream.

Mitch was right in his element. He wasn't laid back, he was really laid back. To be out in a boat on a beautiful lake at sunset with a cooler full of beer and fish to be caught was heaven for him. We cruised out to his secret spot, just as most boats were calling it a night. Mitch set me up like a fishing guide would for a paying client. He didn't get too excited about anything, but he knew his fishing, so I just sat back and enjoyed the night while he put us on the walleye.

The water went on endlessly in all directions around our lighted bobbers. It was cold, but after a few more buds... and a few more buds... I was feeling no pain. I was no longer in a boat, but hovering in mid-air over an infinite chasm to the unknown. The universe extended forever above, below, and to all sides. It was tough to concentrate on fishing. I stared at my bobber so long that it ceased to exist; then I realized it was under. Mitch lived up to his fishing expert reputation, but by midnight our teeth were chattering so loudly that it was time to go in.

Back to the cabin for a nightcap, I got a chance to meet all of Mitch's fishing buddies. His pal, Craig, made a thick deer stew that we scarfed down between gulps of beer. I had only been gone for a week, but was already in a different world.

I don't remember crashing out on the hide-a-bed in the cabin's living room. Suddenly, I woke up in a panic. I had lost the river. No longer could I hear its soothing flow or float along its lovely waters. Where was my canoe? Where was I? How would I get back? It was very strange being away from the river. It was my first night in a real bed, and I couldn't even sleep. Although I found the break from paddling that I needed, I had seriously tainted the purity of my trip. Sure, I had a great time, but felt as if I'd taken a serious detour from the path I'd been so diligently following, and was afraid I wouldn't be allowed back on. I vowed never to leave the side of the river again.

DAY 8

Mitch brought me back to the river early and waited around long enough to help me portage the Blandin Dam in Grand Rapids. I was drained, but my goal was to get as far downriver as possible before the next wave of storms hit. The radio was advertising a ninety percent chance of strong storms.

A few miles south of Grand Rapids, I met Al Rudquist, a world champion canoe racer from the area who was training for his next race.

"I'll bring you donuts tomorrow," Al promised as he paddled away gracefully. I loved watching his canoe cut through the water like a dagger. It was a treat watching him disappear on the horizon. He had found his thing in the world, and I envied that.

The river was really flooded, and had widened and accelerated since the dam. The young, growing river was making its own rules, taking shortcuts through the trees as it moved toward Brainerd, my next goal. I was way ahead of schedule, and really starting to get tired. Storms were on the way, so I quit after only a few hours of paddling.

After setting up camp and stashing plenty of dry wood under the canoe, I spent the rest of the day in the tent, napping, reading, and playing solitaire. Although it sprinkled all day, the big storm never hit, and I felt a little guilty for wasting half a day of paddling. It was a cold night, but I stayed up late by the fire listening to live sets of the Grateful Dead, a real find on my little radio.

Everything seemed so perfect as I stooped over the little fire trying to stay warm, keeping my hand on the antenna so as not to lose the music. I stared at the flames and allowed myself to forget about everything.

The music ended, and I began thinking about the miles ahead. The partying from the night before was unexpected, and made me feel guilty. I thought that by getting on the river I would be able to get away from the things that had consumed me in the past. Rather than come to a conclusion about how to handle the future, I decided to just let the river take me where it would. Even so, I was afraid that if I got too far away from it again, I might not be strong enough to come back.

DAY 9

It was brutally cold with a biting wind from the north. More rain was on the way, and a foggy mist hung over the water. Putting on my coveralls and setting out, I soon discovered that although it was too windy to keep the canoe straight, the current had become strong enough to carry me along at a pretty good clip.

My canoe was getting lighter as I ate my supplies, but I was completely out of snacks. Much of the morning was spent looking back, hoping to see Al Rudquist for some conversation and donuts. Water zipped through groves of trees on the flooded shoreline. At Beer's Landing, I passed two skinny old guys who were standing near a pickup truck at the landing.

"Highest I've ever seen it. You've gotta be crazy to be out there in that little canoe." I spent a few minutes talking to the locals who were out killing time on their lunch break.

"Damn, it's cold out for May," the other shivered, regretting he had moved up there from California to marry the other guy's sister a few years back. They were too cold to talk long, and had to get back to work. Before long, I was back in the fast current heading toward Jacobson, where I could replenish my water and snacks.

After staring around every corner, eagerly anticipating the bridge to Jacobson, it was finally in sight, and I watched it appear bit by bit. Trudging all over town in my coveralls and yellow raingear, I looked like a deep sea fisherman who had just found land after being lost at sea for days. I had so many clothes on that it was nearly impossible to walk, and after spending so many days in the canoe, my legs felt like rubber.

Jacobson wasn't as big as it looked on the map. I found a store, but it was closed. Walking another half mile south, I stumbled into a bar. Everyone looked at me funny as I piled up my warm clothes on the barstool beside me. Several beers later, with Me and Bobby McGee cranking out on the jukebox and the Spurs putting away the Lakers, I'd made many new friends and lost track of time. I spent most of the time talking to two ladies named Sandy, and there was also an old hippie lady who communicated to me without talking. Her glazed eyes wandered over to mine as if she was reading my mind, but every time I thought we were going to talk, she'd get distracted and wander away. We seemed to connect in some silent way, but I never had the opportunity to talk to her.

"I guess I just wandered up here one day and forgot to go home," one Sandy explained as I wondered why she had left the city for a town of forty-four people in the north woods. Everyone in the bar was super friendly, and I was having a blast hanging out with them, but after a few hours, it was raining again and starting to get dark.

Sandy had an awesome new truck, and volunteered to give me a ride back to my canoe. Her daughter's four foot tall Barbie sat between us in the cab. She smoked skinny little Virginia Slims and offered me one when we got back to the bridge. They were the same kind of smokes I used to get from the waitresses when I was a fifteen-year old busboy. I had a good beer buzz going, so I smoked one for old time's sake.

Feeling good, I drifting into the current backwards, rearranging my stuff with the spindly little cigarette hanging out of my mouth. I puffed on it furiously to keep the rain from putting it out. Sandy honked from the bridge, and I paused for a moment to wave.

I never saw the tree of moderation. It nailed me on the back of the head, nearly flipped my canoe, and its branches grabbed my best fishing pole and flung it into the water. I paddled back to shore and tried to retrieve it by casting a heavy weight on my other pole, but the current was too strong, and I slipped on the edge of the bank and got soaked in the water up to my waist.

It was forty-five degrees, I was soaked, it was pouring, I was losing my buzz, and it was getting dark fast. To top that off, I had just donated my best pole to the Mississippi River. At least my cigarette stayed lit. I had forgotten it was even in my mouth. Angrily, I threw it into the wet canoe as if it was to blame, and paddled furiously, looking for the first high ground outside of town. Two miles later, I was searching in the dark. I found a high clearing and set up my tent as the rain finally stopped. It had rained eight of my first ten days. Although the rain had made the current fast enough for me to make thirty-eight easy miles on the day, I was sick of being wet and cold.

In the middle of the night, something woke me up, something that sounded big. People at the bar had warned me about bears, but I joked and said I was hoping to see one. In my haste, I had forgotten to empty my garbage, and the front of my canoe was filled with empty chili cans. I wasn't so brave anymore. Something stomped around in the woods, and the cans in my canoe were being rattling around. I was scared as hell. I thought I heard a growling noise, but was too paranoid to be able to tell. Afraid to unzip my tent and attract attention to myself, I just sat there frozen, and prayed that whatever it was would leave. I wished it would start pouring again. I wished it were light out. The noises stopped, and I sat there in my tent feeling stupid, listening to every little crackle and imagining a bear was about to tear through the seams in my tent.

I'd done things half-assed lately, and it showed. I languished a bit that I'd tarnished my trip with alcohol again. It dulled me both mentally and physically, and made me susceptible to making costly mistakes. Nature has its many dangers, and I was facing them daily, but it was the ways of man and his interference with the natural order of things that could ultimately bring me down. The river was not something to be beaten. I was lucky enough to be allowed to ride on it, and if I didn't give it the respect it deserved, I knew it would take me.

DAY 10

Cold, cold, cold. It was thirty-three degrees when I woke up. It was too cold to sleep, and too cold to get out of my sleeping bag. At 7:00, I finally braved it, and pulled coveralls on. It wasn't too bad once I started moving, but my fingers were frozen from the layer of frost on my tent.

Steam rose off the water as I headed downstream. I thought about my thoughts as I fell asleep the night before. Alcohol was a demon that disconnected me from the infinite loop. My goal was to go completely without it on the trip. I'd treat myself to a coke from then on. In addition, it would help me stick to my three dollar per day budget (I'd spent thirty-eight dollars in ten days). My mind needed to be extra sharp and my body extra strong, or next time it would be more than my fishing pole going overboard.

With that choice made, I felt great. Although cold, the sun was heating things up, my hands were thawing, and I was making great time. Cutting across the water like a dagger, I took a break from paddling at 9:30, having already covered ten miles. With less weight I was faster, but more susceptible to wind.

South of Jacobson, the landscape changed, and most of the shoreline was used for grazing cattle. What were those cows thinking as they watched me glide past? They looked up from chewing grass long enough to stare at me indifferently, but didn't seem too interested. They reminded me of some people

I know, content to waste away their days in one spot without ambition, as long as they had plenty of grass. I mood at one, and set the whole herd into a mooing frenzy.

The majority of the day was spent drifting, by far my most effortless one. Although it was cold and brief heavy rains blew over every few hours, the current was very swift, and I was able to drift along at three miles per hour. Leaning back, I cracked open a book and relished in my laziness. I was feeling very good about making it to Brainerd by Friday to meet friends, in fact at that pace I was worried about getting there too early.

My biggest problems in life were that I'd lost my fishing pole, the reel on the other one was not working, and I was down to only a few lures. I could still troll, but every time I trolled, I ended up getting snagged, couldn't turn around, and lost another lure. My last Rapala was gone, and I was down to one spinnerbait. Fishing was poor with all of the high water anyway.

After thirty-four miles without seeing a single person, I arrived at Scott's Rapids. Every new site felt like my favorite. Those north woods were so pristine. There was no peace like cooking a meal over a crackling fire, while sitting and watching the river flow and listening to the songbirds say goodnight to the forest. There was nothing to delude my senses that didn't come from God. I closed my eyes and traveled away to a million places, but I loved where I was.

A Minnesota Campsite

MAY 25, 1999 DAY 11

Up early, I was on the river before 6:00 in order to make it to Palisade by 10:00 so I could catch my dad on the phone before he left the office. I daydreamed about towns downriver and people I'd meet. A friendly toot-toot from an old pickup truck on a rare corner where the river met the road was my only human interaction in over thirty hours.

By 9:15 the water tower was in sight, and twenty minutes later I was hiding my canoe in the weeds under the bridge. Walking down some lonely highway, feeling like a cowboy, I passed a little green sign that read: Palisade pop. 144.

Stopping at a store to make a few calls, I couldn't help but be completely distracted by the pretty blonde gal inside. She was petite, in her early twenties, and had bright blue eyes that seemed to scream, "get me out of this little town." I was a little embarrassed, having gone two weeks without a shower, dirty, and needed a shave. I must have looked pretty silly walking in and asking her to fill my canteen, but she just smiled and gave me a reassuring look.

I lingered in the store a few more minutes pretending to shop, but really just waiting for the other customers to clear out so we could talk. I was sure she was either married or engaged. How could a girl like her slip by the men in that little town?

Customers cleared, I approached. She smiled warmly and her eyes, sharp and alert, darted about as if she was sizing up the situation, seeing if I was safe, and always returning to lock onto mine. They smiled on their own and waved hello every time she blinked. I knew it was the critical moment to initiate more than small talk, but I chickened out due to lack of self-confidence, bid her farewell, and walked out the door, feeling her eyes sting my back.

After cleaning out the granola bar section at the grocery store, I sat at the town diner eating country-fried steak and potatoes, my first meal not out of a can or the river. Back in college, I could have gotten a date with her, I reassured myself, but I was still upset. It was supposed to be my ultimate adventure, a time to savor each moment, not to sit alone at some diner saying what if.

After finishing a great meal, I wrestled a paper away from a local lumberjack, and caught up on sports. Meeting twelve of the 144 people in Palisade who'd surely tell the others what they'd missed, I marched back to the store, and discovered the name of that blue eyed angel was Sarah.

Explaining that I needed to get back to the river, but couldn't leave without pursuing her, I asked if she might be interested in getting together later. The expression on her face changed quickly, her cheeks got a little red, and she smiled and said, "Sure." Finding out she was off by 2:00 and was definitely single, we spread my map out on the counter and found the perfect rendezvous point, a boat landing twelve miles downstream.

"I'll be there at four-o-clock and wait until four-thirty, and you do the same." I thought about the old romance novel where the two were supposed to meet on top of the Empire States Building, and one got hit by a car on the way. She insisted on giving me her number and address just in case, and I told her if she changed her mind for any reason and didn't show up I would understand.

I started immediately in order to make it on time, and flew through the door with a new spring in my step. I wanted to yell "yee-ha," but there were people around, so it would have to wait for the river. How could I clean up a bit? Boy, did I stink.

The liquor store sign seemed to call out my name. No, I didn't need that, but man, a little flask for the ride there would really calm my nerves for when we got together later. I turned away, then turned back. I must have changed my mind five times. I felt like I was just so boring when I was sober, and I was always calm and smooth after a few drinks. I wanted the night to be exciting, and didn't want to act all reserved. What the hell? I was twenty-four, and you only lived once.

A few pink vodka lemonades later, I was feeling mellow and closing in on the boat ramp. This was living, I thought, pretty sure she'd show up. I washed my hair over the side of the canoe, soaped up, and used the water from my canteen to rinse off with. I put on the one set of clean clothes I'd stored away in a plastic bag for special occasions. After throwing on some deodorant and cologne, I was ready for the prom.

She must have been running late. She'd come. She'd be there. Maybe I gave bad directions. Maybe she'd gotten lost. Yeah, I was sure she was just running a few minutes late. At 4:25, I was starting to get a little nervous, and walked up to the highway in case she didn't see me. There it was, the black Chevy Blazer. A wave, a smile, a laugh, she was twice as pretty as I remembered her.

We picked up right where we left off. It was obvious it didn't matter where we went, so we just sat on the landing and talked. After a half-hour, we climbed into her truck and headed into Aitken. It felt strange to be going sixty. She had total control over me, and I could care less where I ended up.

We found a little bar, and she schooled me at pool while we played our favorite songs on the jukebox. I stared into her eyes with intrigue as I tipped back beers and she sipped Dr. Pepper. The conversation never dulled. She shared with me a poem she'd written, and I told her one of my own. She was witty and intellectual.

Was I dreaming? We were in our own little world; the waitress would come in and leave as if she was interrupting. Things were moving fast, and I was leaving forever in hours. Everything felt so perfect, and it was only 5:30. (I was hammered).

As the evening progressed we were still getting along great, and the growing buzz in my head was really intensifying things. We both realized that it would have to end soon, and gradually she started letting go on her side of the link. We made a lot of promises about meeting again, but I think she sensed I might never again come back to Palisade. After putting away a few stiff drinks in the canoe and several beers in the bar, my self-confidence may have been higher, but the look in my eye was probably not as sincere, and I think she was quick enough to sense that. Anyway, we cooled things off, and she started to grow a tad distant. (I was hammered).

Sarah brought me back to the landing at sunset, and we made the agreement that if our meeting was meaningful, we would meet again another day. As she dropped me off, my heart did the same. I was ready to settle in Palisade and raise a family, but for then, all I could worry about was finding a campsite in the dark and not capsizing. Everything grew so quick and faded so quick. She was gone, and I was alone again.

I drifted downstream in the fading light, feeling a tinge of sadness. Everything started out so perfectly, but I'd ruined things somehow. When I was drinking, I guess a lot of what I showed to others was actually bullshit, and she could see through that act.

"Hey, you in the canoe. Are you the guy going to New Orleans?" Two guys fishing in the dark with a little lamp brought me out of my daydream.

"Yep."

"We heard about you upstream. You got a long ways to go man."

"I know. You guys catching anything?"

"Just a buzz." Conversations on the river were the best, short and simple.

I found Hassman Campsite by the light of the moon and fumbled around in the dark to get my tent set up. In a bit of a cranky mood, I wanted a fire to help me think. Branches whipped me in the face and spider webs stuck in my hair as I bulldozed around the forest with my fading flashlight looking for firewood, still in my good clothes. Now I didn't want a fire, I wanted a big fire.

As it blazed, I stared at the flames intensely and tried to remember the universe was big and I was small. Recollecting myself, I found my peace again as the fire healed me. I sat around the fire until my big stack of wood had all turned to ashes. The sky was getting gray, and I was ready for another adventure the next day.

DAY 12

I slept in until 10:30, and awoke in good spirits. Rather than another day of doing everything the same, I decided to try to shake things up by taking the Aitken flood diversion channel. I couldn't tell exactly where it led to, but guessed it must eventually rejoin the main channel. Approaching the dam, I heard the fearful raging of the spillway as I read a series of signs on the right bank. Danger Do not Approach Dam. Stay on Main Channel. Never being one to believe everything I hear, I attempted a portage around the dam. If it came out where I guessed, it would really save some time.

It took me three trips to carry everything 300 yards through heavy brush without being discovered by the three men working nearby. After fighting through the undertows and fierce cyclones of water in the eddies below the spillway, I was on my way again.

The diversion channel was very exciting. I wasn't sure how far it went or where it led to, but knew it must eventually reenter the main channel. Where else would all of that water go? My rule of thumb when lost had been to follow wherever the majority of water was flowing, and that principle definitely held true in this case.

The diversion channel was one big long canal. Identical banks rose up steeply on both sides, and the thing seemed to go on forever as straight as an arrow. I felt as if I had entered a warp zone. Time stood still in the Aitken flood diversion channel.

As I coasted along the celestial holding tank, my thoughts drifted back to the night before. When I'd taken trips in the past and stopped along the way, I could always go back on the way home. This trip was different. I had a one way ticket, and could not waste time looking back. The current carried me downstream, and I needed to look forward to the next adventure. It would have been very difficult to paddle upstream. Down the channel I drifted, unsuccessfully trolling a line as I went.

Trolling along, I ended up getting snagged and lost all my line on the pole with the broken reel. I wanted to yell and curse, but knew it wouldn't do any good. I didn't have to worry about fishing anymore. I'd been on the diversion channel for a few hours, but there was still no end in sight. What if it didn't go back to the river? What if it was used for irrigation, and drained into the fields?

In my attempt to get clean, I had used my drinking water to clean up with, and had forgotten to refill the canteen. Although I kept thinking I would run into someone or a place to fill it, the diversion channel was desolate, and I was thirsty and out of luck.

The channel finally turned a quick corner, and after shooting through a small set of rapids, I rejoined the river. Cows on either side of the widened river welcomed me back, but I was parched, extremely tired, and the muscles in my back and shoulders were sore. Rather than keep pushing on and trying to find some drinking water, I decided to camp early at Lone Pine Creek.

I had no energy whatsoever and felt extremely drained and weak. I hadn't had a drink of water in over twenty-four hours, and a night of drinking was not helping me out much. I wished there was a sofa I could have just melted into and watched a game or a movie. There was no resting out on the river. I'd spend all day paddling, rush to get a fire going for dinner and set up camp before dark, and then sleep uncomfortably on the hard ground. The closest thing I could find to a sofa was a well-shaped tree stump if I was lucky. I had no appetite, and was about to collapse.

I was very dried out and dehydrated, and having no other options, had to resort to drinking river water. Finding an old bucket, I cleaned it out, taped it up, and filled it full of water from the creek. Using my long underwear as a screen, I poured it into my pan and boiled it. After straining it again with my long underwear, I poured it into the canteen, mixed it with lemonade, and cooled it in the river. It tasted funny and had an ugly brown color, but at least it was drinkable. It was a long process, but a necessary one. The next time I turned on a faucet I was more thankful.

It was kind of a special feeling when the only cares I had in the world were finding water, a safe place to camp, and getting my next meal somehow. It was a lot of work to get all of the simple little things in life done that I normally took for granted. When a day of paddling was over, the chores were all done, and I got an hour or so just to kick back around the fire and let my mind roam, it was a priceless feeling, and made up for all of the day's hardships. I was completely drained, but still felt content. Even so, I hadn't talked to anyone all day, and was looking forward to Brainerd.

I had hit my 300th mile, and would be in Brainerd on the following day. The trip was starting to seem doable. I took a black magic marker, and wrote 2,552 miles, Lake Itasca to New Orleans on the sides of my canoe in big bold letters. For the first time on my trip, I felt as if I could actually make it, and by writing on the canoe, I was crossing a line of no return. It always made me more eager to go on after people heard about what I was doing and got excited about it.

Although tired, I had found a new level of confidence. I sat around the fire watching the sunset as I scanned my little radio for baseball games. The hardest part of the trip was behind me, and a fun Memorial Day weekend in Brainerd awaited me. Things were really starting to come together.

CHAPTER 4: BRAINERD

DAY 13

With each new day, I was becoming more perceptive to my surroundings and the beauty all around me. Most people walk out their front door every morning and see the same old scene, drive to work on the same old road, and look out their office window at the same setting. I realized a new world was opening up in front of me every five minutes, to be in my life once and then gone forever. I enjoyed watching the sun set on a different horizon every night.

The boiled water in my canteen was really stale. If I mixed it with enough pink lemonade mix it was drinkable, but I was really getting sick of it. Just before the highway six bridge, I saw a bar on top of a hill my right, and walked up the rickety old wooden steps. It appeared to be vacant. An eighteen-hole croquet course was set up in the yard, and the whole place was decorated with Vikings and Packers regalia. I was starting to think it was actually a house. No one was home, so I borrowed some water from the hose and walked back down to the canoe.

A vehicle pulled up as I was setting off, and I went back up the steps to say hello. It was a house after all, but had developed into quite a party place. A sign on the shed boasted its nickname, Rivershack Greens. Monica Moore told me a whole bunch of crazy stories about the place, gave me a tour of the inside, and even played Eve of Destruction on her jukebox for me. She was about thirty-five, with curly blonde hair and thick glasses, and from talking to her and seeing her place, I guessed that her mission in life was to make sure everyone around her was having a blast. She was very friendly, and could really tell a story. My favorite was about two old retired guys from Alaska named Bud and Kermit who pulled up one day in a small boat and partied there for almost a week. She even showed me where they had carved their names into the wall. She and her boyfriend were really having a blast with life.

Back in the canoe, my morale was high again. I had my first interaction in two days, the canteen was full of fresh cool water, it was a nice warm day, and I was heading into Brainerd. My heart felt very pure, but I realized that with Brainerd would come sin and gin. Out on the river I was uninvaded by malicious thoughts, but get me into the city and my mind schemed almost as fast as my eyes wandered.

With the added current, the canoeing was easy and I felt stronger than the day before. I looked forward to meeting my friend Brad Eller on Rice Lake the next morning, and seeing my sister later in the day.

The river entered a narrow valley with high bluffs before it entered Rice Lake. The beautiful area was known as French Rapids, and was the first drastic change in landscape I'd encountered. I found an island in the middle of Rice Lake, hid my tent, stacked some wood for later, and paddled into Brainerd to enjoy the evening.

At Lum Park, I stashed my canoe in the weeds and walked into Brainerd. It was my first good-sized town, and I walked all over looking for a fishing pole. I was empty handed, and had a secret campsite about a mile away. I felt like I was on a secret mission or something. My canoe served as a conversation starter, and I was naked without it.

I didn't have any luck finding a pole, but ran into some interesting people. My favorites were two stoners playing Frisbee golf in a park. One looked just like the famous U.S. soccer player with the bright red hair and wild Go-T, and the other had so many hemp necklaces on I couldn't see how he even held his head up. We talked for five minutes, and no matter what I said, one or the other would reply, "Right on!" I guess "right on" was all inclusive stoner lingo that could be used to answer any question.

After walking all over, I was about to give up when I met some folks on their porch having a picnic. Three guys and three ladies were all dressed in black, and three Harleys sat proudly in the driveway. They seemed surprised when I interrupted dinner to ask to use their garden hose for water, but when they found out I was canoeing the river, we got into quite a conversation. One of the guys told me a story about how he and a friend had built a canoe in Brainerd and set out for New Orleans. It took them their whole senior year at Brainerd High School to build it in a shop class, and it was their pride and joy that was to take them on the adventure of a lifetime. The problem was that they packed it so full of beer that it broke in half before they made it to St. Cloud.

The guy who told the story went into his garage, got out one of his old poles and sold it to me for five dollars. It wasn't much, but would do the trick.

I passed a few bars on the way back, and although they caught my eye, I decided against it, wanting to make it back to my hidden spot on the island before dark. I called up some of my friends from a payphone, and got a chance to make plans on meeting Brad on the island either late that night, or early the next morning. After spending the morning fishing with him, I'd meet my sister Laura and her friend Paul at the dam at 2:00. With my plans in place, I fetched my canoe out of the weeds and set off.

The sun had just set as I began paddling toward my secret island. That was good, because it was practically in the middle of town, and I didn't know if I was supposed to be out there. By the time I pulled the canoe up on shore and got a tiny little fire going, it was pitch black. The wood was still damp from recent rains, and when I finally got it lit, I felt like I'd smoked out the entire town of Brainerd. I was sure the sirens would start ringing at any time, but eventually the wood dried out and the flames burned cleaner.

All settled in at my new home, I was lucky enough to find a radio station playing sets of the Grateful Dead. I looked out over the water at the million dollar homes straight across from me. My smoke was drifting right over to them, but they were probably all inside sleeping with their curtains pulled up anyway. I was hidden in the woods with a teeny little fire, cooking chili and listening to The Dead. I stared at the full moon silhouetted by my smoke, and sang along a bit to Ripple. The words seemed fitting.

> *And if you go*
> *No one may follow,*
> *That path is for,*
> *Your steps alone(G.D.).*

Looking out at all fancy houses with their rich, sleeping owners as I sat on my lifejacket and gobbled chili straight out of the can, I felt much more wealthy than anyone in the biggest of those houses could possible feel. I felt the tingle one gets during one of life's defining moments. No matter how hard things got or how much I felt like quitting, everything was worthwhile. I wasn't sure why I was out there, but deep inside my soul, I knew the river would lead me to something.

I stayed up late sitting around a small fire and watching the moon casually drift across the sky. After the music program was over, I listened to sports talk radio, but they started talking about pro wrestling, so I found Art Bell. He was saying something about the end of the world coming. I kept the fire going most of the night in case Brad showed up. He was unpredictable, and could show up any time between 11 p.m. and 11 a.m.

DAY 14

By 5:45 I was up in order to break camp and get ready for Eller. I built a fire, cooked breakfast, got my new fishing pole rigged up, and put all my expendable cold weather gear in a separate bag to send home with my sister. I was down to five cans of food to last until St. Paul, and would be depending more on fish for a few days.

Still waiting, I scanned the boat ramp with my binocs to see if I'd missed him, but there was no sign of his truck. I decided to be appreciative and cordial no matter how late he was. Although we were both stubborn and had silly misunderstandings in the past, he ranked right up there with Dale Radcliffe as the best fisherman I'd ever seen, and I loved fishing with him. That's the thing about guys, we could spend ten hours standing right next to each other and never really talk. You didn't have to worry about feelings and all that stuff, but may need a little help netting a fish.

Still waiting... that's why I liked traveling alone. "The man who goes alone can leave today, but he who waits for another must wait until the other fella is ready." I think Thoreau said something like that once. By noon I gave up, but at least I salvaged some solitude out of the day without paddling my ass off.

Sitting under a tree, I read for awhile, but was constantly interrupted by two little fox squirrels playing a game of who could get closest to me. They were getting braver and braver, running up, chuckling, and then running away to brag about how close they'd got. The wood ticks were thick on the island, and I had to roll up my pants and sleeves to keep them off me. I'd picked off over thirty since getting to Brainerd the night before.

At 1:00, I left for the Potlach Dam. Laura and Paul were meeting me on the right bank at 2:00, and I knew they would be on time. The right bank was covered in barbed wire and was all private property. It was 1:30, so I hid the canoe in the woods, grabbed my backpack, bag, and fishing pole, and walked up to the road hoping to catch them.

Sitting on the edge of the road in the hot sun with my bags spread out all around me, I was dirty, impatient, hot, frustrated, and felt like a vagabond hitchhiker. I hadn't had a shower in over two weeks, and it was by far the hottest day of the year so far. I wasn't sure what kind of car they might be driving, and I stared intensely at every driver so as not to miss them. It was remarkable how the people in every car averted their glances when I looked at them. They were probably afraid I needed help or something, and as long as they pretended like they didn't see me, they wouldn't have to feel guilty about breaking the Good Samaritan law. Most people are too afraid to ask a man if he needs help, especially when it is most obvious that he does.

As 4:00 rolled around, I had been sitting on the hot pavement for two and half hours with all of my earthly possessions spread out in front of me, and no one had even made eye contact. I'd been waiting for twenty-four hours. That darn Thoreau was right. Meanwhile, I was frying in the sun and still picking off ticks. A phone would have really came in handy, but I was out in the middle of nowhere, and had no idea which way to go. There was a highway in front of me, and a little road broke off and went down a hill away from the river just a few yards to my left.

Abandoning my things in the woods, I ventured down the little road to look for a resort. After walking about a mile, I finally found a lodge and reached Paul's cabin on the phone. By the time they showed up, I was dead tired, but it was my own fault. I had said the "right" side of the river. Any normal person would look at a map and take that to mean the East Side, but I was heading downstream, and was thinking of the West Side.

It was a relief to finally see them. Laura had a million things planned, but all I wanted to do was crash on the couch. "Don't you want to take a shower," she asked.

"No, I'm all right."

"Maybe you should take a shower." I got the hint, and after taking a shower and leaving a dark ring of grime on the white of the shower floor, I felt better and so did they.

We spent the evening fishing, relaxing, and talking, and they cooked me a big birthday meal of steak, corn, and watermelon. At dusk, Paul and I had a blast catching bass and northern while wading in the shadows of the lake. With the first hot day of the season, they were nailing anything that moved on top of the water.

Later that night other guests arrived, and as we sat around the picnic table, I found myself having a very difficult time relating to the conversations about work, cars, fashion, movies, and other everyday things. I had completely severed from all of those meaningless things, and it was impossible for me to carry such a conversation. It was great having people to talk to again, but I felt like a foreigner. I couldn't understand anything they were talking about.

After being as social as possible, I went to bed early. It was my first night in a nice, soft bed with blankets, and I couldn't sleep at all. Every time I closed my eyes I imagined drifting slowly downstream. When sleep overtook me, I dreamt I'd fallen asleep in the canoe, and woke up suddenly, looking around and wondering where I was.

DAY 15

After some early morning fishing with Paul and a big breakfast, I was completely rejuvenated, and craved the river again. My birthday was the following day, and it was nice to have my sister and Paul there to celebrate. Every year on my birthday, my sister bought me one new shirt. They made up my whole wardrobe, and if it weren't for her, I would have worn my old lucky flannel every day. I opened presents of Slim Jims, granola bars, and fishing lures. It was the first year she didn't give me a shirt. Paul even pulled some buzzbaits from his own box, since he knew how I loved fishing topwater.

After an easy portage, I was back in the water by 11:00. I fought a strong south wind all day, but was fully replenished and re-supplied, and felt peaceful and patient.

Before I left, I made the mistake of looking at maps of both Minnesota and the United States. I'd been paddling for two hard weeks and hadn't even dented the state. A look at the national map was even more depressing. The map was two feet wide, and I couldn't even fit my thumb between Lake Itasca and Brainerd.

Paddling out of Brainerd against a stiff south wind, I couldn't imagine making it all the way to New Orleans. The wind was really working me over, and I would've stopped for the day if I hadn't lost a full day of paddling the day before. I took consolation in the fact that I was over half way to Iowa. After sweating out another long counting cycle, I made it past Fort Ripley. The wind was still strong, but the current had picked up tremendously. I could finally drift without paddling, and for the first time, the river was starting to look like the mighty Mississippi as I knew it.

The sun slowly set as several deer stood along the rocky shoreline to drink. From one hundred yards away I locked eyes with one. Our eyes remained deadlocked as I drifted in to him, all the way to ten yards away. He stared at me as if to see if I could answer any questions in his young mind, and I looked at him as if he might be able to do the same for me. I tried to telepath everything I knew about being a human, and in the same moment tried to imagine being a deer. We were starting to drift away from one another, but he still hadn't flinched, and neither had I. The sound of a car approached in the distance, and the moment it came into view on a nearby road, he bolted.

I made it to Fletcher's Creek by dark. Happy voices carried over the river from campfires on the other side. It was Saturday night and I was restless to look for a good time at the campground, but I knew it would be better to stay and chill out. I welcomed in my twenty-fifth year at midnight, enjoying the solitude around the fire.

MAY 30TH, 1999 DAY 16

Waking up, I realized I'd been labeled with another year of expectations. At twenty-five, I was still young enough to get away with acting a little irresponsible, but those times were slipping away with the river. At twenty, I figured that in five years I'd be married and making the big bucks. I was so much older then. Maybe it was my last hurrah after all. Then again, maybe it was just my first.

I wanted to be a better person during the next year, not sin so much. Not sinning was like balancing a dictionary on your head. It could be easy for a few minutes, then try going to a party with a book on your head.

Although the current was swift, the south wind was even more overpowering than the day before. I wasn't sure if I had the strength or ambition to fight it all day again.

At Little Falls, the dam was raging. Little groups of people were all enjoying the little trees and paved walkways. Quite the wilderness experience. They all looked at me like I was insane as I struggled to make the long portage in two grueling trips. I took the canoe off my shoulders to rest a few times and looked around at all the people, but they seemed to be doing a good job of ignoring me. I struggled to load the canoe with all of my gear as it was being pounded on the rocks in the flooded water. Several people were sitting just a few yards away, yet nobody was bold enough to initiate a conversation. All I wanted was to talk to someone on my birthday, but the body language of all the little subgroups of people screamed at me to stay away. All eyes watched as I launched, gambling on if I would capsize in the turbulent water. I wanted to stop for lunch, but could only spend one dollar in the next week in order to get back on budget.

Flying along on top of the fast water out of town, I passed a field of geese with their new goslings. They strutted around the field with their new offspring, usually between four and seven young ones. The scene reminded me of the people in the park. A couple in the corner stuck out like sore thumbs. They only had one gosling, and it was small, deformed, and hopped on one leg. They took a few steps and waited patiently for it to keep up, but were obviously separated from the rest of the group. Were they ashamed? I paddled away, wondering if the young goose would ever make it.

The south wind was brutal, making the day before seem like cake. It took me three tough hours of paddling to make five miles on the wide part of the river before Blanchard Dam. The last mile before the dam was nearly impossible. It felt like trying to paddle through cement, and if I stopped, I went backwards. I couldn't feel my arms. Why didn't I stop? I could see the dam. Why didn't I just quit? It would get easier after the dam. I wasn't even moving. It was pure hellish pain on my back and shoulders, but somehow I made it to the dam.

After a tough portage over slippery rocks, I took a break before braving the dangerous currents below the falls. Water flew ten feet in the air. The place looked like the middle of the ocean during a typhoon. I was afraid to put my canoe into the water, but it was the only place to begin my portage. After planning a route in the dangerous water, I got thrashed around for ten seconds before struggling forward to smoother water.

Just south of the dam, I caught my first fish in several days, a huge nineteen-inch smallmouth bass. I never would have even considered keeping such a beauty, but I was very hungry. I had set out in the morning with the intention of having fish for dinner, and it was my only bite all day. Reluctantly, I tied it to the canoe, where it became my paddling companion for the next ten miles. I kept looking down into the water, expecting it to be belly up, but every time I looked down it was swimming right along beside the canoe, as if it was helping me paddle.

The wind was still relentless, and besides a few granola bars, I hadn't eaten all day. At 6:00 I stopped at an island to rest and have dinner. I'd spent the day admiring that beautiful bass, and it was hard to kill it. We had been moving along side by side for so long that it was a partner to me. I thought about throwing it back, but the fire was stoked, and I was hungry. After thanking the fish for allowing me to eat it, I cleaned it, wrapped it in tin foil, and threw it right in the fire. It made a delicious shore lunch.

It was still windy, and I thought about camping for the night, but I was in hardcore mode. I had come to the conclusion that no matter how hard it was or how much it hurt, I was going to make over thirty miles each day. Back on the river, it was still windy, but there was good current. I was too tired to do much paddling, so I drifted most of the final ten miles before dark.

Approaching a campground, I stayed close to shore, hoping to talk to some friendly people on the eve of Memorial Day. All I got was ridicule from drunk after drunk. One guy threw a few rocks, not trying to hit me, but seeing how close he could come without hitting me. I hoped someone would invite me over for a beer, but they were hesitant to even wave, and if they did, it was without smiling.

Storm clouds moved in, and I paddled like a madman for the last mile in order to beat the rain to a free campsite near Stearns Park. I had to walk a few hundred yards back to the park in the rain to get water, but it felt good. I'd paddled a tough thirty-two miles, had broken 400 on the trip, and was closing in on Minneapolis. There was a new confidence growing in me. My body was getting stronger and my mind more focused. The day was one of my toughest, but as I sat in the tent and listened to the rain pound the top of my tent, I felt like it was all worth it. If I had made thirty-two miles against a brutal south wind, how far could I go on a calm day?

DAY 17

It felt like a truck ran over me as my body ached from the exertion of the previous two days. I paddled myself numb in the cool light mist to make ten miles to the Sartell Dam in a record time of two hours. I was down to crumbs for food, and could only spend a dollar all week. After spending the morning considering pushing my budget up from three to four dollars a day, I decided against it.

The Sartell dam was enraged, and after a long, tiring portage, I started out below. I faced fast and furious water that

54

pounded into the rocks on the right shore. The river made a quick turn to the left eighty yards downstream and a point jutted out. The water was quick, but if I could paddle out far enough to avoid the point I'd be on my way.

Starting out with all I had, I soon realized my feeble attempts to paddle were not working too well. I could not keep the canoe straight in the swirling water. Eighty yards became twenty as I headed straight for the rocks. Paddling with all my might, I made it around the point, only to be swung sideways in the downstream back eddy. I went over a big roller sideways, and was finished.

As I flew out of the canoe, I didn't even think of my safety. I needed to save my gear. In one fast motion, I righted the canoe. The gear was all tied down, and nothing was lost, but I was being thrashed downstream in the rapids. My legs and knees bounced off rocks as I clung desperately to the canoe, trying to keep it from flipping over as we raced downstream. After about 100 yards the current slowed, and I swam with the canoe back to shore. Somehow, my paddle found its way to me, and I snagged it as it went by.

Draining the water from my things, I realized how lucky I was. Although I was soaked and freezing, and all of my things were wet, I was unhurt and hadn't lost anything. I felt like quitting for the day and drying off, but had to get through Sauk Rapids and St. Cloud first.

Two miles downstream, I came to the part on my map that said: Danger. Class III Rapids. Warning. Can be Treacherous in High Water. Scout Before Proceeding. As I approached Sauk Rapids, the ripples were soon upon me, and I skillfully maneuvered around them. Reaching the end, I let out a little victory shout, and took a much-needed break. It wasn't nearly as bad as I expected, and I congratulated myself for getting better.

Looking up from my book, I noticed an orange sign I'd passed that was getting smaller and smaller. Pulling out my binocs, it was hard to read because of my shivering, but it appeared to be a warning sign. A roaring sound stole my attention. I was within one hundred yards of a bigger set of rapids than the one that had flipped me. I was smack dab in the middle of the river, closing in fast, and had no chance of turning back.

Trying to remember everything I'd ever learned about canoeing all at once, I sped forward, feeling like Nikolay Rostov charging to Napoleon's front line. I raced past huge boulders just over the surface that created small waterfalls behind them. Any one would surely rip my canoe in half. At times the water went left, then spiraled into an eddy and raced to the right. Waves larger than Winnie crashed into my canoe, filling it full of water and spraying me. My entire trip depended on keeping my canoe straight, a little to either side and I was cooked.

Soon I saw the final obstacle. I faced a wall of water from the right bank to almost the left shore with water crashing down below it and cycloning downstream. I paddled hard to make the left bank, but it was no use. The front end submerged for a split second as I went over, then shot straight up as the rear dipped. The canoe wanted to back up in the eddy, but I spent every ounce of energy to propel it forward. Then it was all over. Looking back at the whitewater and listening to it get quieter was chilling.

I paddled two miles to the St. Cloud Dam with my canoe full of water, where I met Wayne and Henry. They both had that young, intelligent, corporate, wheeler-dealer look, but were unbelievably friendly and genuine. Their family was having a Memorial Day picnic, and when they saw me get out, they got up from their picnic table to say hello. I was dripping wet and shivering. After filling me up on chicken, helping me dry out and portage, and restoring my hope in humanity, they waved goodbye as I maneuvered some turbulent water below the dam and disappeared around the corner.

For the rest of the day the river was ideal. I was done pushing myself; the current was quick enough to do most of the work. The river was no longer a little crick that winded around in circles in northern Minnesota, it was a major river moving in a straight line to the south. A big map of Minnesota revealed marks where I'd camped every night, and the gaps between black lines were starting to grow as I inched my way toward Iowa.

At Clear Lake, I met some people on shore and spent some time answering questions about my trip and talking to their kids about fishing. The adults were savoring the end of their long weekend and lamented going back to work in the morning. They felt sorry for me for being alone. I explained that while they were all in the office, I'd be drifting down the river reading, fishing, listening to the radio, and watching wildlife. They filled me up on pizza and sent me on my way.

I paddled hard to make Monticello before dark, covered forty-four miles on the day. Everything was damp, but I shivered myself into a dreamless sleep after ten minutes of clanging teeth.

JUNE 1ST, 1999 DAY 18

It was rainy and windy with an expected high of forty-seven. I wished I still had my coveralls. I stopped at a Holiday store in Monticello and grabbed a few donuts with my last dollar, got out of the rain, and warmed up. I wore my twelve-year-old lucky flannel, army pants, three-week beard, and carried my canteen around. The store manager watched me with his beady little mouse eyes, and when I lingered awhile to eat my donuts, he pointed me to the picnic table across the street at DQ, in the rain.

Back in the canoe shivering, a light rain turned into a drenching mist that never subsided all day. After being wet for so long, I couldn't have gotten any wetter. If God would've given me one wish, I'd have wished to see the sun. I constantly surveyed the sky for specks of blue, but they never came.

At Anoka, I stopped at a hotel to warm up, but the manager was an angry old prick and chased me back out into the rain. I wanted to make a few calls at the payphone outside, but I was too cold to dial and felt unwanted. My only ambition was to make it past the Coon Rapids Dam, crawl into my damp sleeping bag, and try to warm up.

At the dam marking the entrance to the twin cities, I finished a muddy portage but sliced my hand open on a lid trying to scarf down a cold can of a chili. I was so tired I heaved all of my things into the canoe in a big pile. My stuff was filthy and so was I, but I didn't care. Some guys were wetting a line in the mist below the dam.

"How's fishing?"

"It's fun, haven't you ever tried it?" The other guys laughed hysterically at the wittiness of their fearless, beer-guzzling leader. I was sick of running into assholes, and kept moving. "Hey, you're goin' the wrong way. Row row row your boat." The words trailed off as I paddled away.

Just south of the dam, I found a little island, and after checking it for pirates, I hung up my clothes to dry and set up the tent. Curled up in a ball in my sleeping bag trying to get warm, I could hear the sounds of the city. Hidden from shore, listening to the hum of the interstate, I felt like an escaped convict.

I listened to my favorite Minneapolis radio station, but the alternative music I loved just weeks before didn't have the same ring to it. It was all part of the cesspool that the downward spiral led to. It was the darkness I was paddling away from. After a miserable night's sleep, I was looking forward to morning, and hoping for sunshine.

Chapter 5: Minneapolis/St. Paul

Day 19

With everything I owned still dripping from the rain and recent capsize, the weather was cruel enough to dip down near freezing. Too cold to sleep, I turned on WCCO radio before dawn, hoping for a favorable forecast. By 7:30, it was still only forty degrees, but they were expecting a warm-up later. After doing some push-ups to get the blood flowing, I broke camp quickly and paddled into Minneapolis.

It had warmed up to forty-six degrees as I entered the industrial heart of the state. Big hunks of iron were dropped into barges by a big crane, followed by the delayed sound of the clank as it hit the target. After spending nearly three weeks and rarely seeing anyone on the water, I was dodging my first towboats. I felt like Tarzan on his first trip to the city. From there on, I'd have to share the river with commerce, and already felt like I was in their way. My first glimpse of the skyline was a big rush. It was perfectly silhouetted under every bridge I crossed and the buildings grew with each mile.

At St. Anthony's Falls, I went through my first set of locks. The lockmaster guided me right in and gave me some information about dealing with barges and locks.

"Don't see too many guys canoeing this river alone," the old river veteran said, "Why don't you get a dog or something?"

"Gotta feed it." Our conversation was short as the lock was being emptied and I sunk away from his platform. At fifty-five feet, the first lock had the biggest drop on the whole river. Alone in my canoe at the bottom of the giant chamber, I swore the slimy concrete walls were closing in on me. A few minutes later, a horn tooted, the gates slowly opened, and I was back on my way. Lower St. Anthony's Falls was also quick, as the lockmaster from the upper falls radioed ahead to let them know I was coming.

Being a small town guy, I hoped there'd be no rough areas of the city I'd have to paddle through. An old homeless man was wrapped in a blanket under the Hennepin Avenue Bridge.

I'd heard horror stories about the street and its drug dealers and prostitutes, and wasn't about to stop and ask questions.

"Comeer," he requested as I closed in. "Where ya headed?" He was very old, and had sharp, prickly, gray hairs covering his protruding chin. He was very frail and looked harmless, so I treaded water and held my ground.

"New Orleans," I answered, surprised at my own firmness. I had been asked that question from the start, and was usually pretty hesitant to claim I was destined for New Orleans. Often I'd replied with some non-descriptive statement like "as far as I can get," or "until I quit having fun."

"Yes!" He flashed me a dirty toothed smile, reached into his pocket and pulled something out. I didn't know what it was, but for some reason I felt like I could trust him. "You'll need this more than I do," he predicted, flashing a handful of change. He wouldn't take no for an answer, so I took his only fifty-three cents and headed down river, remembering his kindness and generosity.

At Lock and Dam #1, I had a bit of a wait, so I tied my canoe up to the ten-foot wall on the shore of the City Park. I had been waiting all morning to find a secluded spot to use the bathroom. There was a ledge on the side of the wall to stand on, so after making sure no one could see me, I climbed onto the narrow ledge and pissed while balancing precariously on the side of the wall.

"Whatcha doin down there." Interrupted in midstream, I jumped so quickly I nearly fell backwards into the river. I was shocked to look up and see two ladies above me on top of the wall with city worker shirts on. They were as startled as I was. After getting over the initial suddenness of our chance encounter, we had a conversation, I in my canoe and them on their wall. Cheryl and Mary looked at me like I was an orphaned poodle as they asked question after question about my daily activities. I told them the story of the homeless guy under the bridge and how he had given me his last fifty-three cents. It must have touched their charity buttons, because they wished me luck and threw thirteen dollars into my canoe from the top of the wall.

Putting graffiti on the side of the canoe wasn't a bad idea after all. Since Brainerd, people had read it, flagged me down, and helped me out. Did I really look like I was in that bad of shape? It was time to retire the old lucky flannel and give myself a shave. Even so, I had made nearly a week's worth of spending money and was elated to be back on budget. The wheels in my head spun in anticipation of future donations.

After Lock and Dam #1, the river carried me through a string of city parks where I was bombarded by questions.

"Where to?"

"All the way."

"Yeah!"

"Great trip!"

"Best of Luck!" The questions were all the same and the answers similar, but the shouts of encouragement made me feel like a new man. I no longer hesitated to declare my intentions for New Orleans. I'd paddled 500 miles and knew I could make it.

Traveling through the Twin Cities, I must have seen hundreds of friendly waves. They may have been just being cordial, but for me they had become part of my adventure, and their faces and kind gestures would be etched in my mind forever. My trip was building momentum, and I was becoming stronger with each friendly wave, each passing mile, and each yell from shore of encouragement. With all the yells of "good luck," I must have been the luckiest guy in the world.

At Harriet Park in St. Paul, I met my parents for lunch. Although I was mentally sound, I was dirty, had lost a few pounds, and looked like hell. The worry I'd caused them reflected on their faces. We had a quick lunch, the conversation focusing on everything I'd missed while I was away. The problem was that I'd destroyed all of that in my mind. My slate was wiped clean, and I was only nineteen days old. My father had convinced himself I was only going as far as the Iowa border and was taking the trip as a fun little break from the stresses of reality. I thought of it as destroying everything artificial in my life and facing the ultimate reality. He pictured me back home in some cushy little corporate job within a month, and kept making references to spending the rest of the summer golfing together and going to ballgames.

"Just think. What an accomplishment, seven hundred miles on the river." It was no surprise we were not exactly connecting.

Winding between barges through the industrial section of St. Paul provided a quick dose of reality. Moored barges covered the entire shoreline, and it was hard to predict the movements of the heavy towboat traffic I encountered for the first time. It was not my river anymore; it belonged to commerce. Everywhere I looked I was surrounded by iron. Airplanes buzzed over me, trains whistled by, barges chugged along beside me, and the constant hum of the interstate covered the noises of nature. I felt like a mouse among men, as if I was in the way and about to be squashed at any second. How could I survive another 1,700 miles?

That familiar smell of the river was back. It was a combination of birth, death, and oil. I was afraid of the barges a bit, but always tried to get their attention when they powered past. I waved like a stupid little kid, hoping they would remember my little green canoe for the rest of the summer as I made my way south.

Elated to be dry and through the Cities, I camped on an island chain ten miles south of St. Paul. Three dogs on a nearby island kept me up all night barking at their own echoes bouncing off the limestone bluffs of Grey Cloud Island.

DAY 20

It was tough going in the morning. With the locks, the river was no longer free, but had become a series of lakes. Approaching Lock & Dam #2 at Hastings, the wind was so brutal that if I stopped paddling I went backwards. The current was non-existent in the wide stretch of river before the dam.

It was really tough to move. One inch at a time I moved forward. I had to make it to the dam. I set a tree on shore as a goal, then a rock, and then a buoy. Every time I reached a new goal, I rewarded myself with a cracker and set a new one. If I could get to the dam it would be all right. Keep paddling. I was almost there. As I was in the height of my pain, I suddenly imagined I could smell a carnival going on. I could definitely smell cotton candy, but there was nothing around, and I had no idea where it might be coming from. It must have been just my imagination, but it was so distinct.

I tried using the shoreline to my left as a windbreak, but the wind was plotting against me. After paddling like crazy for two hours, I rested on the only sandy spot along the riprap. A ladybug balanced vicariously on a stick, nearly getting swamped by the waves as they crashed onto the sandbar. What in the world are you doing out here little lady bug? It looked up to me as if it was asking me the same question.

After paddling four furious hours to go ten miles, I made it through the locks. It wasn't much easier on the other side of the gates. The wind had gotten even stronger, and the little bit of current I had was not enough to let me drift without paddling.

Joining the St. Croix River was a big milestone; I had made it to my second favorite state. Prescott, Wisconsin was full of fancy pleasure craft, and I slipped through the constant flow of huge boats to make it over to the gas docks to get water. At the dock, I met a girl named Katie. She had bleached spiky hair and a ring through her nose. Katie took a break from lounging on her lawn chair long enough to peak over the top of her dark sunglasses over her romance novel to give me a look of indifference.

I put on my best alternative approach, but came off sounding negative and cynical. She ended up being highly intelligent and ambitious, just real laid back. We chatted awhile but never really clicked, so I waved goodbye and hit the rough river again, feeling the throes of rejection.

It was a painful day of paddling, but I filled my thirty-mile quota and made it to Treasure Island Casino to meet my parents. Looking forward to the monster, all you can eat buffet, I had starved myself all day except a few crackers. I ate so much food I could barely walk away from the table to get up to the hotel room. I'd lost ten pounds, but gained all ten back at the buffet. I thought my stomach was going to explode.

I didn't like the idea of staying in a hotel, but it made my parents happy, so I obliged. They went downstairs to gamble, but I couldn't move. Watching the weather to prepare for Lake Pepin, I was disappointed to discover major storms were expected in the next few days, with constant winds from the southeast. Pepin was going to be bad. Lake Pepin was five miles wide and about twenty-five miles long. The bluffs on either side had the uncanny ability to funnel the wind, giving it the reputation for eating small boats.

I scanned stations, hoping for a more favorable second opinion on the weather, but my thoughts drifted back to the river. I thought about all of the big boats at the Prescott Marina, staring at me like I was in their way. I thought of all the big shots down at the buffet and in the casino. I remembered walking through the hotel lobby barefoot with my backpack, and the kids who were my age looking at me with condescension.

I felt sorry for most people my age. Graduating from college, most thought they had to run out and get that high paying job, and have it all wrapped up by June 1st. Then they spend the next few years as clones in some big city's safe suburban areas, working all day behind some damn computer with a job title nobody understands, wishing it was 5:00 so they could go to happy hour. Then they go home, sit in their new Lazy-Boy, watching the same feeling-robbing television shows as everyone else, thinking the same thoughts, getting fat and old.

> *I love my neighbor,*
> *Long as he*
> *Be not better than me.*
> *Or drive a better car*
> *Or have a better job,*
> *For we all know*
> *That is what makes the man.*

My generation is the only one in the history of the planet never to face a major life-threatening catastrophe or worry about going to war. They are safe and snug in their little computer cubicles, answering to some fat-ass boss who has been kissing butts for twenty years by saying all of the properly programmed things, yet can barely bend over to tie his own shoes. The boss was on cloud nine; his two weeks of annual vacation were coming up. It's off to the beach with his nagging wife. That year they'd decided to go to the more elite club. No riff-raff, just highly distinguished individuals like themselves, highly schooled in manners, etiquette, and other general falsehood. These thoughts swam through my head as I drifted off to sleep before 9:00.

DAY 21

Awake at 5:00, I looked out the window to discover it was already gusty from the southeast. Pepin ran straight southeast, so it was the worst possible direction the wind could come from. With no need to rush to Pepin only to wait, I went back to sleep. By 9:00 it was already raining, and the forecast called for storms and strong winds for the next two days. By 11:00, it let up a tad. I started off, hoping to get to the edge of Pepin before dark where I could set up camp and wait for calm water.

I tried to look as skillful as possible as I left the friendly people at Treasure Island Marina who had let me store my things for free. It was tough paddling, and nearly impossible to keep my canoe straight in the wind.

Getting pounded in the stiff south breeze and taking in water from the waves, I finally made it to Lock & Dam #3 in Red Wing. It was an ugly day that promised bad weather. Using my hands to work my way along the concrete wall to the signal chord, I nearly jumped out of my skin after coming face to face with a six-foot snake. It hung from the red ladder at the locks, and had draped itself over the rope I needed to pull to signal to the lockmaster. I had no clue what kind of snake it was, and no intentions of finding out. After five minutes of flailing my arms, I caught the attention of the lockmaster, and he let me through.

After the dam, the waves hammered me so badly I was forced to bypass Red Wing, and go down a chute on the Wisconsin side which offered the day's only refuge from the wind. I wanted to see the town, but it was near home and I'd been there before.

A chain of islands on my right shielded me from the wind as my narrow chute gradually opened up to Lake Pepin. I came around the end of the last island and was nearly swamped. Huge whitecaps covered my entire field of vision. It was the end of the line. Backtracking the island chain, I watched for high enough ground to set up camp. Everything was either swamp or mud. After paddling around inside the flooded timber and debris of the island until it got too shallow, I set out on foot and tromped around in the mud. I finally found sand on the south side of the island, just off the main channel.

My 200-yard portage took three squooshy trips through the mud. Both shoes got stuck in the mud and I walked right out of them. My hands were too full of gear to stop, and it was too muddy to put it down, so I made a mental note and continued on with bare feet. After setting up, there was nothing left to do except sit frustrated and wait. With strong storms on the way, it looked like I'd be stuck for awhile. Déjà vu of Winnie. I felt like a convict trapped on Alcatraz.

What in the hell was I doing there? Where would I be if I wasn't there? Probably just somewhere else I hated. I couldn't find anything in life I loved to do. Everyone on earth was put there for a reason, but they must have forgotten about me. Everybody walked around with those stupid smiles all day, and I just didn't understand what there was to be so happy about. What in the hell was wrong with me anyway? I'd sit around in my canoe alone and look around at the pretty trees and clouds and get all peaceful and happy and jolly until the world was just one big sweet fucking cupcake, and then I'd get around people and I hated everyone. I'd look at them and think of their pitiful lives and how meaningless everything was, but then I looked at myself. What was I doing to help anybody? Why was the earth any better because I happened to dwell on it? I was just like them, but a million times worse. At least they could walk around and pretend, but I was nothing but a grouchy old hypocrite. What's the fucking point?

Imprisoned on my muddy island, I imagined the world was over and I was the last man alive. A call from my parents on the cell phone shattered that illusion, but it wouldn't keep the signal long enough for them to hear me. After finding a spot on the island where the phone worked, I found out they had pinpointed my location, and were on the mainland straight across from me waving their arms up and down.

Selfishly, I was a bit perturbed at the security break to my inner world, and was less than cordial on the phone. I realized I was acting immature and defensive, but when you're pretending you're the only man alive and look up and see your parents waving their arms on the other side of the river, it takes something away from the whole idea. I realized they were worried and just want to be part of the trip, but seeing them every day for the last three days had become overwhelming. They'd given me a lot and helped me in numerous ways, but I didn't know how to show any appreciation.

I pretended the trip down the river was my new life, my new reality, and that everything before May 15th did not exist. My whole life depended on getting to New Orleans, and when it seemed so hopeless I had a hard time coping. I came into the world and would die, but I needed to do something to make my mark. I needed to do something great, something meaningful, something that could never be taken away from me.

> I'm gonna find my way
> To the sun.
> If I destroy myself
> I will shine on (Bush).

I was completely miserable. I'd bitten my fingernails since I was a little kid, but had gone three whole weeks without touching them. I could peel off tape; I could scratch an itch on my back; I could pick a woodtick out of my scalp.

I gnawed off three weeks of fingernails. I chewed and chewed and chewed until three of my fingers were bleeding. My whole body was full of mud and blood, and my mind was choked in desperation. I hadn't touched a drop of alcohol since Palisade, ten full days. Had I ever gone ten days without drinking? The streak was over, and an empty bottle of vodka lay at my feet. A storm was on the way, and I could care less if a tornado came down from the sky and took me away. I had lost each and every scrap of peace I'd ever acquired. Why did people like me all die so young?

I had brought along a cigar that had been reserved for the Iowa border, but it seemed like the time to smoke it. After being ready to jump in the canoe at 11 p.m. and say, "who cares," my head began to level. JD Salinger once wrote something about being foolish and dying nobly for a bad cause, or deciding to live humbly for a good one. I guess I wasn't as scared of dying as I was of not getting to New Orleans, and I had to stay alive at least long enough to do that. As for living humbly, that seemed like quite a leap.

Getting a fire going long enough to cook chili, I put a log into the fire, only to see ants scatter and die in the flames. They ran in circles panicking, when all they had to do was run back down the log to safety. I felt bad for killing so many ants, and decided I'd choose my logs more carefully, so as not to cause any more world-ending cataclysms.

I was making too many rules for myself. After averaging thirty-five miles in each of the last eleven days, I was only able to make thirteen on the day, and the fact I missed thirty was killing me. It was time to slow down and enjoy myself. What did it matter if I was stranded on Pepin for a few days? Where the hell did I have to go anyway? What did it matter if it took me a year to get to New Orleans? I needed to chill out and enjoy the ride. Still, it really sucked to be stuck in the middle of nowhere. I wished I was on shore, and man, I wished I had a beer.

DAY 22

I was up by 4:00 in the morning. It was still pitch black, but I could already hear the wind. Scanning the radio, they promised a major storm was on the way. It hit at 5:30 with tremendous rain, wind, thunder, and lightning. By 6:30 it was gone, the water had calmed slightly, and I was on the river. Making it to the Minnesota shore offered some protection from the increasing wind; I'd go as far as possible until it was too dangerous.

"Hey there! How'd you survive that storm?"

"Barely."

"Where ya headed?"

"New Orleans."

"You got a long ways to go son." By his tone, the way he emphasized the word long, it was like telling me I had no idea what I was getting into. Waving the old nameless fisherman along, I was soon at the Old Frontenac boat ramp. Although it was only 9:00, the wind was picking up, and I knew I couldn't get much farther. By Long Point, I turned a corner, only to be stopped by huge whitecaps and overpowering winds. I was stranded again. Calling my parents on the cell, we decided to meet for lunch.

After stashing my canoe on Long Point and getting lost in stinging nettles and heavy brush, I made it to Highway 61, just as they were completing their half-hour drive. Trying my hardest to avoid confrontation, I lasted five minutes. The trip had become "my mission," and I was too stubborn to accept any caution, worries, or advice. Claiming I was obsessed and about to get myself killed, we had it out in the restaurant. I couldn't handle the meteors crashing into the atmosphere of my fantasy world.

After promising not to put myself into any life-threatening situations, I needed to be left alone for awhile, and walked back in the woods near Frontenac. Finding a trail through the swamp, I ran into a man named Trapper who'd lost his dogs.

"They're like my kids," he explained as he gave me a collar, some favorite toys, and promised me fifty dollars and a steak dinner if I found them. I spent three hours walking through swamps, streams, and poison nettles calling "Gretchen," "Hunter," before I gave up. On the way back I came across a newborn fawn that was too small to move and just stared at me, wondering if I was his mother. By 6:00, the wind was stronger than ever, the area was under a tornado watch, and I was too tired to walk around the woods any longer. The day of unsuccessful searching was tough on Trapper. I couldn't help but compare him to my parents, and me to his dogs. The look on his sad face helped me to empathize with their worrying.

It was Saturday night, I was stuck in the middle of nowhere with a tornado bearing down on me, and I was lonely as hell. I called my buddy Rob Gilbert in Alma, and he arranged for Brian (Richie) Cunningham, my college roommate and friend from Winona State, to pick me up on the way from the cities for a night of partying at Rob's.

We set up a time to meet on Highway 61; I stashed all of my things, chained the canoe to a big tree, and headed down the mosquito-infested swamp toward the road. It was nearly dark, and the mosquitoes were so thick they nearly carried me off. Smacking my face with my hat to fend them off, I ran the whole mile back through the mud.

By dusk, the rains hit. Lightning filled the sky, and I was sure a tornado was going to whiz me away to Oz at any moment. I paced the side of the road in the pouring rain, wondering if he would see me in the dark, wet night. It was pitch black, and I felt silly and afraid of getting run over by a car, yet the defiant words of Bon Scott filled my mind as cars whizzed by and splashed me with water.

> *Well you can stick your nine to five living, and your*
> *.... collar and your tie.*
> *You can stick your moral standards, cause it's*
> *.... all a dirty lie.*
> *You can stick your golden handshake*
> *Stick your simian rules*
> *And all the other shit*
> *.... that they teach the kids in school*
> *Cause I ain't no fool (ACDC).*

A horn honked, and Richie pulled up. We drove to Alma amidst the heaviest part of the storm as the radio warned us about tornado touchdowns in bordering counties. We always played tricks on Richie because he was such a good sport. He had a knack for finding the action, always had something up his sleeve, and no party was the same without him. He was always on the lookout for something crazy to do, and the ladies were quite fond of him.

We pulled into Rob's, and were warmly greeted by a couple of cold beers. Rob was the perfect party host. He was unselfish, listened to great music, and would truly be upset if anyone weren't having the time of their life. If he threw a bash, he pulled out all the stops, buying a million unnecessary things, and never accepting any contributions.

At Rob's, we pounded beers, shot the shit, and watched an amazing lightning storm illuminate the dark river. We were all up for a mellow night, so we strolled over to the Red Ram, a local haunt conveniently located across the street, and spent the night playing pool, drinking, and unsuccessfully looking for women. The pizza Richie bought made a great Frisbee in the wet streets, and although the toppings were a bit lopsided, it saved my life at 2:00. Too bad for Richie, he fell asleep while it was cooking. We must have forgotten to wake him up. I forgot about the river for a night.

DAY 23

Struggling to peel myself off the couch as my head pounded furiously, I awoke to strong southeast winds with more heavy storms on the way. My friends had treated all night, and I drank a lot more than I hoped to. I wasn't going anywhere, so I decided to be a bum. We hung out all day on the couches, watching movies and vegetating. After watching Saving Private Ryan, I thought about how cake my life really was.

I'd had hangovers before, but this one wasn't normal. I could barely move. By 5:00, I was starting to feel guilty from being away from the river; it felt like I was cheating or something. When Richie headed out for the cities I was ready to catch a ride with him back to Pepin, but Rob convinced me to stay due to my ailing condition and another tornado watch. We decided to drive to Winona and go see the new Star Wars. I had lived there for six years, and had been looking forward to a triumphant entrance into Bullseye Beerhall. Instead, we went to the movie incognito. I felt like I was going to die.

It was hard to concentrate on the movie, but I took one major thing from it. It may sound corny, but I needed to learn how to use the force. I needed to meditate on being connected to the eternal source, the divine love embracing everything. I was so confused about everything I was bouncing off walls. My life was so patchy and inconsistent. I didn't have any clue what I was even doing half the time.

The ride back to Winona was hell. I wasn't sure if I was going to puke or pass out. My head was swimming to stay awake, my fingers were tingling, and I couldn't feel my legs. Rob had to return a keg to some guy's bus from a bachelor party, and we drove all over Fountain City looking for the bus. Fountain City was a typical river town, nestled between the river and the bluffs. It was only about two blocks wide. How in the hell did they lose a bus? My whole body was in agony, and my energy level was down to zero. As we searched sidestreets, I kept thinking about the force, and looking for the bus. What was the point of drinking like that?

The last thing I remember was struggling up a few flights of stairs. I was sleeping in my shoes within seconds of hitting the couch.

I awoke in my canoe. It was pitch black, there were flashing lights all around me, a bell was ringing, and I was overwhelmed by a terrible roaring sound. It felt like I was being sucked into some sort of hydraulic tunnel in the river, and was about to be minced. I couldn't find my paddle anywhere. There was nothing I could do to avoid being drawn into the empty blackness. I yelled, then the train went by, the street lights out by the river stopped flickering, and I realized I was still in the apartment on the couch.

DAY 24

6:00 came too quick, as Rob needed to bring me back to my canoe before he went to work. I snoozed the whole way to Frontenac. Before I knew it, I was hiking through the mosquito-ridden swamp in a daze, hoping all my gear was intact.

The wind was very strong again, but luckily it was straight at my back. The waves were treacherous, and I couldn't stay pointed straight without my backend swinging around sideways. I paddled as long as I could, but it was so frustrating I spent most of the day slowly drifting with the wind. The waves were growing by the hour, and I learned that if I kept my canoe straight for long enough and paddled hard, I could catch a big wave and ride it very fast, just like a surfboard. It was extremely dangerous, and after two close calls where I nearly capsized, I decided not to risk a third. Although I would have stopped for the day if I were smart, I was so sick of being stranded I hung on tight and let the wind slowly push me across the killer lake.

After seven nervous hours, I covered the final fifteen miles and was out of Lake Pepin. It felt unbelievably great knowing I had just passed another major obstacle. Pepin was the scene of one of my worst moments. It was the bully in school that haunted my mind for the last three years.

In August of 1996, I hastily stripped the motor off of my Alumicraft, and was dropped off on Pepin by my friend, Tim. I was sick of my dull life, and on the spur of the moment had decided to use the oars on my boat to row and drift my way to New Orleans. There was no planning involved, and all I brought along were some beans, Ramen noodles, a couple of gallons of water, a tent, a rifle, fishing equipment, sleeping bag, and a fat bag of weed. My plan was to depend on total self-sustenance. I never said a word to my boss, and was planning on skipping a few semesters at school. I was going to disappear for awhile.

Launching at Reed's Landing, I felt total freedom. One hour later, I was fifty yards upstream from where I'd started. The wind held me up and pushed me back, and the current I had been depending on was nowhere to be found. I rowed myself silly until my hands were blistered and bleeding. Two hours later, I was still within sight of the boat landing. It took me six hours to row the first five miles. The trip ended up being a total nightmare, and I only lasted five days.

Although that hazy experience didn't work out, it taught me the importance of preparation. I was so happy to finally get off the lake and into the current. As I hit the same spot, the last three weeks didn't seem so hard after all. I was still averaging almost twenty-five miles per day. In the makeshift rowboat, my best day was fourteen miles.

After Pepin, I had an easy ten-mile drift past Wabasha and into Alma, where I paddled up to Rob's backyard. Rob and his neighbor Mike spoiled me with dinner at DQ, showed me the town's famous scenic view, and we spent the night watching ESPN.

JUNE 8TH, 1999 DAY 25

It was hot and calm, the perfect summer day. It was exactly how I'd envisioned the river in my daydreams. So many days in the last few years when I had found myself stuck in some office or feeling trapped, the vision was my escape, and I was there. It was total bliss. The day was perfection. I paddled lazily through the glassy water, soaking up the rays from the sun, soaking up everything, feeling everything.

Paddling by the confluence of the Zumbro River was a thrill. I grew up on the shores of that muddy crick, and learned everything I knew in life on its banks. The brown water that mingled with the Mississippi was the same water that went by my parent's house, and was now connected to Lake Itasca, New Orleans, St. Louis, Memphis, and the ocean. In fact, all water in the world was connected somehow together, and if that was true, I was connected to everything also.

> All rivers run into the sea,
> Yet the sea is never full.
> To the place the rivers come from,
> There they return again (Ecclesiastics).

If the breath filling my lungs came from the wind, how could I die? Everything was eternal. Everything was boundless and forever. Everything was connected.

Then the storms hit. Finding a three-barge wait at Lock & Dam 5b in Winona, I paddled back around an island to portage the spillway. It was rainy and windy, and rather than take everything out of the canoe, I attempted to lower the boat over the concrete spillway and ease it into the water below. With my paddle in my right hand, I let the canoe slide down with my left. I slipped on the rocks. The canoe went down hard and sideways, and I landed on top of it as my paddle flew out the topside of the spillway.

The canoe took on water and some of my things bounced out. Scrambling around in the rain, I gathered my seat cushion and spare paddle. My bags were tied down, but both of my poles were on the bottom of the river and my paddle was on the topside of the spillway. The green paint scraped on the side of the spillway drew a perfect arrow to where I could find my poles, and luckily it was only five feet deep. Struggling to keep my chin above water, I shuffled my feet on the bottom, starting near the spillway and methodically worked in straight lines, trying to feel every square inch of the bottom with my toes. I found the pole with the broken reel below the green skid line. Rain fell harder and lightning move in. I couldn't risk my life looking for a pole, but I needed the paddle.

The slimy spillway was impossible to climb. I wedged my fingers into a crack and scaled up the wall by swinging my feet up over my head and pulling myself up. The winds had pushed my paddle straight out into Polander Lake, fifty yards away. It was against my better judgment, but I decided to swim for it. I swam out into the turbulent water, grabbed the oar, and pulled myself back onto the spillway, exhausted. I gave myself five more minutes to find the other pole in the dreary, drenching rain.

It was scary trying to stay above water and feel the bottom with my feet. I'd been fishing in the same spot when I was eighteen, and witnessed the Winona Dive Team recover the body of a drown victim. Feeling along the bottom with my toes, I thought of their dragging efforts and it gave me the creeps. I found the pole as I made my final pass.

I paddled hard to make it to Latch Island by 6:00, where I was meeting my friend Bryan Madsen. I was dragging my canoe up through the mud when his white jeep with Alaskan plates pulled up. As he shook my hand and helped me with my things, we both could barely contain our grins. Experienced in various outdoor pursuits, he'd been instrumental in helping me prepare. Bryan could crawl through a tunnel of shit and come out smelling like a rose. Genuine and honest, he was most at home in the woods, but had a boyishness to him, like Opie Taylor with an edge.

We took off toward the place my buddy Dale Radcliffe works, and were having so much fun sharing stories we forgot to pay attention to where we were going, overshot it, and went right out of town. I was eager to tell him about the trip and he was fired up to hear every detail. Every time we got together we started talking about cross-country road trips, moving to Alaska, starting adventure businesses, and other crazy things until we were both ready to pack our bags and quit our jobs. I don't think I'd even have taken the trip if it weren't for our know-no-limits, free-spirited talks that kept me fired up. After driving to his place in La Crosse, I tried to get hold of Dale. Madsen and he were both new in town and living just a few miles away from each other. They were two of my best friends and I wanted to introduce them to one another.

Dale hurried over after work. It was impossible to have anything but a good time when you were around Dale Radcliffe. He knew how to make a trip to the dentist a good time. He even had a fun job. As a pro walleye fisherman, he was published in several magazines and had his own guide service in the La Crosse area. He had nerves stronger than the ice on which he drilled holes, and was cooler under pressure. His unorthodox fishing methods were unbelievably successful, and he'd do anything to help a guy.

The three of us spent the evening shooting the breeze, and Dale and I set up a meeting place on the river for the following day.

DAY 26

I was up by 5:30, and we were on the road shortly after as Madsen went out of his way to bring me back to Winona before work. Although tired, I paddled my ass off to make sixteen miles by 10:30, and met Dale and his girlfriend, Jess, south of Trempeleau. For the first time in my life, I didn't really care if we caught anything. I was completely spent, and it was a relief to be out of the canoe and amongst friends. I was more interested in the lunch Jess had packed than in fishing, but nobody fished with Dale without catching anything. Man, that guy never stopped smiling. I wished I could look at life like he did. After nailing some walleye, sauger, and bass, it was back in the canoe.

I had no energy. The last few weeks had really taken their toll on me. I'd felt weak since St. Paul, but the night of drinking in Alma really wrecked me. I wasn't eating right, wasn't getting enough sleep, wasn't drinking enough water, and was working myself too hard. How would Dale handle the trip? He'd make it, but it would take him over a year because he would stop in every town and talk to everyone he saw. What's wrong with that? Who cares if it took me the whole year to get to New Orleans? I didn't see how I could make it.

I'd been on the river almost a month and was still in Minnesota. I hadn't felt so drained since my row boat disaster. My mileage average had taken a hit on Pepin and I wanted it back to thirty.

After drifting a mile with the paddle on my lap, I decided to make some changes. I would eat when I was hungry, sleep when I was tired, drink a gallon of water every day, and not worry so much about mileage. For the time being, however, I had to keep pushing. I was meeting Madsen at his boat slip on French Island Marina, and although I'd love to have called it a day, I wanted to get there. Entering La Crosse gave me a little second wind, and I gave it my all to paddle up the Black River a mile to get to his slip.

We spent the evening zipping around in Bryan's Bayliner, and stopped at the Bikini Yacht Club, where we ran into some guys we went to college with. They drank beer, I stuck to pop, and we all dug the live music and waitresses.

Back at Bryan's, I talked to my dad on the phone as the Knicks went up a game on the Pacers. He'd called the Corp of Engineers about maps, but instead had received nasty letters from several southern states, claiming I was suicidal to be out on the river in a canoe. He was worrying himself to death about me, and it showed in his voice.

"I've never asked you to do anything for me, but I'm asking you to do one thing for me now. Please stop." The long silence that followed precluded the end of our conversation. I was drained, there were storm warnings for the next day, and I was caught in a catch twenty-two, torn between my dreams and my father who loved me. Although frustrated, I couldn't keep my eyes open.

CHAPTER 6: IOWA BORDER

DAY 27

It was pouring when I woke up at 5:00, but after a few minutes it let up into a sprinkle, and everything was dead calm. More storms were forecast for later and Bryan suggested I stay another day, but I was yearning for solitude, and needed to get back to the river. I appreciated my friends and family, but I'd rather be in my tent on an island feeling the storm than looking through trails of water on someone's patio window.

I felt stronger, better than I'd felt in two weeks. I couldn't understand how. It must have been because I was heading into unfamiliar territory for the first time. I'd spent my whole life on the Mississippi River, but never south of La Crosse. I was moving away from everything I knew. There would be no more friends' houses to take refuge in, and no more dinners with my parents. I was heading south, had no one else to rely on, and everything I needed to survive was within arm's reach.

For as long as I could remember, I've had this enormous amount of energy bubbling away inside me, but had nothing to do with it. It became painful, so I had to kill it. There was nothing like getting annihilated to dull my senses and make everything simple and easy. I needed that energy for the first time in my life. It was overpowering.

Paddling out of La Crosse in the foggy mist, I planned on going only about ten miles before the next wave of storms hit. I paddled hard, the sun came out, and I whipped off my shirt. I hadn't seen that part of the river before. Everything was new and beautiful, and I had nine more states besides Minnesota in which to explore the summer. In a burst of strength, I paddled twenty-one miles before noon. The words of my father, "please stop," kept coming into my mind, but I forced them out and lost myself in the bluffs that enveloped me.

The river was dead calm and everything was eerie. At Brownsville, I broke all rules of common sense and went on a two-hour, eight-mile crisscross over the wide lake caused by Lock & Dam #8 at Genoa. There were no safe havens, and storm clouds were moving in. I paddled harder and basked in it. I was fully exposed to nature's wrath and completely vulnerable. I was alone in the middle of the lake, and there was nowhere to hide if the storm moved in quickly. Staring at a red barn, adrenaline pumping through me, Wisconsin grew slowly as Minnesota shrunk away behind my wake. It was starting to sprinkle, but still dead calm. Distant thunder boomed as I paddled toward the dam. The red barn took on an ever-changing angle over the reflection of the darkening clouds.

Passing the Genoa Dam, the rain was steady, but I tasted Iowa. A violent storm ripped into me as I crossed the border like a sprinter hitting the white tape. I hastily made camp in fierce lightning and heavy wind just a stone's throw past the Iowa border.

DAY 28

The raw, sunburned skin on my back and shoulders was brutally sore, and it was difficult to sleep. After paddling four weeks and 678 miles, I was only in Iowa, but it felt like a foreign country, and the novelty made me stronger.

I met my parents for lunch under the Lansing Bridge at 10:30, praying I could act appreciative and patient. In order to look as healthy and happy as possible, I shaved for the first time on my trip. I felt strong and wiry, and the act of shaving felt symbolic of a new feeling growing inside of me. When I began the trip, I originally planned on going to the Iowa border, but I knew if I could make it to Iowa, I could make it to New Orleans. My confidence level was at an all time high.

The time with my parents went well; we spoke openly, and they bought me some snacks at the grocery store. I was done portaging, so they brought the rest of my food and my cooker. I was done eating cold chili. My dad explained in carefully chosen words how he was frustrated about my lack of preparedness for the southern part of the trip. I'd depended on him to get maps, but instead he'd received nasty letters from three states. With a sad and solemn look, he handed them over silently, and I began to read:

I hope you have your personal affairs in order and waterproof ID attached to your body, because that's what we'll need to identify you once you make it to St. Louis... I lost track of the bodies I pulled from the river there... is your personal adventure worth the agony you're putting your family through or even your very life? No personal adventure is worth your life.(Missouri State Water Patrol).

I have pulled far too many lifeless bodies from the currents of the river not to have these concerns... these currents form tremendous eddies and undertows... washes with up to five foot swells that put boaters in great peril... it is my professional opinion that a trip of this type is a very risky proposition, even with the best of training, equipment, and physical ability... you should reconsider your plans south of St .Louis (Louisiana Dept. of Wildlife and Fisheries).

I do not recommend traveling on the Mississippi River by canoe... From Missouri to the Gulf Coast the river takes on the nature of an uncontrolled beast... treacherous even for twenty-four foot power boats... once swamped it's impossible to escape... even as a professional in the boating field, I am hesitant to go boating on the Mississippi River (Arkansas Game and Fish Commission).

I read the letters without commenting, but for the rest of the day my dad talked about "getting to Hannibal," "a victory celebration after Hannibal," and about doing things together later in the summer. My heart was in my throat, but I didn't say a word.

The bluffs outside Lansing were beautiful, but I was too depressed to enjoy them. Hadn't people made it down the river in a canoe before? If it was possible to do it I'd do it, but I felt guilty for causing my parents so much grief. It was ruining my peace and solitude knowing that attempting to attain my goal was causing the people I loved so much pain. The thought of stopping at Hannibal killed me. Why not just quit right then? It felt like there was a dead end on the river and a dead end to my dream. I felt stuck.

I paddled until 9:30. It was too nice to quit. Even with my long stop in Lansing, I broke thirty miles on the day, and 700 on the trip. From my muddy island I watched the Friday night fireworks at the Miss Marquette River Boat, seven miles away.

One thing that had come easy for me was sleeping, but I had too much on my mind. Even though it was after midnight, I called home and woke up my dad. Although it made me feel selfish, I explained to him that it was my life long dream, and he needed to trust my judgment. He tried to talk, but I interrupted him and finished. I couldn't put any limits on the trip without finding out for myself, and I needed his moral support. I told him I would go as far as I could without getting myself killed, but I didn't want to die, and wouldn't put myself into any bad situations. He was either with me or against me, and if he were unable to stop worrying, I would have to sever communication for the balance of the trip. I felt like a real prick, but it was the only way I could make it work.

We both spent the conversation yelling, and he got so mad at me his mouth was too dry to talk. I asked him if he thought I would die, and he said yes. I had caught him off guard in the middle of the night, but would not let him go until he chose between giving me full command or severing communication. Knowing he was too loving to let me go, I gained my objective and he was forced to give in. I felt like a real asshole, but it was the only way I could finish my trip. The hidden control that a father has over is son is so powerful, and I could not go on without his blessing, even if it was extorted.

I felt much better and could sleep, but the muddy island was full of beavers and their gnawing kept me up all night. It sounded like there were thirty of them surrounding my tent. Every few minutes I yelled to scare them away, but they kept coming back.

DAY 29

Sleeping was difficult due to sunburn, beavers, bugs, and heat, but I dozed off near morning. I hadn't touched a beer since Alma, it was Saturday, and I was looking forward to meeting Bryan at Wyalusing State Park that night for some partying.

A beautiful blonde girl working at the Miss Marquette distracted me. Canoeing the length of the river is a good conversation starter, and I used it to my advantage whenever possible. I pretended to be interested in learning about the boat and the city, but was really just waiting for her obtrusive boss to quit giving me maps so I could set something up for later. By the time I left, I had two pink wristbands to listen to Ronnie Milsap that night, a phone number, and a date for later to see Angie and some of her friends at the Sawmill bar in Prairie Du Chien.

It was a rush to see Bryan's white jeep pull up at the beach. I knew he'd be amused at the connections I'd made for us that morning. After setting up camp, we drove around town carefree, stopping wherever looked good. We pounded screwdrivers and talked to several good looking women. The world was our oyster.

At the gambling boat, I tested out my keep doubling your bet until you win theory on the tables. It never even came into play. After winning my first six hands, I walked away with more than enough money to cover the night's expenses. Ronnie Milsap cranked out country music as we dangled our toes in the river and chugged beers.

When the concert was over we headed to the Sawmill. I was pretty juiced. Angie was a terrific hostess, and introduced us to hoards of girls, telling them all about my trip. We had such a blast it felt like I was in college again. With the fatigue I was going through, my tolerance for alcohol had dropped in half, and I didn't remember much. We closed down some dance club across the street; I was so tired I could barely keep my eyes open. The end of the night found me withdrawn and unsociable, and we were unable to find any camping companions to bring back to the park.

We arrived back at 3:00 under the close scrutiny of a park ranger who pulled us over at the entrance. He gave us a quick look over, but after seeing we were registered campers and checking out Bryan's Alaskan plates, he let us go. Still, flashing red lights at 3:00 can make a guy a little jumpy. Back at camp, we cooked some chili over the fire, reflected on the evening, and I guzzled a half-gallon of water to combat the next day's hangover. I slept soundly, but woke a few times in the night with my head spinning, wondering where in the hell I was. I was angry with myself for drinking again and spending the evening clueless. I wished I could keep my edge, but every time Saturday came along I just couldn't wait to kill accountabilities.

JUNE 13TH, 1999 DAY 30

I awoke at 9:00 feeling much better than expected, but had developed a scary case of jungle rot on my feet from being wet for a month. We relaxed until 11:00, then hit the beach. I was pissed off to discover someone had stolen my spare paddle.

I lingered awhile before launching, partly because I would be alone from then on in, partly to look for my paddle, and partly to check out three women sunbathing nearby.

A young girl tried to get her mother's attention, but she was too relaxed to look up from her lawn chair. Feeling neglected, the little girl pulled herself through the mud on her belly, completely caking herself in mud yelling, "Mom, look mom." She ran up to her mother and smudged her arm in wet sloppy mud, finally succeeded in her mission.

Three drunken guys were swilling beers and being very obnoxious as I shoved off. They all stared at me, trying to think of something smart-ass to say. I beat them to it.

"What the hell? It's not even noon yet, way too early to drink beer."

"Never too early man. It's six-o-clock somewhere." They raised their beers to that and gulped. All three had belligerent looks on their bully faces. "Where you headed man?"

"New Orleans."

"No shit!" They hooted and hollered, and gave me the outstretched pinky and pointer finger, like kids did at concerts.

"Right on bro."

"Have a beer."

"Sorry guys, gotta jet." I paddled as swiftly and skillfully as I could among the Sunday pleasure boaters, knowing the eyes of the beach were on my back. Feeling a tinge of loneliness, I never looked back.

After paddling a few miles, I looked through my stuff to get a book and take a break. I stumbled upon my little Bible, which I'd forgotten I had even packed. It was the first time on the whole trip it had been in my hands, and had a special glow to it, seeming to call out my name to be opened. I read the entire book of Matthew as I drifted, and the words jumped off the page like poetry. Never before had anything made more sense to me. It filled me with hope and happiness, and everything around me looked beautiful. I decided to start every day with it, a decision I soon forgot about.

Near Guttenburg, I ran into a guy in a bass boat named Todd. He was about my age, tan and muscular, with an Iowan freshness to him. He looked like a football player.

"Smallies staging up on the rip rap yet?"

"No, high water has 'em all scattered." We drifted together for a half-hour, talking of fishing, women, adventure, and river lore. We both knew the same girl in La Crosse, where he had gone to college, but her name alluded us both.

Todd showed me his homemade spinnerbaits that were guaranteed to pound the bass, and insisted I take one with me. He also told me about a bar in Glenhaven called Wack's Bar, and told me I was crazy if I paddled by without stopping in. He sped away, and just as he disappeared, I remembered the name of the girl from La Crosse.

Although worn out, I decided to head to the Wisconsin side to check out the bar. I was on no time constraints anymore, and wanted to enjoy every moment and stop whenever I felt like it. I took the trip to be free, and had forced rules on myself. Taking a break from paddling, I turned on some tunes and decided to chill out.

It seems to me I could live my life
A lot better than I think I am.
I guess that's why they call me

They call me the working man.
I guess that's what I am. (Rush).

The song played the night I decided to quit my corporate job in Detroit, and the significance of what it once meant for me gave me chills. I was happy to have made that decision. Drifting along through a slough in Wisconsin, I tested Todd's spinnerbait, and nailed two bass and a northern right off the bat. I was at peace, and my wheels were spinning with marketing ideas.

Wack's Bar was an insane circus. I was the only guy in the bar who didn't ride up on a Harley. Shuffling my feet through an inch of beer on the floor, I grabbed a stool near the least dangerous looking characters I could find and sat down, trying not to look at anyone for too long. Several drunken women bore their breasts, and one guy walked in the front door and mooned everyone. It was 4:00 on a Sunday afternoon, and I was told that Sundays were the only day they didn't let the women dance on tables naked.

I felt sober and alienated from all the uninhibited behavior going on around me. It took everything I had to keep myself from drinking. Everyone was annihilated, but I just minded my own business and ignored the bikers who kept bumping into me as I devoured a huge burger, grilled cheese sandwich and several cokes. The owner, Jerry, shook my hand, and paid for my meal. He told me about some guys from Tennessee who'd come in the other day on some sort of a bicycle-propelled raft. It had started to rain. I was craving beer, so I decided to take off before ruining my new Christian ideals.

Paddling downstream in the rain, I looked back to what I'd seen at Wack's, and it seemed ugly to me. I hadn't been in too many situations where I was sober and everyone around me was peeled. I'd spent most of my life living recklessly, and wondered what I looked like to others. It was depressing that everyday life could be so rough I needed to ruin myself to forget things. I didn't want to lead that kind of life anymore, but the nine to five American dream thing didn't work for me either. It was a no win situation.

Feeling low and praying for answers, I was happy when the rain stopped and the sun popped back out before setting. Turning a corner, I was greeted by one of the most brilliant rainbows I'd ever seen. It started on the left side of the river and made a perfect arch over to the right. It was surreal as I paddled under it.

Suddenly, I had an overwhelming feeling that everything was going to work out perfectly. I felt like God was watching over me, and would keep me safe for the rest of the trip. Thinking about the scriptures I had read, I knew that if I stopped worrying about everything so much and stayed in touch with the good in my heart, everything would work out. Who needed alcohol and drugs when I had so much beauty and freedom at my fingertips? I felt very fortunate to be where I was at that point in my life.

After passing under the rainbow and watching an amazing sunset, I paddled past Cassville and onto a beautiful sandbar on the head of Jack Oak Island. While setting up camp, I received a call from my dad, who called every Sunday night at 9:15. He had been at church, and told me about the sermon on Matthew. He told me how he wished I could have been there, and had prayed I could hear the word. That was at the same time I picked up my Bible. I'm not quick to label coincidences as miracles, but the whole day was full of strange occurrences.

It had been my best day. I had learned many things about myself and found a new faith within me. From there on in, I had a hunch that things would be easier and more meaningful. I felt very happy about the way things were going, and I was getting closer to reaching the state of mind I was looking for when I started out.

I camped just three feet from the river, and spent a long time looking out at the reflection of the stars on the calm water, savoring the moment. I felt so content about everything, and the river was more beautiful than any night I could remember. I didn't know exactly what love was, but it must have been something like the way I felt when I looked out at the stars over the river and felt shivers down my spine as my whole body tingled to behold the beauty of that night.

Free Meals

DAY 31

I lounged around the campsite until 10:45. With a steady current and a brisk wind at my back, there was no need to hurry; I spent the morning drifting and reading. Drifting along at a good clip, I floated right into JD's Landing in North Buena Vista.

"You goin to New Orleans?"

"Yea, how'd you know?"

"I heard about you from some boaters. C'mon over and get something to eat." JD was a tough looking guy of about forty. He'd spent his life as a trucker, but always dreamt of owning a place on the river. He was excited about my trip, and filled me up on burgers, chips, pop, and ice cream. We were both living our dreams. After spending an hour talking about Detroit, black jack, and crazy river voyages, I untied.

I couldn't eat again until Lock & Dam #11 was in sight, and I'd covered twenty miles. I had to read ten chapters of my book and see three more barges before turning on the radio. I was still abolishing rules used to push myself. Why did I need to push myself anyway? It was hard to get used to being free. Instead of waiting, I ate a big meal and spent the day moving freely back and forth between reading and listening to tunes.

I was alone on the wind swept river. JD was the only person I saw. Solitude was rare for most people I knew. They could go a whole day and never be alone. I couldn't see how anyone could live like that. Traveling alone, my experiences were much richer. When thrust into a new environment with people I already knew, I spent my time talking to them, and didn't grow as a person. As a stranger in a strange land, I was forced to shed my complacency, step up, and be my best at all times. I was more attentive to others, more alert, and more ready to show who I was.

Approaching Dubuque, I felt like I would miss Wisconsin. Illinois was unfamiliar to me, and all I could use as a reference was Chicago. At least I had the simplistic right bank of Iowa to cling to. I loved Iowans. They moved so slow and talked so slow, and everything seemed so simple and easy for them.

I waited at the Dubuque dam while they let the Mary Lynn through. It was gone at 9:20, and although I pulled the signal chord several times, I didn't have any lights and the Lockmaster couldn't see me. Clinging to the sidewall, I was swarmed by bats before a guy walking the railing finally heard me yelling at him and let me through.

It was pitch dark. It was too dark to look around Dubuque, so I claimed the only muddy little flat I could find. I sunk up to my knees in mud setting up and was distracted all night by the flashing lights of milemarker 581.5. I had paddled 765 miles.

Day 32

My muddy little island looked quite different in the daylight. After sinking up to my knees again getting out, I headed into Dubuque. Stopping at a small marina, I walked up to a place called Tugboat Willies. My rugged appearance was not warmly accepted at first, but soon I spotted the man with the proud look of ownership and approached him.

Mike Walsh had bigshot written all over him. He would have looked natural in some movie as a nightclub owner in Miami. Mike treated me like a king, buying me lunch and parading me around like a celebrity. I had my picture taken several times, one with us shaking hands in front of my canoe, like they did with famous people. I wasn't sure if I liked all the attention, but enjoyed the river lore and free food. It had been so long since I'd paid for a meal I began to feel like a dog that lived next to a park and had discovered family reunions. Mike gave me his card, warned me about St. Louis, and wished me luck. I was heading into Illinois.

The Issaquena was being assisted through a railroad bridge on the Illinois side and back under the highway bridge on the Iowa side. It was my favorite tow thus far. I recognized some of the crewmembers I had talked to back in La Crescent, MN, especially the huge guy with the long blonde hair and Go-T who looked exactly like a pirate.

It was a slow process for the assist tow tugs to guide the Issaquena around the obstacles, and I passed it easily and headed out of town, where I met the Dubuque River Boat. Hoards of elderly people eagerly listened to the booming voice of the captain.

"And here comes the Issaquena. Five long and three wide, pulling so many tons of cargo and burning so many gallons of fuel per day." I paddled as close as possible.

"How's fishing?"

"I'm not fishing, I'm paddling to New Orleans."

"How long you been out?"

"Thirty-two days. I've come seven hundred eighty miles." Everyone on board stared over the side of the boat, and the captain repeated what I said. They snapped pictures and shouted bits of encouragement and questions, but the boat soon passed and the voices faded away. The Issaquena was coming, and I had to get out of the way.

It was moving slowly downstream, using the current to conserve fuel. I hoped they would remember me. I paddled quickly to get off to the side and let it pass, but soon realized I was keeping right up with it. Feeling like a young dolphin on the side of a cruise ship, I tried to race it. Starting dead even with the front barges, I paddled five miles in nearly one hour before it overtook me. I kept waving, but the crew wouldn't come on deck to say hello. They didn't want to encourage a canoe to play with barges.

Clinging to the Iowa shore, I was still treating Illinois like the kid who moved into my best friend's old house. The long race with the barge tired me out a bit, and I was distracted by peeling layers of skin off my back and shoulders from my sunburn.

The Tete Des Morts Creek reminded me of Winona's Homer Trestle, which had always been one of my favorite fishing spots. I wanted to stop and sniff around, but, but what? It was the only chance in my lifetime to see the Tete Des Morts Trestle, so I paddled up the creek a few hundred yards. The water looked like it was unsure of which way to go, and I experienced a haunting sensation that gave me shivers up my neck. I hustled back under the old rusty bridge and back into the river. There was something spooky and morbid about that place.

By Bellevue it was starting to get dark, so I figured I'd camp before the dam and leave the town for exploring the next day. There was only one island between me and Lock & Dam # 12, and I gambled it would have a suitable place for a tent. The front had nothing, and the right and backsides were muddy. I paddled upstream to check the left side, knowing I'd have to settle for whatever the little patch of trees had to offer. I felt like a businessman checking into his hotel, opening the door and turning on the light to see if it met his approval.

Luckily, there was a small beach perfect for my tent and canoe. The high water made it difficult to find a good place to camp, and I rarely stopped for the night soon enough. I'd done all of my cooking in the canoe and hadn't had a fire since Pepin. Usually, I finished paddling at 9:00 and got in the tent and fell asleep. On this night, however, I felt like spending a few hours soaking up life around the fire.

Sitting on my lifejacket on the edge of the river around a symmetrical little fire, I felt more peace than I could remember. There were no distractions in my life. My brain wasn't dulled by anything unnatural, and I looked at the world with childhood curiosity and newness. Every corner was a new adventure as I remembered who I was before my soul became diluted with all the world's bullshit. I was losing my cynicism. I pictured myself back in society functioning like a normal person, maybe even holding a job.

Looking ahead, I was eager to experience every small town between there and New Orleans. There was something great about going into a town for the first time, getting a feel for what it would be like to live there, and then leaving. I'd lived in twenty different places in the last three years, often just driving through a town, liking it, picking up a newspaper and finding a cheap place, and living there for a few months without signing a lease. If not, a campground on the outskirts would do. I wanted to treat every little town like I was going to move into it. I wanted to know every little river town intimately and learn about the people there.

DAY 33

The forecast called for rain, but a beautiful, sunny day greeted me as I paddled into Bellevue. There was a long wait at the locks, so I stashed my canoe along the inside wall and climbed the grassy bank into town. I always got butterflies walking into a new town. I was eager to explore, but didn't know what kind of a reception to expect.

I peeked my head into every business in town, trying to start up conversations whenever possible. It was my first and last time in Bellevue, and I knew I could be bolder than normal. I already had a formula; to find the person in charge was to find a free meal. After devouring free cookies and cokes at the Frontier Bar, I talked to a nice old lady at the hotel who insisted on getting the newspaper. I wanted to lock through first, but promised I'd be back for lunch.

Noticing two boys hanging around my stuff, I hustled down to the canoe to make sure everything was intact. They sat along the ledge on the inside wall of the locks with their bare feet hanging right in the water, looking like Huck Finn and Tom Sawyer.

"Hey guys, thanks for watching my stuff for me."

"Is this your canoe? We didn't know how it got here." The boys had a million questions about where I had come from and where I was headed. Mitch and David told me everything there was to know about the town of Bellevue. After a quick conference between the two in which they discussed whether or not they could trust me, they explained how the hidden spot between the locks and the bank was their secret clubhouse. They came there every day during the summer to get away from everyone and make big plans. I locked through, thanking them and telling them I would be at the hotel if they wanted to stop in and talk more.

On the other side of the locks, an old fisherman and his wife were fishing, and volunteered to watch my things. She watched in admiration from her lawnchair as he proudly hoisted a little smallmouth bass from the ripples. "Largemouth bass," he declared to everyone around. "I catch 'em here all the time." Some youngsters nearby tried telling him it was a smallie, but he'd hear nothing of it, so they left him alone. After pulling out a chunkier smallie, he turned to the three boys who were fishing to his right and looked at them with a real serious face. "I've been catching these here largemouth in this spot for sixty years. Don't none of you little squirrels try teaching me about fishing."

The old man was getting agitated, but his wife was kind enough to watch my canoe, and I didn't want to correct his sixty-year mistake. The old man pulled several more bass out of the water. He didn't say a word, but made enough of a scene to let the kids nearby know that he was outfishing the daylights out of them. Mitch and David came flying past on their bikes like a couple of private detectives.

"We've been waiting for you inside the hotel, but they won't let us in there no more." Instead of getting a chance to respond, I was bombarded by questions by the pair.

"We went home and looked in the Janus Book of World Records. You can beat the record."

"The farthest is one thousand and five."

"It must be fun."

"Do your parents know where you are?"

"Do you ever get scared at night?"

"Where do you sleep?"

"Don't you miss your friends?" They asked me questions so fast I couldn't tell who was asking. They pushed their bikes next to me along the side of the road as I walked, but were soon distracted and started fighting over a piece of driftwood as Mitch snatched it right out of David's hand.

"I got it first."

"Yea, but I'm the one who saw it."

"Any of you guys ever read Huck Finn?" I asked, trying to distract them.

"No, but I saw the movie. I don't read nothin' less my teacher makes me. I went into the hotel, but the boys were forced to wait outside. Soon the newspaper guy arrived, and I was doing my first interview. Nathan was a college student at Northwestern, and it was obvious he was dedicated and thorough, and would be a big time reporter some day. Mitch and David rode their bikes around in a big triangle between the library, bookstore, and my canoe, researching Guinness records and making sure my things were safe. Occasionally, they poked their heads into the door of the hotel yelling in reports, until the proprietor got mad and shooed them away.

After some pictures, I was back on the river. I'd miss Bellevue. Gosh, I loved Iowans. I paddled right by the Twilight Riverboat on my way to Savanna, and everyone waved and smiled. I was making excellent time, and decided to hit Savanna rather than wait for the following day.

Turning the corner before town, I anticipated the appearance of the bridge. Paddling along the edge of town looking for places to explore, I found a riverfront bar, tied up to the docks, and ran inside. Stepping onto Illinois soil helped me to remember how far I'd come. I would spend the next month in the state, and it felt like I was meeting my betrothed for the first time. The bar was dark, and my eyes had a tough time adjusting to the lack of light. Before I could make out faces, a scratchy female voice from one of three shapes at the end of the bar greeted me. The lady's voice spoke very loudly to overcome the loud rock music on the jukebox.

"Beautiful canoe. Are you going all the way?"

"Yep."

"I told you he looked like he was going all the way," the bartender said to the lady, leaning over the bar and giving her a friendly tap on the shoulder. "We've had em stop in before, but they're usually in pretty rough shape by the time they get this far.

"Well I guess I'm just not working at it too hard anymore."

"What's your name sweetie?" asked the lady with the scratchy voice.

I introduced myself as Matthew for some reason. I always went my Matt, but sitting in front of her, I felt like a Matthew. Besides, as a stranger in a strange land I could call myself whatever I wanted.

"Let me get you a beer honey."

"Let me get his next one," offered the man sitting next to her. There were only two people in the bar besides the bartender, but they carried on like it was a party, and everyone seemed a little sloshed.

"I'd rather have a pop." A giant mug of beer with was filled and its foam was sliding down the side of the glass and onto the bar in front of me before I could even get the words out.

"C'mon, have a drink with us. A few beers ain't gonna hurt ya. You deserve them." It was hard to turn down free beer, and I didn't want to offend anyone. They were an interesting bunch and played excellent music. There were no lights in the bar except a few hazy rays of day coming through the window overlooking the river.

Al and Maggie were from Chicago. Both had the appearance of weathered regal elegance, like they were once on top of the world but had fallen on hard times at some point. Al had been a nightclub singer and performer, and Maggie, still at his side, was still very pretty, only now she was beginning to show her age. Both were full of spiritual and life advice, and looked straight into my eyes as if trying to connect with me in some special way. They'd moved from Chicago to start a bed and breakfast called The Palisades.

Greg was the eyes and ears of the town. He told me about the lack of money around, how he couldn't keep good help, and how all the girls in town left when they turned eighteen. He alluded to his many girlfriends, and told how eight topless girls came off the river one day and strutted up into his place. He told great stories, but it was hard to tell how much was true. He fed me beers, played me Creedence Clearwater Revival, and taught me how to play a horseshoe type game called washers.

Beads of water formed on the window. It was raining, but I was buzzed and didn't care. Maggie kept calling me Matthew, honey, and smiling at me, and Al told me how envious of me he was. The rain let up and Al and Maggie left, but not before Maggie gave me a big hug and kissed both sides of my face like some long lost aunt would. Both kept smiling at me and wished me well. It was sad to see them go.

I couldn't afford to get loopy, so I left soon after, but not before Greg warned me of the dangers of Pool 13 coming up south of town. It held more water than any pool on the river, and if there was any wind I was screwed.

Stopping at a gas station to make a few calls, I got into a conversation with the lady working there, and told her about the bar I'd come from. "Don't go in that place. No one goes in there anymore. They're goofy in there. Go to the Home Port across the river in Sabulia. They're boater friendly. I just can't believe you went in that place."

A little buzzed and looking for another warm welcome, I paddled across the river and downstream to Sabulia in a light mist, and walked into the highly touted bar. My stuff was soaked, and I only had a little light left, but I never worried when I was in buzz mode. Everyone in the Home Port Bar watched through the big window as I pulled up.

"Whatcha doin?" I was grabbing a stool when a guy at the end of the bar who was slouching over his beer began interrogating me.

"I'm heading to New Orleans," I declared proudly.

"I've seen people try that before, they're all a bunch of idiots." The drunken sloucher did all the talking, while his friends laughed at everything he said. "I got some bad news for you boy. You're goin the wrong way. Ain't now 'Nuolens' round here." I tried giving him a laugh to be a good sport, but he kept firing away at me. "What the hell you want to paddle to 'Nuolens' for anyway. Are you stupid or something?"

His look challenged me, and the blood began to boil inside. I looked around the bar to scan the potential of the situation, but realized there were five other guys looking at me with the same hateful stare he was. Fighting was definitely a bad idea, so I sat there trying to keep my cool. Rather than thrash the guy, I laid low and swallowed my pride. I ordered pizza and a beer, and looked for a second opinion on the place.

Hoping he would find out about my voyage and volunteer to pay for my drinks, I fired into a conversation with the owner. He looked lit, and was too busy playing video games and drinking Old Style to talk. Meanwhile, the prick at the end of the bar hurled something smartass my way every few minutes. It was obvious he'd spent every night of his life in the same barstool at the end of the bar. I was over my initial adrenaline rush, and could see nobody in the bar was probably going to start a fight with me unless I did something to initiate it. I could hang with those guys, and relished the thought of the challenge, but knew I'd get hammered in the process.

Slamming my beer down, I cancelled my pizza order, waived goodbye to the asshole at the end of the bar and hit the river without sticking around to listen to their complaints about my leaving. It was better to distance myself from such belligerence, avoid trouble, and get a good start on Pool 13.

Paddling out of town, I was a little miffed at my naiveté. I'd started thinking a hero's welcome would await me at every stop. I'd gotten a big head, imagining everybody would think what I was doing was so great they would buy me things and pat me on the back. I had forgotten about the element of contempt.

I crept into the big lake called Pool 13. It was dead calm, and if I hadn't wasted so many hours in bars, I could have put it behind me that evening. My only hope was for a calm morning. Memories of being stranded on Winnie and Pepin filled my mind. Reaching back, I put my hand into my backpack to discover my sleeping bag was soaked. The radio forecasted scattered storms and record lows. I made a rule never to go into another bar after 4:00 p.m. unless my tent was already set up.

Realizing there was a chance I may be stranded in the morning, I found a perfect sandbar two-miles south of town. Although it was already dark, I draped my sleeping bag over the tent in order to dry it a bit, but it was pretty useless. I wanted to get a fire going, but all the wood was saturated from the day's rain.

I lay in my damp sleeping bag shivering, taking consolation in the fact it had been a memorable learning experience. It was all part of my adventure, both the good and the bad. I slept terribly. Everything was soaked, and water leaked out of my bags causing a pool on the floor of the tent. To make matters worse, it was raining again.

I tried to sleep, feeling like a dog that had been kicked. My ego was bruised from the people at the last bar, but it was deserved. I knew I might get stranded on the island for awhile, and part of me wanted to get stranded. I'd used people too much to get free food and boost my ego. A little solitude was what I needed to get back in touch with things. Remembering the good people I'd met in Bellevue and Savanna made me feel better, but I fell asleep humbled.

Mitch & Dave In Bellevue, Iowa

DAY 34

After suffering through a teeth-rattling evening, I was up before the crack of dawn. I couldn't sleep, and wanted to get past the lake. Pool 13 was huge, but it was dead calm. I paddled hard, covering twelve miles in three hours and putting distance between Sabulia and me. By 9:30, I was at Lock & Dam #13 in Clinton. The lake was wider than Pepin and had ended the journeys of others before me. I hit it during ideal conditions and was fortunate to be through so easy. The wind picked up as I entered the locks, and a giant chop formed as the lake woke up for the day.

After stopping at the Mississippi Belle and feasting on free cookies from the ladies on break, I left Clinton and headed toward Albany. People on the Illinois shore all looked up from whatever they were doing long enough to give me a friendly wave.

"Where's your motor?" I held up my paddle. "That won't get you far."

"It's gonna get me to New Orleans."

"You got a long ways to go." Of all the expressions I heard on the river, that was by far the most common, and the one I hated the most. Why couldn't people say, "you've come a long ways"?

Albany was a beautiful little river town with an excellent riverfront. I walked around town talking with exceedingly friendly people. The Postmaster insisted I talked to Merlin Howe, an old river vet. She called him and told him to meet me at Julie's Café.

"How will I know who he is?"

"You'll know."

I walked in, ordered a pop, and started writing a letter to the girl I met in Palisade. A thin hand was placed on my shoulder as Merlin found me before I spotted him. He shook my hand with vice-like grip and sat next to me. At eighty-six years old, he was full of energy and stories.

Merlin told me about fighting the flood 1965, about the time the Delta Queen crashed into high wires right before his eyes, about his radio fishing show, and about his grandfather who officiated the wedding of Ronald Reagan's parents. Memories burned in his eyes as he spoke. He had individually taken several large manufacturers to court for polluting the river, and as a lifelong conservation officer he nailed anyone who ever did anything to harm the river. The walls of the café were plastered with framed articles of him in different stages of his life doing heroic deeds to help preserve the river.

"You gotta be a sneak to catch a sneak," he revealed, shaking a finger at me with a wry grin. He told me how people had rammed his boat, tried to run him over with their cars, and assaulted him, all for doing his job.

"That Merlin Howe is a crook," they would yell in court. His eyes misted as he looked back on life and spoke. He'd been going to battle for the river his whole life and fought to make Albany a beautiful river town. All around him were friends and family. Although retiring had been rough on him, he'd found the thing in life he loved and made a difference. Not many people could honestly say that, and I hoped that someday I could. After complimentary peach pie and ice cream from his daughter, Julie, I hit the river again, feeling good having talked to Merlin, and glad I was living my dreams.

Two pretty girls lounged on a dock as I paddled into Comanche. Naturally, I pulled up to say hello. Both were college athletes, and had the physiques to prove it. Amy was cute and shy, while Lisa was tall, freckled, and outspoken. We talked awhile, and had friends in common at University of Iowa. They told me about LeClair and Port Byron. The two towns a few miles south had a big tug of war every year with a giant rope stretching across the river. I normally didn't go for six-footers, but I saw something I liked in Lisa. I tried to set up a rendezvous, but she was already hitched with some Iowa baseball player. I should have read the cues a little longer and gone for Amy, but it was too late. Undeterred, I gave them a quick tour of my canoe before conceding to tainting the innocence of the chance encounter. Happy to have given it a shot, I paddled away.

A guy could afford to be more aggressive on a trip, as long as he was willing to accept some rejection. Like my good friend Dale once told me, if you talked to a hundred girls and got shot down by ninety-eight, you've just met two girls you didn't know before. I didn't have to worry about feeling silly seeing them at work or school or whatever, or feeling like their friends were laughing at me every time I saw them. I'd just hit the river again and look for another town.

I spent the next few hours reading, drifting, and admiring the evening. By 9:00, I felt so tranquil I didn't want to leave the canoe or the river. I had learned to love the freedom of the river so much I wished it would never end. After thirty-four days, it felt like the canoe was an extension of myself. Rather than legs, I had a canoe. I paddled in the dark, halfway looking for a sandbar, but not too excited one way or the other. I listened to the Stars and Sabres in the Stanley Cup playoffs and threw a buzzbait at the moon's reflection on the water.

I found a grassy point one-mile upstream from Cordova. I was having such a good time I almost paddled by it, but I needed to save some towns for the next day. I was approaching 850 miles and having a great time. I slept freely without the impending threat of being torn away by the rude buzzing of an alarm.

CHAPTER 7:QUAD CITIES

DAY 35

I was on the water by 9:00, and despite a stiff south wind, it was another nice day. The radio said something about a ballgame in the Quad Cities. They were a class A affiliate of the Minnesota Twins, and their right fielder, Michael Restovich, was from my hometown and destined for stardom in the majors. I called the radio station to get information about the game, and they invited me in for a live interview.

My dad was a teacher, and had Restovich in class. He always talked about going to see him play, and it seemed like the perfect opportunity. My mother and he decided to drive down and meet me in Davenport. We had been getting along better than ever on the phone, and I was fired up about seeing them. The thought of being on radio made me uncomfortable. I rehearsed what I'd say, but everything felt so contrived. It was a phony thing to do, so I didn't call them back.

After winding through some pleasure boat traffic, fighting the wind and waves, and dodging a fleet of barges, I happily made it to Lock & Dam # 15 in Davenport where I met a few guys my age. We tied up together, shot the breeze, and they fed me a few beers during the wait. It was impossible not to get offered beer everyday. On a Saturday, I could be sociable and drink one beer with everyone I met, and end up drinking enough to be swilled by the end of the day. It was so damn hard to say no. My parents waited for me at a landing within sight of the stadium. We stashed my canoe in the weeds and went straight to the game. It was fun spending time with my folks. We had fully reconciled after not seeing eye to eye before. I loved minor league baseball, and it made my dad's day to talk to Restovich.

A little boy and girl sitting in front of us peeked over their chairs and smiled. Only a guiltless kid could lock eyes with a total stranger and smile with a completely clear conscience. It was hard looking back at them without feeling a combination of envy and self-doubt over my own lack of innocence. I smiled quickly and made a funny face, then looked away to avoid their honest glances. It was frustrating. Why did I have to complicate life so much? I should have been able to smile and look at anyone without reservations, but I'd built walls. It was so difficult to break through and connect.

We gambled after the game. My double your bet until you win strategy worked again, but having my entire trip fund in front of me in chips had me sweating bullets. It was tough to lose seven in a row but not impossible. After betting eighty to win back five, I retired my strategy for the rest of the trip. We had a great time together, and stayed at a hotel in town. It was sweet having a few good meals and cleaning up.

DAY 36

It was hard for me to get comfortable in a bed. It made me feel guilty, like I was cheating or something. After a great omelet breakfast at Monica's Café, we were back at the landing. Several boaters came to the docks wondering what the deal was with the canoe. The most interesting was a great big man who introduced himself as Mr. Shoe. He gave me a bunch of his fish scent, which smelled exactly like strawberry jam but was guaranteed to catch lunkers. After waving goodbye to my parents and their new friend Mr. Shoe, I was back on the river.

With a very strong south wind and heavy Saturday boat traffic, the going was slow and treacherous. The beaches of Buffalo Shores were stacked with people and fancy boats as I paddled close by. Everybody was piss drunk.

"You're goin the wrong way."

"Hey kid, you're going to get yourself killed."

"There's that dumbass in the canoe again." Several people pointed and laughed or had something smartass to say. No one waved or said hello. I felt like I was in enemy territory. A big fat guy with a stupid look on his face saw me coming and stumbled out into the water with his beer tilted sideways in his chubby hand, spilling it as he went.

"Hey Gilligan! Where's Skipper?" He repeated it and turned around to see if his friends had caught his cleverness, but they were busy. One was pissing while the other two pelted him with empty beer cans. "Hey Gilligan!" I wanted to explain to him that Gilligan never found a boat and never moved 1,000 miles across the water, but was stuck in one place his whole life, never able to escape, just like him. I hoped I didn't act like those baboons when I drank, but looking back at college, I supposed I did.

The fun that they were having made me feel angry and alienated, and I didn't feel like talking to anyone. The chaos and drunkenness didn't thin out until I was fifteen miles downriver from the Quad Cities. They were the dangerous ones, not me in my canoe. I made a mental note to avoid all large cities on weekends. There were true river people, and there were others. I'd seen so many loud, drunk assholes lately that every time I saw group of people on shore, I automatically assumed they were the same. Part of me wanted to join them, but seeing their big power boats and watching them throw cans in the woods, I wanted to get far away and just find my own little island to camp on. It was a little frustrating when I thought about it.

After a few beers I'd be acting just like them, in fact, I'd be the worst of them all. I knew it was wrong but I did it anyway, and I loved it. Why?

Big puffy white clouds slid slowly across a deep dark blue sky. It was endless. I couldn't even start to understand it. I was lonely, confused and tired of fighting the wind.

At Clark's Ferry, I found a boat landing to rest from battling the wind and waves. An eerie feeling swept over me, like there was a divine presence around. After saying hello to some kids, I was drawn toward an old man at a picnic table.

Ernie was frail, with fading eyes and a gaunt face. I had a strong feeling he was very sick and living out his last days. He looked at me as if I was the grim reaper who had come off the river to take him away. When I sat down next to him and said hello, he smiled sadly, tilted his head to scan me over, and started telling me about his life.

He had worked every day after school to help his mother buy groceries for the family. He spent forty years doing manual labor at the Arsenal. Ernie used strange expressions to define everything. His age was four score missing one, and he spoke of me being older than he was. We connected in a strange way. He looked at me seriously as if about to tell me a secret to live by, but his face started to tremble and his eyes welled up with tears and he stopped. He was afraid to cry in front of me, and whatever he wanted to say, his pride would not allow him to say it. Using his cane for support, he got up to leave, but not before looking at me with the saddest look I'd ever seen.

"Keep the man upstairs with you. You'll need him more than you could ever know." He let out a gasp, and the tears came streaming down his face as he turned his back and slowly hobbled away.

The wind had died down to nothing, and it was a gorgeous Saturday night. I passed a huge party on shore at Fairport. They looked like a nice group of people, so I paddled by and waved, lingering awhile and hoping to get invited over, but no one talked to me. After treading water for a moment or two, I kept moving.

There was a wilder party going on at a beach a few miles down. A bunch of stoned kids were on a beach packed with junky boats and one kayak. The entire shore was covered in empty beer cans, and several floated in circles in the foamy eddy out front. The loud sounds of Metallica lacerated the fading evening sky, and the smell of weed lingered in the still air. A skinny guy with tattoos all over his back slammed down the last of his E & J bottle and launched it into the river with a victorious howl. His friends all howled back. A guy with a beer bong was the only one who noticed me.

"Hey where you headed?"

"New Orleans." He ran over to the edge of the shore to get closer.

"Right on man. You better hurry, record is eighteen days."

"Well jump in and help me paddle."

"Hey, I'm all about that man. Believe me, I've had many conversations. See that kayak, that's mine man, someday I'm gonna do it too" The guy was really smashed, and he stumbled along beside me for several hundred yards with bleeding eyes, asking me questions about the trip.

He looked like a promising young man who had made a few bad moves and was now heading fast in the wrong direction. I saw some good in him, even though he was FUBAR (fucked up beyond all recognition). I paddled closer to him on the sand as he walked away from the party and along the beach beside me. The party raged on, and no one noticed he was gone. Tiny drops of beer flew from his bong and danced on the surface of the calm river as he twirled it in the air as we talked. He stopped at the end of the island and flashed me a bowl he pulled out of the pocket of his black cutoff jeans.

"You wanna catch one?" It was tempting, but it looked like a pretty rough bunch he was with, and the ratio sucked anyway. It was hard to say no, but I'd been so good lately, and didn't want to mess with the purity of mind I held at the moment.

"Thanks for the offer, but I've been sticking to beer nowadays." He offered for me to come back with them and party, but something inside me thought it was a bad idea, so I wished him luck, encouraged him to do the river, and paddled on down the line. I was leaving when he yelled back out to me.

"Dude, go to The Brew in Muscatine tomorrow. We go there all the time, man. It fucking rocks." I paddled another mile and still wasn't out of earshot of the wild party. It was hard to believe I had passed it up, but I'd felt kind of weird after my strange encounter with Ernie. He was so sad when he talked to me, and thinking of the guy with the kayak made me sad too. The sun was setting and I was looking for a place to camp when a bunch of guys drinking beer in a flat-bottom passed me.

"Ha Ha. That guy's in a fucking canoe. What a moron." They were definitely bound for the same party. I was almost two miles away, and could still hear music and yelling. There was nothing worse than listening to guys yell, girls shriek, and music roar when you weren't there. I was starting to understand what it felt like to be old and boring, and it kind of pissed me off.

I was almost to the Muscatine Dam before the voices trailed away. It sucked being alone when they were having such a free for all, but I found a nice little sandy point to set up camp. I named it Saturday Night Island. I sat up late listening to the Stars win the Cup in three overtimes and thinking about my life, the world, and the decisions I'd made. Everything was finally getting clearer, like I was done heading in circles and finally going in a straight line. Although I felt left out, I was glad to be by myself on Saturday Night Island, instead of on some sandbar losing myself in a crowd of people.

JUNE 20TH, 1999 DAY 37

After staying up nearly all night listening to the hockey game, I slept in until 9:00. Muscatine gave me a bad feeling. Maybe all the good folks were still at church or something, but everyone at the launch was frowning, and I didn't receive any friendly looks as I tied to the docks. The line of people waiting to load their fancy boats for a day on the river looked at my canoe condescendingly on the crowded docks, as if it was in the way. I found a cheap little café and had pancakes, but ate fast because I didn't like where my stuff was. On the way back, I watched a nice looking gal in white shorts and a sleeveless top get out of her car and head for a walk. I tried to make our paths meet, but she didn't notice me and headed the other way.

It was slow going as I faced another day of wind from the south. I was paddling along the Iowa shore next to a park and saw the same pretty girl I'd seen walking earlier. She was even with me, but elevated forty feet on top of the levee on a trail, and didn't see me. She was trucking along at a pretty good clip, walking like she was on a mission.

"Do you wanna race?" My voice startled her from below.

"No, you'd probably beat me."

"Are you walking anywhere in particular?"

"Just walking. How about yourself?"

"I'm heading to New Orleans."

"That sounds exciting."

"Hop in then." She laughed, but walked briskly, still not really looking at me. The levee was further away and it was getting harder to hear each other as I maneuvered around some barge docks, trying to keep up with her. "Are you from Muscatine?"

"Actually, I'm from Michigan and just moved here."

"Me too." It turned out we'd both lived in East Lansing at the same time while she was getting her Master's at Michigan State. She loosened up and even looked at me.

"Well, I'm at the end of the line here," she informed me as the trail ended. I treaded water awhile and we yelled up and down to each other, but it was hard to hear.

"Do you want to get a cup of coffee or something?" I repeated it twice before she heard.

"Sure, that would be great," she yelled back. I looked for a place to stop and stash my canoe, but it was all riprap. Although I knew it was bad for the canoe, I pulled it up on the rocks and walked up to her. She was pretty, with auburn hair and an athletic body. It was a little ways of a walk to get back to town, and there was no where safe to keep my canoe. I wanted to leave it on the rocks and walk back to town with her, but she had just finished biking, and wanted to go home and take a shower.

Looking at my map, I saw what looked like a boat landing five miles downstream at Fruitland, and asked her if she wanted to meet there at 1:00. "Yes," she said with a shy smile, "but I'm really not much of a coffee drinker."

"Me neither," I admitted, "I just figured that's what people do on Sundays in Iowa. By the way, my name is Matthew."

"Nice to meet you," she said politely, extending her hand, "I'm Rachel."

"Why were you walking so fast, are you mad about something?"

"Just a little mad at the world sometimes."

"Me too, but I'm getting happier every day." We could have talked all day, but it was smarter to split up for then and meet at the landing later. I watched her attractive figure disappear down the trail, knowing I would be seeing more of it later. I was pretty fired up about the potential of the rest of the day, and paddled toward Fruitland in a great mood. After jumping in the river with some soap on a rope and getting the closest thing to a bath the river could offer, I changed into my clean clothes and got ready for our date.

Reaching what was supposed to be Fruitland, there was nothing showing any resemblance to a boat landing, just a few old guys sitting in a flat bottom boat fishing for catfish. "Where's the Fruitland Landing,"

Both men laughed for awhile before one looked at me like I was stupid. "Shit, there ain't been no landing here for ten years, and there ain't no water in Fruitland. If you wanna get to Fruitland, that's about three miles off the river." I felt about as stupid as the look on his face intended for me to feel.

It was already 12:40. I did some quick calculations in my mind. What was my fastest time in the mile? How fast could I run three miles? It was hopeless. After hiding the canoe in the weeds and grabbing what I needed, I started hiking toward town. After running through a tiny patch of woods, I crossed the corner of a field and hit a gravel road. There was a grain elevator there, and an old farmer was just getting into his rickety pickup as I ran by. Gasping for air, I told him I was paddling the length of the river, had met a girl, made a date, and given her bad directions. He was a little suspicious of me, but was heading to Fruitland, and allowed me to hop in.

"I don't know what kind of a story you're trying to tell me, but I'll drive you as far as Fruitland, and you'll have to find your own way back."

We were pulling into town when I saw her drive by us going the other way. "There she is," I exclaimed, pointing at the white car. Without any prompting, the old farmer whipped a U-turn in the middle of the road. Gravel flew into the ditch as the tires of the truck spun madly to grip the surface of the narrow road. We got up behind her, but she was heading out of town fast, doing seventy and stopping for nothing.

She was new in town, had never been to Fruitland, and must have wondered who the two wacko farmers were in the truck behind her. He gave the old truck all it had until the whole thing was rattling, yet we still were not gaining.

"Just like the movies," he explained with a wild laugh. I was a little nervous as the race car wannabe stranger hit eighty, slowed down enough to spin around a corner, and finally got right on her tail. Doing eighty-five, he pulled right up beside her. I waved frantically and yelled, but her windows were up, her face was pale, and she was afraid to look. Finally she peeked over and I flagged her down. I thanked the farmer for a wild Sunday drive and hopped in with Rachel.

There was nothing open except Herky's Harley Bar, and we spent a few hours in there drinking beer and getting to know each other. She was older than I was, professional and single, and although she enjoyed her beer, she was already sick of the singles scene and men of Muscatine. Bikers were waiting in line to talk to her, making me feel silly and small. We were getting along good despite the distractions, and the strange circumstances by which we had met had us feeling like destiny's buzzed children.

After a few hours of getting comfortable with one another at the biker bar, we took off, found a quiet park, and laid down on a blanket with a six-pack of Bud Light for our own little picnic. She peeled the skin off my sun burnt back in sheets, and made fun of my legs, which were burnt crispy on the insides, and snow white on the outsides. We burned the whole day away at the park, and it was getting dark before we knew it.

We had an awesome time together, but I knew I'd never see her again, and I didn't want to ruin a good thing. She took me back to the canoe, and after a memorable goodbye, I was back on the river again, looking for a sandbar in the dark.

Calling Bryan Madsen on my cell phone, I discovered he'd run into two guys in Winona and again in La Crosse who were doing the same thing as me. Chris and Geoff had left Lake Itasca on June 1st, were averaging over thirty miles a day, and were on pace to catch me somewhere near St. Louis. The two had been staying in some of the same spots I had, and had been talking to some of the same people. I was very excited about meeting them, sharing stories, and paddling together for awhile.

DAY 38

I slept like a log until being rudely awakened early in the morning by someone yelling. "Get up, get up you sleepy heads. Get up, get up get out of bed." Peeking out, I saw a bunch of guys yelling at my tent from a passing barge. I had camped at party central. Beer cans and bottles littered the entire island and a huge bonfire still smoldered from the day before. A rusty keg lay in the grass and had been split open and turned into a grill. I went back to sleep for a few hours and didn't get up until 9:00.

I wanted to drift, but the brutal south wind wouldn't allow it. After a few hours of paddling I took a break and gorged myself on bananas, strawberry bars, licorice and Tang, while the wind held me hovering in one spot for five minutes. The rest of the day was spent on chutes off the main channel where I could escape the wind. I had a blast trying not to get lost in the mazes of side channels, but was always afraid I'd miss something when I left the main river, like the Delta Queen would go by or something.

Where was I? I was canoeing down the Mississippi. No I wasn't. Yes I was. Was I dreaming? Was I stoned? I drifted along, paddling every once in awhile, my pace being dependent on that of a dead carp I was trying to keep up with. I recalled past vacations. Usually, I didn't even realize I was there until I was on my way home. I'd been out for thirty-eighty days, and it was still hard to believe I was doing it. I was free, and everything I needed to survive was right there.

The proud faces of people holding up their prized catches filled an Illinois fishing magazine. They were fish killers: to sacrifice an animal just to hold up in front of a camera to show their friends. Was I taking the trip just for pride? I had done some pretty selfish things myself, and had no right to judge what anyone else did.

Approaching Lock & Dam #17, I was disappointed to find several barges in line. It looked like a very long wait. The gates of the dam were wide open, and I wondered if I could shoot it. I wasn't sure if I could fit, and had no idea how big the drop was. With my binocs looking for danger, I drifted in, checking to see if it was possible. My heart started pumping as I glassed over several warning signs that said Restricted Area. A horn started blasting at me continuously from the locks, the signal for danger. It was too late to turn around. I was indecisive, the current picked up, and I had no choice. It looked scary as hell, but I was lucky enough there was only a small drop and just enough headroom to squeeze through. The adrenaline rush didn't hit me until it was over. I'd saved several hours and shot my first dam. At New Boston, I decided to kill some time, and stashed my canoe in the woods in case anyone was looking for me.

The sidewalk up a hill led straight to the Portside Bar. It didn't even look open. The heavy door slammed behind me as I walked into the dark room. Everyone stopped talking to stare at me. Six tough looking farmers sat at the bar, and I sat at the only open stool, right between the two biggest guys. They looked at me, waiting for me to talk.

"ID?" the bartender commanded, holding out her hand sternly.

"I just want a coke."

"You gotta be twenty-one."

"You gotta be a certain age to drink pop in this state?" The big man on my right stared at my canteen as I pulled my wallet out of my plastic bag. He started whispering something to the guy on his right, obviously referring to me. I heard southern accents for the first time on my trip.

"What in the hell are you supposed to be? Some kind of road warrior or something?"

"Nope, just canoeing and wanted to take a break."

"You canoeing that river out there? What are you, nuts?"

"I took a canoe twelve miles once," the farmer to my left slowly reported.

"Yea, in the back of your pick-up."

"Boy, if you're headed to St. Louis, you'd better be damned careful. Those tows down there got twenty-foot waves. You don't even take boats down there." The advice came from a man at the end of the bar who'd fixed his eyes on me since I came in. Jay looked just like Martin Sheen.

"I could make it with my flat bottom and Gene's thirty horse Johnson," the man on my left who had taken the twelve-mile canoe trip slowly predicted.

"I'd rather have a sister in a whorehouse than a brother in law with a Johnson." Everyone roared, as the men on either side of me seemed to be related by marriage. The big guy on my right was Ron, and he was the mayor, DNR, part time police, and county coroner. He did most of the talking, usually to the slow talking Freiden on my left.

"Here, let me stick this thing through your ear and carve your name into it," he said, holding up a fork, "so they'll know who you are down there when they find ya."

"Abe Lincoln designed this town," Freiden interjected abruptly.

"Yea, he was on a seven day drunk," Ron explained. Jay and Gail at the end of the bar chimed in with advice, and although Jay started out trying to scare me, he soon became friendly.

"You're having the time of your life, aren't you? Best time to do it. Good for you." Jay bought me a beer, and Ron and Freiden claimed my next two. They gave me shit, but ten minutes later I had three beers and a steaming hot pizza in front of me.

"You don't got fleas do ya?"

"Your canoe down by the river? That's private property. If the cops ain't already got it, them boys down there will steal it for sure."

They spent the whole afternoon razzing me, but I kept my mouth shut, ate their pizza and drank free beer. They slapped an "I love New Boston" pin on my chest, and when I got up to go, Jay got up with me, shook my hand, and slipped me ten bucks.

"Hey, I want you to have this. Get yourself a pizza somewhere downriver, and be careful." I was lucky to have come across such nice folks. I felt guilty for accepting so many gifts, but it helped me out, and apparently it made them feel good to help someone.

The river had narrowed, and was faster with the open gates from the last dam. I was feeling good, but wanted to feel better. After a quick paddle to Keithsburg, I beached near a waterfront bar as two grizzled fishermen pulled up from downstream in a flat bottom. Ken and Cy were both about fifty, but that was the end of their similarities. Cy was real amiable. He smiled constantly and was looking for one good time after another. He joked about everything, and acted real goofy. Ken was a tough guy with real serious, piercing eyes. He looked like an old river man. The two were on vacation, running up and down the river in their boat drinking beer in every town along the way. The bar on the beach was closed. They argued about what to do next for awhile, then the three of us decided to walk into town and look for another bar.

Keithsburg was old and deserted, and looked like a ghost town. The flood of '94 had nailed it. We stumbled into a bar like we had found a desert oasis, and the two ordered three beers, one of which was for their "new little buddy." The wild-eyed bartender was talking to a portly farmer about a billy goat that ran away because they'd forgotten to water it. He was wearing only one shoe.

Ken and Cy bought me several beers and paid for my meal. Cy kept trying to convince Ken to run up north and cook up some pork chops on the grill, but Ken just wanted to order another Old Style and eat burgers at the bar. The two bickered back and forth for ten minutes, drinking two while deciding to stay for one more. The one-shoed bartender was talking like a duck, and was still quacking something about a lost billy goat. Every once and awhile he looked up from flipping burgers long enough to let out an unprompted hysterical laugh. He was drinking faster than anyone. Ken and Cy got up to leave, but not before buying me another beer. I felt bad, but Cy explained it was what the Indians did for the Voyageurs back in the 1600's. I finished my beer and hit the river.

It was a hot muggy night, and I barely got set up on the first sandbar below town before a wicked storm moved in. I was shit-faced, and felt propelled to take a swim in the river during the worst of the storm. It rained so hard I couldn't tell if I was under water or above it. I swam out into the current as far as I dared, watching storm clouds envelop the moon as lightning flashed in the distance. It was a strange trip. I felt like an invincible wild savage.

DAY 39

After sleeping in until 10:00, I spent the next two hours drifting toward Oquawka, unsuccessfully trying to sew up a hole in my tent with a fishhook and line. I stopped in town and had the first meal in a week that I paid for. The southern accents of the conversations going on around me made me feel farther away from home.

"Ya catch anything this mornin?"

"Just one gill, but he wuzza good one. Thought I'd get me a mess of 'em, but that was my only nibble. Had the little bugger in the live well, but let 'em go, and he looks up at me and says 'thanks fer lettin me outta jail. Yer the nicest fisher I ever met.'"

The newspaper wanted a story, so I waited around my canoe and talked to a lady named Helen who let me tie up to her wall while she did yard work. She was a ninety-year-old Irish lady, and knew more about the river than anyone I'd met. She knew every tow ever to pass by her house, and told me stories of pollywogging when she was a girl. When she wasn't hunting clams, she was fishing cats, and knew every beach, island and milemarker on the river.

I waited awhile for the paper, but after twenty minutes they hadn't shown up, so I kept moving. I didn't feel like paddling, in fact I would have killed somebody to lie on their couch. A big lunch and two days of drinking made me lazy, and I felt like finding a sandbar and calling it a day.

People kept asking me how I could go on the trip alone. I couldn't imagine going with another. It was great spending a whole summer without asking anyone anything or answering to anyone. I did whatever I felt like. From the time I started kindergarten, it seemed like there were no such thing as individual decision making. Schools didn't seem to teach it. Instead, it was group work and group thinking. No one wanted to bend the rules or rock the boat. Corporations took bright young kids out of school and turned them into policy following zombies. It made me sick.

There were barges all over Lock & Dam #18, so I beached it and walked up to talk to the Lockmaster. He told me it would be a two-hour wait, so I made some calls. My dad had been doing research for me and found the names of a few guys who had made it through the lower parts of the river. The tone of his voice showed no worry, and he was more excited than ever about my trip. To know he was on my side really fired me up. We were finally thinking on the same wavelength, and I felt like there was absolutely nothing holding me back. I felt like a big gill that had finally been let out of the livewell.

The lockmaster saw me on the phone and walked over to tell me he would let me slip through between two barges. Catching the day's second wind, I ran full speed back to the canoe, eager to get past the locks and continue making my way south.

The captain of the Ed Renshaw seemed to take a special interest in me as I paddled past. He tried yelling questions down at me, but it was too hard to hear over the idle of his engine. All I could do was wave as I cut in front of him and entered the locks. The fact his big barge full of cargo had to wait for my little green canoe made me feel guilty, but he didn't seem to mind.

Near Burlington, a big bully looking guy in a duckboat motored up to me. At first I thought he was going to kick my ass or something, but he ended up just being curious as to why I was traveling by canoe. The tar all over his face and shirt revealed he was a roofer from town, and he asked me tons of questions about my trip between big gulps of Old Style. We tied up together, he tossed me a beer, and we spent a few minutes shooting the breeze. Although he knew several dirty jokes, he spent most of the conversation telling me stories about the railroad serial killer. Apparently, some Mexican hobo was going nuts killing people and was rumored to be in the area.

With my own painting of the serial killer permanently etched in my mind, I passed up several nice sandbars out in the open for a dark little island off the main channel where I felt hidden and safe. I wondered what it might be like to be the serial killer, having everyone in the country looking for me, and constantly hiding out alone.

After six weeks in the canoe, I was finding myself acting without thinking, with big gaps in the spaces in between. One minute I was in the canoe, and the next thing I knew, my tent was up, the wood was stacked, the fire was going, and I was whistling some old tune while staring up into the stars. I had quit thinking so much and started feeling. A primitive feeling was slowly taking over me. My mind was empty and clear, and I did everything quicker and more efficiently. My instincts were taking control. My body was stronger than ever, and my mind was reaching a new level of sharpness.

It was a nice night when I went to bed, so I didn't bother putting up my rain flap. A quick storm moved through in the middle of the night. Wind whipped at my tent and rain sprayed in through the top. My flashlight was dead, and I scrambled around barefoot in the dark in pouring rain, waterproofing my things and putting my rain flap up. The inside of my tent got soaked, and I lied there uncomfortably listening to the thunder for an hour before I fell back asleep.

The River Widens

CHAPTER 8: NAUVOO, ILLINOIS

DAY 40

The rain let up, and I headed into Burlington for breakfast. The first two places I stopped catered to business types. After walking inside and seeing high prices and no possibility of a free meal, I abruptly left them both. A long search brought me to Deb's. It was family owned and had just opened the day before. Deb and her daughter slaved away behind the counter, scanning their customers with curious glances, hoping everyone was enjoying their meals. Deb struggled to contain her smile as a deliveryman came in with fresh vegetables.

Freshly hatched mayflies hovered over the entire riverfront. Some were already dead, and the rest were dying. Skipping down the steps, I slipped on a stinky mess of them and lunged for the railing to keep my balance. White bodies covered entire cars and buildings. They were dead in slimy masses on the sidewalk. Mayflies lived for less than twenty-four hours. How did that compare to my life on the planet? In one glorious day, a mayfly was born, grew up, acclimated to its environment, bred, and died. What had I done with my life? I wanted to live with the sense of urgency of a mayfly.

Rather than return to my canoe, I found a colorful bar on the river and went in. Instantly attracted to the pretty young blonde bartender, I made every attempt to talk to her, but she avoided me like crazy. I sipped my beer and admired the way she looked, talked, and even smelled. She was wearing some sort of odd oil that was only found in a record store in Houston. I hadn't shaved in a few weeks, and probably had dead mayflies stuck to me. Although I could picture myself flying out my mayfly life in Burlington, I decided to jet while I could still attribute her avoidance of me on being busy.

Within ten minutes, I had forgotten about her and was battling rain and a brutal south wind. The rain died, but the winds remained strong. The rest of the day was spent exploring side chutes. I was off the main channel and couldn't find where I was on the map, but where water flowed, it had to go out somewhere. Severe storm warnings and a tornado watch were broadcast on the radio. I wanted to set up camp but was lost in an endless flooded slough. I paddled on, trying to find my way back to the main channel and higher ground.

A solid line of black appeared on the sky and thunder boomed in the distance as the clouds burst once again. I frantically looked for a place to hide, but was surrounded by water on all sides, including up. It was raining so hard it felt like I was drowning, and sideways hail stung my face. I hustled over to what appeared to be a clump of trees on my right. It didn't look like much, but was the closest thing to shelter I could find.

The clump was a giant heap of dead trees and reeds that had been hallowed out and turned into a duck blind. I crawled inside. It was dark, smelly, and swarming with mayflies. It felt like I was entrapped in a coffin, but I was safe from the storm. The bad part of the storm moved through quickly, and although it was still raining, I vacated my rotting refuge in favor of the deluge outside, scraping dead mayflies off my arms and face as I went. My entire canoe was filled with mayflies in all stages of life.

I was still picking out mayflies when I drifted into Dallas City and floated by a waterfront bar, where I was greeted by a wave from the lovely silhouette of the barmaid in the window. Parking my canoe along with a few fancy boats on the docks, I hustled inside, hoping to get some food and a better look. The place was equally divided between locals and boaters. It was easy to tell who was who by the way they were dressed and the looks on their faces. The locals looked beaten after a long day's work, and looked out at the little groups of happy boaters with contempt. Not feeling much like a member of either, I picked out a stool at the end of the bar. The lady in the window was older than she looked from the river, and although she was pretty, she had a big rock on her hand. Susie gave me a free hat and some beers while we shot the shit.

Three happy looking couples my parents' age sauntered in as we talked, and an important acting man leaned up against the bar next to me to order drinks for the group while the other five grabbed a table overlooking the river. He had the cocky look of "big money" that a guy gets when he's stepping up to be the man and buy the first round. "Man my back is sore," he said, holding it with both hands as if trying to make a joke, "I came boating in all the way from Dubuque."

"Dubuque, no shit?"

"No, I'm just kidding. We came in from Burlington. What about you?"

"I started at the beginning."

"How long did that take?" he asked indifferently as he looked around, trying to make conversation but obviously not paying any attention.

"Forty days so far." The drinks had come, and he left in the middle of our conversation to go disperse them amongst his friends. The loud voices carrying over from the table revealed they weren't their first drinks of the night.

"Which boat is yours, the big one?" He was standing up along the window with his friends, pointing out to a big yacht as he yelled over to me so the whole bar could hear. From the way he laughed when he said it and smacked the shoulder of his buddy, I figured he was trying to make another joke.

"I'm in the green canoe." He didn't say a word back to me, but began talking in lowered voices to the people at his table as he pointed out the window at my canoe.

"He's full of shit," I overheard someone at the table say. "Four days? The kid is definitely lying." People talk louder than they think when they've been drinking, and I could hear them plainly from where I was sitting at the bar.

"Hey," he called back to me, "How in the hell do you expect me to believe that you paddled a canoe all the way from Minnesota in four days?"

"I said forty days." No one at the table believed me one bit, and before I knew it, he and his buddy had walked over and were quizzing me about different towns along the way. After passing all of his tests, I was invited over to meet the rest of the group. The six of them boated together every Wednesday of the summer, stopping there for a few drinks before going to another place for chicken. The rest of the group was quiet, as Tim, the guy I originally met, did all of the talking. He had this "I've been around the block a few times kid," attitude that he used with me, never believing anything I said without challenging me with a million questions. When he wasn't questioning me he was preaching to me. He tried to convince me how unsafe my trip was and told me I "needed" to stop before St. Louis.

"Promise me you'll always wear your life jacket," he commanded, pointing a stern finger at me. "No, promise me, and you won't try paddling through St. Louis, right? Make sure you stop before you get to St. Louis." His words disintegrated into the brick wall behind me as I nodded my head without listening. He'd been on my nerves since I saw the "I'm a big man," look on his face when he walked into the bar, and his domineering presence really bugged me.

When the drinks were gone and they were ready to go, Tim must have figured it would make him look generous to invite me along. I didn't like people trying to tell me what to do, but figured I could ignore him long enough to accept an invitation for all-u-can-eat chicken and free beers.

I tried to keep my distance from Preacher Tim, but he was impossible to escape. I spent the whole dinner answering character testing questions. I enjoyed games of whit, but was sick of playing. I felt like I was meeting my girlfriend's parents for the first time and had to sit there and try to act like a little pansy ass model citizen. They were treating, and I felt obligated to use some manners, so I played along. It was the first time on the trip I felt obligated to do anything. My polite actions and table etiquette felt unnatural.

I lasted half the meal, but could pretend no longer. Rather than spend the evening in submission, I decided to change things up a bit. I allowed my mind to regress into wild savage mode. Pretending I was seeing my first humans after being raised by a pack of wild dogs, I devoured plate after plate of chicken, letting little chunks of scraps and grease accumulate all over the bottom of my mouth and chin.

I kept my greasy face as close to the plate as possible, taking off my hat and allowing my long hair in front to dangle close to the plate. Between pieces, I made the closest thing to a growl I could get away with without looking too obvious. Tim was done eating and was silently watching me as I wolfed down everything in sight. The waitress decided I'd eaten enough too, and when she didn't bring more chicken, I borrowed one off of Preacher Tim's plate without even asking. He seemed to be done, and I didn't want it to go to waste. With a disgusted look, Tim suggested we call it a night, but I pointed out to him that there was still a little beer left in the pitcher. After admonishing the group for being a bunch of Sallys, I drank the end of it right out of the heavy glass pitcher, and proceeded to grab Tim's vacated half-full glass and polish that off too as they all stood there, waiting for me to finish. After spending days of scavenging for food, I could no longer watch things go to waste. Tim didn't try talking to me any more.

We returned to the waterfront, but the six were keeping a good distance from me, and no longer included me in the conversation. They walked in the bar as I slipped away to my canoe. Two huge boats were looking for a section of dock big enough to tie to, and they stared at me with contempt as they waited for me to get my canoe out of their way. I could feel the eyes of the people in the bar, but I paddled away without looking back.

The dusk sky was an assortment of dazzling colors. A storm filled the west with flashes of lightning, while the southeast was a spectrum of pink, orange, and yellow, amidst alternating ripples of clouds and blue sky. It was great to be alone again.

It was getting dark, but every island was flooded. Feeling adventurous, I paddled into Fort Madison and searched for a park to hide my tent in. My flashlight was dead and it was hard to see, but I found a little sandbar under the railroad bridge near town. After setting up my tent in the dark, I didn't want to waste a good buzz, so I strolled into town.

As I climbed up the railroad bridge and walked the rails into town, I remembered the railroad killer. What if he was there? What if people thought I was him?

The mayflies were too thick to enjoy the town, and I was afraid to leave my tent unattended, so I headed back down the tracks toward my hideout, thinking I saw the killer hidden in every shadow along the way. What if he was in my tent? What if the cops came and shot me thinking I was him? Paranoid, I took an alternate route back, sneaking the whole way through the woods. I slept with my gun loaded at my side.

Never sleep under a railroad bridge. Trains felt like they were running over me all night, and I was sure one would derail. A siren blew every half-hour to warn people in town about the drawbridge. When it finally got quiet, every noise outside was the serial killer coming.

DAY 41

By the time dawn broke, I wasn't sure if I'd slept yet. It was 6:00, and rather than get chased out for trespassing, I hit the river again. Stashing my canoe downstream of town, I found a homey diner and had a nice greasy breakfast. It was a tiny little place, and I sat at the bar a few feet from the smoking grill and watched the plump cook silently make my meal. A lady came in that was so fat, she had to turn sideways to get through the door. She sat in the two chairs to my left, and I ate my eggs without looking at her.

It was the calmest day I'd seen in two weeks, and I drifted all the way to Nauvoo. I was starting to look really seedy, so I decided to clean up and shave off my beard. Rather than leave a Go-T, I left just the long hairs on my chin. It gave me a very alternative appearance, and I felt clean and almost like a brand new person.

I stopped for water at Joseph Smith Park, wondering why a place in Illinois would be named for a Minnesota Timberwolf basketball player. The whole place was filled with cars with Utah plates and healthy looking people my age walking around looking at memorials. Soon I realized I had entered the land of the Mormon. A van with Arizona plates and fourteen people rolled up beside me and two attractive girls got out to look at a monument. Allison and Meredith were sisters, and eagerly answered all my questions about their religion. They likened my trip down the river to the Mormon journey from Nauvoo to Utah. I really digged Meredith. She was tall with little piggy tails, and was so sincere as she poured out her soul with everything she said. I felt a real connection as she spoke to me, but soon the people in the van were calling them to go.

Walking down a gravel road with signs of Mormon testimonials along the cornfield to my left, I watched two girls on bicycles with Amish-type clothing go into a church. Naturally I followed. More Mormon girls greeted me at the door. I had become really interested in finding out more about their religion, and they were more than eager to help. When they introduced themselves or talked of others, they always used "sister" as a pretext. The Somoan sister had the most beautiful brown eyes, and when she shook my hand she squeezed it firmly and hung onto it a tad too long as she connected with me. She let me ride her bike to the Visitor Center where sister Arial would find me a Mormon Bible to look at. It was a lady's Schwinn from the early 1900's, provided by the church to all the girls on missions in Nauvoo. After being limited to a five mile-an-hour top speed in my canoe, it really flew.

Sister Arial was Portuguese, with dark, dark eyes and blonde hair. The place was crawling with sisters. I felt like a bull in a glass store. Everyone was all dressed up, contrasted by me in my ripped up, dirty, sleeveless, tie dyed Led Zeppelin paddling shirt. They all looked so fresh and healthy with such bright, captivating eyes. I asked Sister Arial her first name but she wasn't allowed to tell me.

"Tia," she later revealed. "I like Led Zeppelin too," she added in a whisper. After Tia got off work, I rode with her and two other sisters across town in our matching Schwinns to go to their house and find a Book of Mormon. The girls had conservative Amish skirts on, and were so pretty and athletic.

I could hardly keep up over the hilly terrain. It was such a sight; I couldn't help but laugh out loud as I lagged behind.

There was no such thing as small talk with them. It was all spiritual, and the eye contact was riveting. I was being drawn in by the minute, but of course wasn't allowed in the house. Swarms of huge happy families on pilgrimages walked around town, and I used the Book to cover up the naked sexless angel on my shirt as I weaved through them on my lady's bike on my way back to the church. The girls at the church watched me walk in all sweaty with the Book of Mormon, and were so happy they nearly shed tears.

They invited me to watch them perform a play, but I thought it would be best for me to get back on the river. I was very impressionable to new ideas, especially when presented by pretty girls. They'd devoted their lives to their religion, and it made me guilty to think I was using that devotion to get to know them. I paddled away with mixed feelings. I had fallen in love ten times that day, but was pretty sure I couldn't have stayed another ten minutes without getting converted. I had the Book, and if there was any future for me as a Latter Day Saint, that was the best way to find out.

At Lock & Dam #19 in Keokuk, the stagnant water was completely full of dead mayflies. Entering the locks, the nose of my canoe cut right through the stink. I felt a tinge of sadness at the plight of the mayfly. They had lived for one glorious day, and lay rotting in the water. How could a mayfly realize it had only one day to do everything? Was that the end for them? What about my long day of life? Some day would I lie rotting and stinking somewhere too?

I didn't want to live a stale life and then die. I didn't want to be like everyone else. I wanted to live like a mayfly, but I didn't want to end up in a stinky heap somewhere with thousands of other dead mayflies. I wanted to fly away and live like a mayfly, but was afraid to fly too far away and end up a dead mayfly.

It was 8:45 and nearly dark, and I was only a mile from the Missouri border. I had a new rule about not going into a bar after a certain time, but saw one that looked too good to pass up. I wanted one last sniff of Iowa, and besides, I had a lot on my mind. Somehow, sitting alone in a bar full of strangers in some foreign place really helped to put things in perspective for me.

As expected for a non-regular, everyone turned to look at me when I walked in the door, but they ended up being an unbelievably friendly bunch. The man on my right had seen me pull up in the canoe, and before I knew it I was the center of attention and everyone was buying me beers and asking me questions. I spent most of my time talking to Boone, and he offered me a cabin to spend the night in. It was a few miles downstream, but he drew me a map and even went to his truck to give me his own flashlight. I was a little suspicious of his unsolicited generosity at first, but after talking to him for a few minutes and seeing how much everyone respected him, I could see he was genuine. Apparently it was a fishing cabin shared by several local river rats, was unlocked, unoccupied, and filled with food which I was invited to help myself to.

The lady happily bartending was unbelievably friendly, and wouldn't let me spend a penny. Before I knew it I had a shirt, a hat, a pizza, and three beers in front of me, not to mention ten new friends. I still had to paddle four miles in the dark, and left before I started getting too tipsy.

It was a rush paddling the next hour into the pitch-black night. I had no idea if I'd find it, and being after midnight, was the latest I'd been on the water. I lit up a cigar as I hit the Missouri border, thinking of the good people of Iowa, and the good times ahead.

At Alexandria, a bunch of noisy high school kids sat around a campfire drinking beers. I drifted by in the dark silently, and came within thirty feet of them.

"What the hell is that?" One guy stood up from the fire and took two quick steps backward, as if he'd just seen a ghost.

"It's just a big log floating by."

"What the hell is it." His voice was scared, and he was still backing up.

"Hello," I called out. Everyone around the fire jumped out of their skin, and two kids took off running. I could see them perfectly, but the big fire had blinded their eyes.

"Who is it out there?" One brave kid called out, as if expecting Freddy Krueger.

"Don't worry, it's just me, Huck Finn. I'm on my way to New Orleans in this canoe, but it's way too hot to travel during the day." They were over being scared, and the kids who'd run off were trying to salvage the beers they'd thrown.

"Take me with ya."

"Me too." The current was deceptively swift, and in a few seconds they could no longer see me. Their voices faded away as the fire got smaller.

In a few minutes, I arrived at what I thought to be the cabin. Opening the door, I expected someone to blast me with a shotgun. After tripping around in the dark, I found the lights.

The place had only the bare essentials. A stove sat in the center of the peeling floor near a woodpile, a couple of fridges adorned the back wall, a rusty oven sat in a dark corner, and six bunks made up the rest of the furnishings. It was 2:00, and all I was worried about was sleeping. Still not convinced I was in the right place, I fell asleep amidst the buzzing of flies, hoping I wouldn't wake up feeling like Goldylocks.

DAY 42

It was strange waking up in the little cabin, and it took me a few moments to remember where I was. The walls were covered with pictures of guys with beards in flatbottom boats, fishing, drinking, and waving American flags. It was their clubhouse, and I felt like I'd joined a fraternal organization of sorts. Checking out the guest book, I discovered Greg and Janice and their big black dog had left Itasca on April 21st, and were ten days out in front of me. They were planning to hit the Ohio at Cairo, and end up on Lake Kentucky. The thought of catching them was exciting, and after filling up on old bread, peach jam and pickles, I hit the river.

I spent the entire day trying to remember the name of the Samoan sister who lent me her bike. Hertado? Hildago? I wished I could remember. Why did I ever leave?

After stashing the canoe in the woods below Canton, I walked up the railroad tracks into town like a vagabond. I didn't know what to expect. The diner I stopped in first was empty except for a stern looking cop, and he looked me over good. The combination of carp, cops, and no owner to leech from made me hit the street again.

Walking down the sidewalk on the hottest day thus far, I noticed an old guy trying to shove a dresser in a truck. After rendering my services, he asked if I'd be interested in a job for an hour or so. I sweated my ass off lugging fancy furniture around for an hour, and he surprised me with twenty dollars, enough money to last over a week.

After talking to a few girls and asking where the best place in town was to eat, I walked into the place they recommended. The special there was also carp, and they were out of peach pie. A big burly man wearing a black tee shirt and a handlebar mustache glared intimidatingly at me from behind the counter, so I took off. If there wasn't anyone interesting inside a café or it didn't look like I could score a free meal, I always kept moving until I saw a better opportunity.

The sign at the American Legion said there was an ice cream social at the park, so I walked down to take a look. There wasn't anyone under sixty, and they all looked at me guardedly as I walked up to the pavilion. I gave my best Opie Taylor impression as I approached the elderly man who was taking the money.

"Excuse me, sir. I came here to thank you. Men such as yourself have fought to secure our nation's borders, and without such peace of mind provided years ago by men in organizations such as yours, my generation would never have the chances in life that we do today. I am living my life long dream of dissecting this great nation by canoe, a dream only made possible by the sacrifices made by you gentlemen here."

Two minutes later, I was gorging myself on peach pie, German chocolate cake, ice cream, and Kool-Aid, and surrounded by old men asking me questions about my trip, and eagerly telling me the Huckleberry Finn stories of their youths.

After walking back down the tracks and uncovering my canoe from its hiding spot, I was back on the river and in high spirits. It was a great summer day, I had a full stomach, and had more money in my pocket than I had three weeks ago.

I stopped in a bar a few miles down river at La Grange, but the lonely men on either side of me were complaining so sadly about their lives, wives, and jobs that I found it depressing and decided to leave after they had only bought me three brews.

Good old La Grange. My friend Brad and I had come down there in high school and roamed the same streets. We wanted to go off and test ourselves anywhere that seemed like a long ways from home, and Missouri had a nice ring to it. Some girls we had met from this town on a fishing trip had even ran away from home, and showed up unexpectedly in Minnesota with suitcases in hand. It was where we'd come every spring to fish and explore. It was a far away land of mystery, and I'd paddled to the same spot that had been our farthest journey ever from home. We had some wild times in the area, and I spent an hour exploring the town, halfway expecting to run into one of those gals.

I paddled hard to make Pigsback Island before dark. It was rumored to be a top party spot, and it was Friday night. Earlier, I had avoided those types, but I was looking for some action. People were going to be rude, crude, and lewd, but when you went to Rome, you had to act Roman. After a month of thinking of all the people on shore as a bunch of drunken assholes, I was ready to be a little rude and crude myself.

Groups of people dotted the island, and I paddled close by until someone offered me a beer.

After chugging two quick Buds, I put on my best asshole act. I enjoyed being the center of attention, and utilized it to crack jokes about women, beer, and other vulgar things. Hell, if a guy had paddled past in a canoe, I would've given him shit too. I was having a blast drinking and putting on a show as if I was some crazed madman out on the river, until at some point I came to a realization. There were a few drunk guys nearby who were egging me on and having a good time acting like morons with me, but out on the perimeter were a others sitting there trying to enjoy the evening with their wives. Some weren't even drinking, and looked at me like I was a piece of human dog shit.

I had grown so accustomed to labeling people and being a chameleon I'd shifted over to drunk-vulgar mode without even thinking. Why did I act like that? I didn't even believe the things I was saying. Feeling a little embarrassed, I waited for a good time to leave, and got back into the canoe hoping to float into another sandbar by the moonlight.

Although it was already after 11:00, it was a very bright moon, and I found an empty sandbar just up from Quincy. I was angry at how I'd acted lately.

Standing awkwardly alone on the sand on an island in the middle of nowhere, I pondered the last few days. I'd been drinking like a fish everyday and getting free stuff from everybody. I had so much energy and steam I wanted to yell at the top of my lungs. I felt violent and angry. I didn't have any clue what I was doing there. What was the point of the trip anyway? What was I going to do when I got back? Everything was such a waste. My head was cluttered with meaningless thoughts and I wanted to get hammered and kill it all, but I knew that wouldn't do any good either. I was breathing heavy and felt like breaking something. I knew I needed to calm down. I didn't really know why I was so angry. Looking back at the personality that came out of me at the last island, I realized it was all a bunch of bullshit. The things I said to the old man at the park may have been true, but the way I said them was just a bunch of bullshit too. Everything I did seemed like such bullshit, even taking the trip was meaningless. I wanted to climb into the canoe, find some bar in Quincy, and get pie-eyed.

A big sandy hill loomed in the darkness behind me, and I climbed up to the top to try to clear my mind. My brain was cluttered with terrible things and I wanted to erase everything.

I lay down on my back and stared at the stars and watched wicked clouds envelop the moon as I let myself go completely. Closing my eyes, I pretended a giant vacuum was taking everything out of my brain forever until it was completely empty. By the time I opened my eyes up again and looked at the stars, they were all gone as clouds had moved in and blanketed everything completely. I stared at the empty void of sky until I could no longer discern where my mind ended and space began. It was taking me in. I no longer felt my body, as I was empty and part of the sky. My breathing took on the characteristic of a wild animal, but to me it was just the sound of the water as it washed up on the shore below. I was primitive man. I was Adam. I loved everything. I was nothing. Listening to my breathing parallel that of the water below me, I had a sudden urge to become a part of it.

The next thing I remembered was being in the water naked and letting the river take me away. All the worries of before were gone, and my mind was empty and numb. All that mattered were the sky above and the refreshing water surrounding me. I love the sky, I love the water, and I love everything. I'm dreaming. Snap. Where am I? The current was too strong. The lights of Quincy were ahead, and I pictured my dead body washing up on shore. Remembering the dead mayflies, I wondered who would find me in the morning. Fighting the current was useless, so I let it take me, gradually treading water toward the left shore. It was an exhausting process. After walking awkwardly for a quarter mile up the railroad track, walking through the mud, and swimming across a sloppy slough, I staggered over to my tent and collapsed.

CHAPTER 9:HANNIBAL, MISSOURI

JUNE 26TH, 1999 DAY 43

Not quite sure how much of the previous night was a dream, I paddled to Quincy in a light rain. It let up as I landed on shore. An old commercial fisherman recommended the Riverhouse as a good place to eat. I walked into the quaint waterfront bar, promising myself I was done scamming free meals. I took a seat and waited for someone to appear. The wall behind the empty bar was scribbled with funny quotes that regulars in the bar had regretted saying, and I was looking through them when the owner of the bar came in and greeted me. The kitchen wasn't open yet, but after finding out my story, Jim went in and prepared me the best hoagie I'd ever had. He wouldn't accept any money for it. He had recently served Greg, Janice, and their dog Payton, and I was hoping to get a chance to meet them before they hit the Ohio. After eating my meal and thanking Jim for his kindness, I was ready to roll on toward Hannibal, thinking of how nice all the people in Quincy were, even though I'd only met two of them.

It had turned into another beautiful day as I walked out the door and looked toward the pavilion at the riverfront park. A family dressed in matching red and white outfits were having a professional portrait taken in front of the river. Scowling faces revealed anger at having to set aside time in their busy day, as if they wished he would hurry up and get it over with. Everyone stood with their hands on their hips or folded on their chests as they impatiently waited for the photographer to prepare. When he finally got ready to shoot the picture and they posed, they became the happiest family in the history of Quincy. Everybody wore huge smiles and their arms rested on the people in front, just like the photographer had choreographed. It was a thing of beauty to see them with their matching outfits and happy smiling faces, and they all seemed to love each other so much. By the time the last picture was taken, they couldn't get the hell out of there fast enough. Cars peeled out of the parking lot in different directions like crazy.

At Lock & Dam #21 south of town, a big yacht pulled into the locks behind me. They must have figured they'd have to wait for me on the way out, so they maneuvered around me and then slipped back in front of me in order to get going again faster. Sunbathing on the front of the yacht like she'd never worked a day in her life was a good looking lady of about forty. Her teeny bikini struggled to hold her enormous chest. The captain of the boat was a rich looking guy of about sixty-five wearing a gay-ass sailor man type shirt. The old guy couldn't drive the boat worth a shit, and he was having a hell of a time trying to slide it around me so the lady could grab the rope.

The situation started out funny, and ended up in total chaos. He lost his cool and yelled at the lady to reach over the side and grab up for the rope, but it proved to be a major task for her. Every time she put up her hands to grab at the rope her big boobs started popping out of her little bikini, and she had to put one hand down to try to shield them. She was so conscientious of the lockmaster and me watching her, she wasn't leaning out far enough to get the rope. The lock was still open in the back and the current was swift. She couldn't reach the rope, and yelled at him to keep the boat straight. He got impatient, the front end of the boat started swinging around a little too fast, and it looked like it was going to nail the side of the concrete wall and cause some damage. He screamed at her to grab the wall with her hand before she ruined his boat, and she yelled back that he couldn't drive. The old guy was so busy trying to steer he didn't realize the show she was putting on for us. She lay across the front railing trying holding the side of the slimy wall with one hand while shoving her chest back into its top with the other. He was trying to grab the rope too. I was sure she'd fall overboard.

Eventually, the lock closed, the current died, and things stabilized. After the boat sped away, the lockmaster and I laughed so hard together I thought I'd tip the canoe.

Near Hannibal, some guy came running down his stairs and called me over. "Hey, come on and pull in here. We're partying." The guy was like a jackrabbit. He had more energy than anyone I'd ever seen. Within two minutes I was upstairs in his house at a party with a beer in my hand, mowing on a big pile of deer sticks.

"Usually I don't bring strangers in, but I could tell right away when I seen you comin down that river in your canoe with your Zeppelin shirt that you're one of us. When you get between that levee there and the river, the law ends and we start. We do whatever we want and nobody fucks with us. We drink beer and smoke weed and do whatever the hell else we feel like. Do you wanna catch a buzz or what?" The guy was definitely a mad man. All he had on was a ripped up pair of jeanshorts. He was covered in tattoos, and had crazy long black hair that was thick and tangled. His entire body shook when he talked, and he didn't even look at me, just kept pacing the room, literally bouncing off walls. He was sweating profusely.

The living room was filled with guns, animal mounts, a big confederate flag, and bunches of hillbillies in all stages of toxification. One guy was passed out on the couch, another sat at the table staring aimlessly. His eyes twitched, looked toward the ceiling, shut, and started over again. A guy on the porch was pacing in a big circle, doing weird mannerisms with his hands like he was talking to someone, but he was alone. He came in and said something about a ghost who'd came off the river and talked to him the night before. Everyone at the party was having their own trippy experience.

The phone rang and a lady answered it. For ten minutes she stood up facing the wall with one hand cupped over her free ear. There was a shocked look on her face, and she kept saying "no shit," over and over again. When she was done, she sat down, put her hand on her head and looked down for awhile before looking back up and asking to no one in particular, "Who in the hell was I just talking to?" It suddenly came back to her, and she told everyone another of their "dumbass" friends got caught making meth.

I was introduced several times, but everyone kept forgetting who I was and would walk up and ask me all over again. I sat at the table watching everyone and drinking beers while the carnage continued. I felt like I was invisible. A little boy was out on the dock collecting billy-gar minnows and ran inside to show his dad, but his father was unresponsive. They passed a bowl over the kid's head as he cut through the group to watch cartoons. Dejected, the little boy sat in front of the blaring television, shielding his face with a blanket from the confusion around him. I was about to do the same.

When I told my host I had to go, he looked at me like he had just remembered me, then started running around the house catering to me like I was his long lost brother. Getting a cooler out of the garage, he packed in a shit load of leftover food, two gallons of water, and a few beers for the rest of the afternoon. He packed the top in ice and handed over the whole works. "C'mon, just stay for the rest of the day. A bunch of us are gonna pack into my flatbottom, hit the backwaters, smoke some bud, and get lit."

"Sorry man, I gotta make Hannibal before dark."

"I want you to have these then." He took the hat off his head and the coolie off his beer and gave them to me. "I feel like I've known you forever man. I always wanted to take the trip you're taking, and now I'm old and married, but you can do it for me."

We shook hands and I hit the river again, feeling a little touched. They may have been druggies, but they were nice people. Their mode of life was extreme, but I could see how it worked for them. When life's troubles got them down, they just met back at the kitchen table every three hours and passed the bowl around. Man, that Bob Dylan song was true. I couldn't go anywhere without someone trying to get me stoned.

The area north of Hannibal was hard to escape. Everyone waved me over and shoved beers in my face, and although nobody was quite as wild as my first hosts, I did meet several nice people, and stopped for a few minutes at several good parties. I entered Hannibal in rare form. Thoughts of Mark Twain flooded my drowning head, and I felt proud to have made it so far. I felt like Huckleberry himself, and was ready to make a wild homecoming and tear up the town. There was a live band at the edge of town playing some Creedence for a birthday bash, and I stayed until dark partying it up with a bunch of strangers on the side of the river.

I'd stopped for a beer with every group of people I'd encountered. By Hannibal I was pretty buzzed, but it was Saturday night and I was on a mission to find a good time. Darkness was closing in, so I stashed my things in the first patch of woods within walking distance of the town. Near a creek at the south end of Hannibal, I found a nice sandy point with some overhanging trees to stop at for the night. After setting up camp and doing a half-assed job covering my tent and canoe with branches, I grabbed all my essential belongings and set off down the railroad tracks toward town.

It was eerie walking down the tracks at night. They went forever in front of me, and every time I looked to the side, I imagined the silhouette of the railroad serial killer. It seemed like it was darker than most nights. After a short walk, I discovered a light at the end of the tunnel of darkness, and busted through the forest into the city of Hannibal.

I was fired up about a big Saturday night on the town, and already had a good head start. I had no idea where to go, so I walked up a hill toward where the traffic seemed to be the heaviest. It was dangerous walking around in the traffic. I had become accustomed to seeing a barge about a mile in the distance, and having ten minutes to slowly get out of the way. Several times I stepped out into traffic, not realizing the speed at which the cars were traveling. Near the top of the hill, I ran into a nightclub on the right side of the road, and decided to check it out.

As I was heading into Boogie Nights, two great looking girls were leaving, so I struck up a conversation with them. Flashing neon lights reflected off of faces. Tasha had a raw, native look to her, and was very spiritual and open minded. She had dark hair and dark eyes, and wore a yellow tank top. Jenna was fresh looking, with short blonde hair and bright blue eyes. She was always smiling. When I talked to her she listened with an attentive, eager, and receptive smile, and nodded her head affirmatively to everything I said. She looked so open and friendly that it probably fooled all guys into thinking they had a chance with her, when in reality she acted like that toward everyone. An angry looking guy trailed a few steps back, but when they stopped, he kept going.

"That your friend?"

"That's my husband, Greg," Tasha explained, "he's being a lame ass tonight." They'd driven down from Quincy to find some cool bars and invited me to hop into their vehicle and go partying with them.

Greg was already in the driver's seat waiting, and when he saw I was coming along, he stared at his wife Tasha with disbelief. I had my river clothes on, was unshaven, and carried around a big ziplock bag with all my important things. Hopping in the backseat with Jenna, I tried to make conversation with him, but he was miffed at having a homeless guy in his car. He drove silently while I entertained questions from both giggling girls.

Greg was the serious type. His assassin eyes occasionally glanced at me in the rear view mirror. He was wiry; veins popped out all over his arms and neck. I guessed he had a very short fuse. The girl in the backseat who I was trading smiles with was his sister. He had a right to be a little suspicious, but after driving around without finding anything, he finally started accepting me, and actually even talked a few times. With nothing better found, we headed back to Boogie Nights.

Greg and I played pool while the girls danced to a live band. He even played pool like an assassin. One miss and my game was over. He was distracted, constantly having one eye on his wife on the dance floor ready to pounce on any guy who looked at her. The girls were really, really wild. They were the best looking gals in the bar, and always came back every few minutes and tried dragging me out to the dance floor.

I drank moderately and shot pool poorly until I became partners with Jenna, and turned my hat on backwards. I always shot better when pretty girls watched. Jenna and I were really hitting it off. Every time she shot, she leaned over the pool table provocatively, looked into my eyes, and asked me what I'd do. Then she'd miss. I loved playing pool with her.

After shooting a few games of sticks, the girls went back to the dance floor. They were both really open girls, and it was obvious they enjoyed the attention from the guys in the bar. They were the favorites of the guys on stage, and at the request of the band, Tasha dropped her tank top for them. The guys in the bar went nuts, and Greg flipped. He ran up to the dance floor, and I thought he was going to kill every guy in the band, but he just dragged her back to the pool table. She tried denying her flashing, but the looks and yells from every guy in the place betrayed her as they walked past.

By this time Jenna had another admirer, some Marine jughead named Jeff. He followed her around like a puppy dog, and kept putting his hands around her waist. I wasn't too happy to see that, and sensed a confrontation. Jughead's brother was with him too. He was a real drunken doofus, and kept asking me the same questions five times and sprayed spit whenever he talked. He got to be real buddy-buddy toward me and wanted to high-five every ten minutes. He asked me to do a shot of tequila with him if he bought, so I followed him up to the bar. He laid down a twenty, and gave the bartender a thirteen-dollar tip. After the shots arrived, he told me he didn't even like tequila. I wasn't a big fan either, but figured it might help me to deal with Jenna, so I did both of his shots. The guy was goofier than goofy. He was the type that spent over a hundred every night in the bar, and didn't remember a thing. He was real unstable, and between him and his jughead brother and me both going after the same girl, I expected trouble.

Jughead was an awesome pool player. He was very competitive, and engrossed in a serious game. It was time to make my move before it was too late. I got Jenna outside, told her some good gushy lines, and made my move. She pulled away from me, but with a smile, and invited me back to Quincy. It was nearly bartime, and Greg and Tasha had been looking for us. Thankfully, there was no sign of Jughead Jeff or his brother Doofus. We hopped into Greg's car, and headed for Quincy.

Everything I owned sat on a sand bar on the outskirts of town, probably on private property. I ditched it all to chase a wild goose on a half an hour ride to who knew where. I knew I was making a poor decision, and I'd be better off calling it a night. I wasn't sure exactly where we were going, and didn't know how I'd get back. I envisioned all of my things getting either stolen or confiscated. I thought about going back to hide my stuff better, but it was too good of an opportunity to take a chance at spoiling.

It was a long ride back, and a squad car trailed us for a good part of it. Greg struggled to keep the car straight, and Tasha sat in the front seat doing a one-hitter as the cop watched for us to make one false move. I tried not to partake, but sometimes it was really hard. We made it to Quincy, and Greg went right to bed. It was just the girls and me and a good buzz going on, and we partied all night. We were still going strong by morning, and when Tasha went to bed at 6:00, I stayed up until 8:00 with Jenna. By the time Greg got up at 9:00 and volunteered to take me back to Hannibal, I'd slept for less than one hour, and was having a very difficult time figuring out what state I was in.

DAY 44

I was drained on the way back, and hoped my stuff would be all right. Crossing the Illinois bridge into Hannibal, I looked to my left out the car window and saw my tent and canoe in the trees down below. It was dark when I'd gotten in, and I hadn't hid my things as well as I should have. Greg dropped me off at the railroad tracks, and I staggered to my abandoned camp. I loved meeting new people, but it felt good to leave Hannibal behind and get back down the river.

I drifted out of Hannibal in a total daze. Sleep had come for only one hour, and I was still messed up. The details of the previous night were very sketchy, and my mind drifted back to Jenna. She was nearly a ten, and probably out of my league if it wasn't for the mysterious traveler image I had been using lately with girls.

A perfect night for me did not have to include sex. I enjoyed meeting a new girl and getting to know who she really was. Innocent intimacy was my real goal. There was no guilt later. I liked Jenna. She was open, honest, and lived for the moment. I enjoyed the night and morning with her, but knew I would not see her again. We had fallen asleep on the couch together as the sun rose. After waking up a few times and looking at her pretty face, I had moved to the other couch so I wouldn't surprise her brother. As usual, the buzz had either worn off or the connection died.

The Mark Twain Riverboat had seen me the night before, and they made a point of circling me several times. I took pictures of them, and they all waved and took pictures of me. It made me sad for some reason after they left.

I was very reflective on life after a night of hardcore partying. Feeling near-death the next morning always put everything into perspective. Unusually, I felt no guilt over the previous night's worldly excesses, but I sure felt like shit. It was physically impossible for me to paddle, so I drifted until I couldn't stay awake any longer.

Looking around, I realized there was nothing fake in sight. No wires, no cars, no concrete, no buildings, there was only nature all around me. It had been that way for a good part of the trip, but I had recently became ultra aware of it. Then a train chugged past in the distance and ruined everything. I found myself angered at the train. I found consolation in the fact that I wasn't in the city where I could have looked around me and realized every single thing in my plane of vision was fake. What really made me sick was those suburban apartment complexes that planted pretty little trees and shrubbery, trying to go for the natural look while they packed people into little compartmentalized rat houses and raped their wallets. Trains I could live with.

When I was in college I used to love Sundays. We would be so hungover that we would wake up just in time for kickoff and lay on couches all day watching football, eating pizza, drinking more beer, and remembering things from the night before. I was running on empty, but my canoe felt like the old green couch I sat on in college. Heading down a side chute, I laid back against my cushion and closed my eyes for a few minutes.

They were the most psychedelic dreams. The act of slipping away and coming back was a real trip. I was putting my life completely in the hands of fate. I woke up with no idea where I was, looked up to make sure I wasn't about to get killed, and instantly zonked out again.

"He's either dead or drunk." It was someone on shore speaking in a southern accent. I knew I was falling asleep, but allowed it to happen anyway. Since the beginning of the trip I'd woken up at night thinking I was drifting down the river, but when it was real things were a little different. I had really dozed off. Looking at my map later, I had been asleep for nearly two miles.

"Nope, he still ain't movin' yet." Rather than giving them the satisfaction of discovering if I was dead or not, I played possum, not moving a muscle until I had drifted far out of sight. The sleep refreshed me, and I was able to make twenty-five miles.

By late afternoon I cooked up some chili and Ramen noodles, and drifted through a big crowd of Sunday boaters as I was eating. They looked at me cautiously as I devoured my food out of the frying pan, the propane cooker still balancing precariously on my lap. They were especially awed to see me washing my dishes over the side of the canoe in the dirty river, yet no one said a word and none stared for too long. They probably lived in some fancy apartment complex in the suburbs.

After setting up camp on the last non-private land before Louisiana, Missouri, I crashed hard. Although I tried listening to the Cards-Diamondbacks game, I fell asleep with the score tied in the tenth.

DAY 45

I was still drained from a weekend of hard partying. After stopping at the Louisiana Boat Club, a friendly old guy named Elgin drove me in his truck to the only diner in town. I walked back, and stopped in the boat club to say thanks. Three old guys were sitting in opposite corners of the room talking. They were all at least fifty feet apart, and made a perfect triangle. One was drinking near-beer. After talking awhile about big storms on the way, I hit the river again, hoping not to get rained on.

It started sprinkling, so I waterproofed all of my bags. Ten minutes later it was pouring buckets. The lightning was still distant and it wasn't too windy, but it was a very heavy drenching rain. The blast woke me up. Being over ninety degrees already, it felt good at first. After paddling seven miles in the downpour, I arrived at Lock & Dam #24 in Clarksville. The Indian Princess was locking through, and I had a little wait. Initially, the rain had been refreshing so I didn't put on my raingear. I was soaked to the bone. There was a bar nearby, and I walked in to dry off.

There was a tense silence inside. Everyone acted like they'd quit talking when I walked in. I was drenched and looked quite shabby as I dripped a trail of water behind me before setting my canteen and plastic bag on the bar and pulling up a stool. Within minutes the bar came back to life, and I was bombarded by questions.

"Where in the hell did you come from?"

"Where in the hell do you sleep at night?"

"Are you crazy or what?"

"Those islands got cougars and mountain lions."

"It's supposed to rain like this for the next four days."

"Where in world is Lake Itasca anyway?"

"You got a long ways to go until New Orleans."

"Let me buy you a beer."

I settled on a pop from the guy next to me. He was a big Crimson Tide fan named Ace, and was putting away beers at a pretty good clip for noon. The barmaid was very upset about something, and talked heatedly to a guy down the bar. I heard them arguing plainly, and then zoom... the power went out. According to the conversation I was overhearing, it had been turned off by the electric company.

"Son of a bitch hasn't paid them bills in four months."

"Come in with some lady last night, she was takin' all his money."

"He wanted to bet that guy three thousand on one game of pool, kept looking out the window looking for that county cop so he could go beat his ass."

"Shit, I seen him today, he was nuts. Kept sweatin' up a storm. He's gonna get us closed down yet." The bar was very eerie without electricity. It felt like it was either haunted or everyone was gonna turn into vampires and devour me any second. Although it was still pouring, I split, and headed back to the locks.

The Indian Princess was finishing locking upstream. They knew me from upstream, and although they noticed me and talked amongst themselves about me, none was willing to engage in a conversation. They must have thought of my canoe as a nuisance. For them the river was a commercial highway. For me it was playground fantasy world where anything was possible, and time and space no longer existed.

The rain let up and I locked through. The funny looking lockmaster dressed like he belonged in a cough drop commercial in the Swiss Alps. He talked to me in different languages and wouldn't repeat anything he said. A guy at the front of the lock stopped smoking his pipe to yell at me to hurry up, so I left the strange Scandinavian and paddled to the other end. A giant rat ran scurried along the wall next to me.

The pipe smoker warned me there was nothing to see between there and St. Louis.

The barges were getting very, very thick. I was getting closer to St. Louis. A storm front moved in, and I moved near shore and found an isolated beach. A boat shot up out of nowhere and a suspicious looking guy got out. He had the strung out appearance of a guy who was once successful, but had gotten caught up in drugs or gambling. His darting eyes made me instantly not trust him.

"I'm sorry, do you own this island?" It was starting to rain again, but the guy didn't seem to notice. He looked nervous, and seemed angry at me for being around. He was very uncomfortable, and kept looking around behind him.

"No, I've never even been here before. I'm just looking for a good fishing spot."

"What are you fishing for?"

"Yea," he replied, keeping his distance from me. It was pouring now, and lightning was cracking. He pulled three ancient fishing poles out of his boat, and threw the lines out haphazardly. We were in an eddy, and the three lines were going every which way, getting all tangled up. He took a step back and crushed his worm box under his foot. He stayed thirty feet from me, paying absolutely no attention to his lines. He kept looking around and pacing by the woods in the rain. I would have set my tent up if it wasn't for the weirdo, but instead took shelter under a big tree. He was no fisherman.

"Is this a pretty good area for catfish? I was thinking of throwing some lines out myself." The guy paid no attention to my question. He had something to hide on the island, and was either afraid or suspicious of me, and figured the rain would have sent me packing by then. Until the lightning stopped and the wind died, I had nowhere to go.

We stayed under separate trees forty feet away while his unwatched lines continued to tangle together in the eddy. I felt like telling him whatever he had going on there I didn't care, but didn't want to let him know how obvious he was. We were both soaked, stuck in a pointless standoff of silence until he finally yelled over to me.

"There's a few real good camping islands a few miles downstream." He looked very perturbed, and I knew it was my invitation to leave. The worst of the storm had passed, and although it was still raining, I got back into my canoe to leave.

"Yeah, I'm gonna leave now too." He pretended to pack his things away as I quickly disappeared down the river. I looked back with my binoculars. He waited until I was out of view of the naked eye, looked around again, and walked back into the woods toward the place he seemed to have been guarding earlier. I put ten quick miles between him and me, keeping a loaded gun handy in case he decided to revisit later.

The rain let up near dusk, and it ended up being a nice night. I wanted to get as far away from the island guarder as possible, and paddled after dark by the light of the moon, paranoid he would look for me. The current had accelerated, and it was scary paddling. I felt like I was being sucked into St. Louis where all sorts of dangers awaited.

After covering thirty-six miles on the day, I found a sandbar in the moonlight and set up camp. I was far enough away from the guy on the island, that I was no longer worried about him. My tent was ripping again. I'd already sewed it twice, but it was worse than ever. I was missing a tent pole, which was essential for the stability of my little shelter. To make matters worse, all of my things were damp, sandy, and smelly from the storms all day and the toll they've taken from the last forty-five days.

I wanted someone to travel through St. Louis with. The prospects of catching Greg and Janice and their black dog were dim. Chris and Geoff were somewhere behind me, and I expected them to be catching me soon. The mysterious guys in the bicycle- propelled raft I'd been hearing about were out there somewhere too. I fell asleep, proud of myself for going a whole day without drinking any beer.

In the middle of the night another storm hit. Massive winds ripped my rain fly off, collapsed my tent, and sent my cooler rolling down the beach. I raced outside and recovered all my gear during the worst part of the storm. It nearly blew me away. I got everything back, but it was all soaked.

DAY 46

Up early due to discomfort, I made it quickly to Lock and Dam #25 at Winfield. There were barges everywhere and it looked like a long wait. The lockmaster promised to sneak me through, and while I waited, I passed the time by talking to a guy on an assist tow. He sported a huge tattoo on his forearm that said hot and horny. The Missouri headwaters had been pounded with rain, and some major floodwaters were on the way. It got hairy after the convergence, and they'd already had two barge accidents that spring.

I drifted and read, until coming across a restaurant called the Golden Eagle. Everyone watched me out the window as I pulled my canoe up. I sat down and got into a conversation with a guy who was sitting with his two daughters, who were both college students at Mizzou. He did all of the talking, and watched me very intently, probably realizing I was noticing his girls. Two guys at the next table came in to the conversation also. They both had a Jimmy Buffett carefree look to them, and it was obvious from their constant Elmer Fudd laughs they were stoners. We talked about the river near St. Louis, and the dangers associated with the heavy barge traffic.

After lunch, I was talking to my Dad on the phone, and one of the Jimmy Buffett guys came up with index finger and thumb held together to his lips to ask if I wanted to smoke some. Cupping my hand over the phone, I thanked him, but I needed to keep my head clear with all of the boat traffic approaching St. Louis. After getting back into my canoe, he and his buddy came out to say goodbye, and asked if I'd changed my mind about getting baked with them. As if what I was doing wasn't crazy enough, to do it stoned with that kind of current and boat traffic would have been a death sentence.

The river was as swift as I'd seen it, and the boat traffic was very heavy as I approach the suburbs of St. Louis. My orange road construction vest with orange reflective tape helped warn boats of my presence. It fit snuggly over my life jacket. St. Louis really scared me, especially after those letters I'd received. I wanted to stall for a few days, hoping the two canoeists behind me caught up, yet I enjoyed traveling alone. I didn't feel very focused, and needed to be fully aware by the time I hit the Alton Dam. The river was more dangerous each day, and it would only get worse as I moved south.

North of Grafton was a sandbar full of people. A guy my age flagged me over as the River Eagle towboat roared past. Several girls clad in bikinis roamed the dirty sand, and the guys on the barge watched them shamelessly with binoculars. The guy on shore introduced himself as Todd. He had four girls with him in swimsuits. Todd tossed me a beer without even asking. He was a little messed up, but had a spiritual look with really kind eyes, even if they were a little glazed. The girls were all pie-eyed, and they flipped out when they saw the Minnesota license on my canoe.

Todd and I really connected well, and he gave me some advice about St. Louis. I didn't know whether to take the Chain of Rocks Canal or the old channel, and he insisted I take the Canal. An older guy came by stumbling drunk, overheard our conversation, and insisted I take the old channel. He told me it was a piece of cake in a canoe, and it would be a bad move to go through the Canal, where all the barges were. He was really hammered, but seemed like an old river rat. Todd respected the older guy, but told me in a light voice to make sure I took the Canal.

The girls gathered around me asking tons of questions that I was happy to answer. Their manner convinced me I must've beached right after they'd smoked a bowl. Todd asked if I wanted to catch one, and with all those girls around it was tempting, but I'd been living too recklessly lately, and knew I couldn't afford to lose my edge with the most dangerous part of the trip coming. There were a lot of things I found appealing at that sandbar, but something in my mind told me to get the hell out of there before I could no longer resist. Beer, weed, and women really made me lose my focus, and when I got off track, I really derailed. If it were half as bad as those letters from the Corps of Engineers said, I'd be lucky to survive as it was. After finishing the beer I was nursing, I split. As I pulled away from the party, the drunken guy who tried giving me directions broke into a loud off key version of Proud Mary. I paddled away wondering what I was missing. I wanted desperately to get into the same wavelength as Todd's friends, but knew I had more important things to concentrate on.

It was getting dark, and after covering the day's thirty-fourth mile, I found an island near Portage Des Sioux. In addition to the tear in my tent seam and lost pole, the duct tape holding the floor together was leaking badly. I had also broken my third fishing pole earlier. I was filthy, everything I owned was covered in mud and rust, and half of it was broken. My brand new canoe looked ten years old. Besides my canoe, my body, and my paddle, everything else was expendable. I had no idea what to expect the next day, but had a hunch it could get ugly. Regardless, I had to keep truckin'.

Chapter 10: St. Louis

Day 47

My tent was in really rough shape, and it was getting very hard to keep my things dry. My sleeping bag was damp, but I still slept pretty well. It was a misty morning and the forecast called for a total washout. Rather than try pushing through St. Louis, I decided to aim for the Missouri River confluence and save the city for later. The river was higher and faster than I'd seen. A giant statue of the Virgin Mary patrolled the right bank. I wanted to go over and touch it, but instead said a silent prayer and moved on.

I paddled hard to the Alton Dam with the sensation of moving toward enemy territory. It marked the entrance to St. Louis, an area I'd been warned about since day one. There were two sets of locks, and I expected to see a lockmaster, sign, or a signal chord, but found nothing. The swift current became too strong to fight, and carried me into the lock chamber on the right. It was open, and my only guess was that someone had seen me coming and opened it for me. The lock was twice the length of any I'd encountered, and my canoe was completely hidden from view as I clung to a rope on the left wall. There was no sign of life, and the current was too fast to turn around. I'd chosen the wrong lock, and no one knew I was there. I clung to the giant concrete wall for ten minutes, hoping to be noticed, and feeling trapped. I figured a barge would come through at any time and crush me.

A sign said not to climb the ladder up the wall, but I had to get someone's attention. Voices sounded on a loudspeaker, but nobody was in sight. Shedding my raingear for dexterity, I climbed to the top of the ladder and reached a concrete platform. Two men were perched in a tower on the other side of the left lock. After frantically waving my shirt and yelling, they noticed me, and were confounded as to how I'd gotten there. They spoke through the loudspeaker, taking me for either a trespasser or a wacko, but they hadn't seen a boat, and had no idea how I'd gotten there. The river was too loud to hear my responses, so I gave them hand signals to explain.

They finally figured out I was trapped in the big lock, and the loud speaker ordered me sternly to get back in my boat and wait. Within fifteen minutes, I was down the ladder, back in the canoe, and the gates were opening. Although I expected someone to walk over and talk to me, no one bothered. I was scared about what I'd find on the other side of the parting gates, but other than a little more barge traffic and some swifter water, it wasn't much different.

A heavy amount of barge traffic heading upstream forced me to the right shoreline. The current was very fast, and I was soon at the point of the confluence. The dirty water of the Missouri must have been going fifteen miles per hour. Huge waves crashed into the slower river forming a jagged line where the different colored waters met. The Mississippi was dirty, but the Missouri was really dirty. I waited on the point, and although I knew I should've been on the left side, Duck Island was perfectly situated just after the confluence on the right, and was the only spot I could camp before the Chain of Rocks Canal. Waves crashed on the dividing line to my left, but if I paddled hard across the fast water of the Missouri, it would be possible to make it to the island and avoid the rough water at the jagged line of confluence.

I paddled like my life depended on it, straight across the Missouri. I was getting closer to the other shore, but moving faster to the left than I was straight. Fixing on a spot on the far shore ahead of me, I put all of my effort into reaching it, glancing occasionally at the turbulent water to my left I was sliding into. After narrowly missing the rough water, the river calmed slightly, and I gained ground on Duck Island. I was out of danger, and found a little patch of sand to call home for the night.

It was hard to get to, but was the perfect location. The entrance to the Canal was a hundred yards downstream and straight across. I was sitting along the bank of the old channel, just past the confluence. The next day was the one everyone had warned me about, and my heart pounded with adrenaline thinking about it.

It was only 2:00, but I needed to rest and get focused in order to make it through all of St. Louis the following day. I spent the day watching barges go in and out of the Canal, and listening to the N.B.A. draft. If Wally ever became a star for the Wolves, I wouldn't forget where I was when they nabbed him. After listening to the Cards, I secured my canoe, shoved my dirty shoes under the tent, and fell asleep early.

Although I expected there to be people all around me as I entered St. Louis, the only person I communicated with all day was the guy at the tower who I gave hand signals to. Silence was good. People talked too much anyway. They should have made a law that after 100 words each day, your tongue got shut off until the next. People would only say what they meant. We would be forced to listen, be more intuitive, and look each other in the eyes. People would get to the damn point, and all superficial small talk would be eliminated. I always thought of goofy shit as I fell asleep.

St. Louis

JULY 1, 1999 DAY 48

I awoke at 5:00 a.m. to pouring rain and a loud whooshing sound. My feet were submerged in a pool of water. Was it possible it was leaking that badly? Delirious from sleep, I unzipped the door, and water flooded in. The sand below me was caving away, and my entire tent was about to be washed down the river. Acting as fast as I could in the dark, I unloaded the tent, threw my gear as far up the hill as possible, and dragged the tent up. My canoe was being bashed against the shore and was filled with water.

After emptying the canoe of everything, I took an inventory to see what I had lost. Miraculously, the only things missing were my shoes. They'd been washed right out from under the tent. Everything was completely soaked, it was still raining like crazy, and I was freezing my ass off. There was no way to set camp back up, and I couldn't dry my things out. Dawn was just showing herself. There was no other option than to try to cross the river and enter the canal before the water rose any farther. It had rained three inches in the last few hours, and the river had gone up two feet overnight.

Looking across the raging river toward the Canal, I knew I was in trouble. It would have been easy to get across the day before, but the rain had made it nearly impossible. I only had 100 yards to play with before I missed the entrance and was sucked down the old channel. Although I considered trying my luck with the old channel, I trusted Todd more than the drunk John Fogarty wannabe.

Never had I felt more serious then I did then. The flash flood had complicated an already dangerous situation, and I would be allowed no mistakes. I felt like a young warrior who had his first taste of war, but the battle was just getting started. After packing my canoe full of soaking wet gear, I waded through knee high water to pull it upstream another twenty yards until a big flooded tree blocked my way. The effort gave me at least a little better chance to make it across to the Canal.

Spending every speck of energy in my body, I set off toward the Illinois shore at a forty five-degree angle upstream. At the halfway point I was still on pace to make it, but the closer I got to the shore, the further right I was pushed. After two eternal minutes of furious paddling, my numb arms carried me past the rock point that marked the entrance to the Chain of Rocks Canal. I made it by less than five yards.

It was still sprinkling, but the rain had let up considerably as I entered the stagnant water of the Chain of Rocks Canal. Thick fog hung over the damp early morning. I was out of trouble for the moment but would be forced to rejoin the main channel in seven miles. Having become accustomed to being aided by the current, and tired from crossing the old channel, it was really tough moving the canoe down the Canal. It took two hours to reach the lock at the end of the canal. As I approached the river's final lock, the skies burst, and it started raining again.

Paddling toward the lock in the pouring rain, a towboat captain called me over and invited me inside the Helen B. to get out of the rain. He reminded me of Jerry Garcia. I was shivering badly, and jumped at the opportunity for some shelter. The captain radioed ahead, and the lockmaster suggested we tied the canoe to the side and lock through with the tow. After waiting inside the tow for half an hour and being warned about the area after the arch, we locked through. His crew was a rough bunch, but followed every order the captain gave. The gates opened, they untied me, and the captain killed his engines while I paddled out of the way. The rain let up again as I left the locks, but it was very windy.

A few hundred yards downstream from my twenty-ninth and final lock, I rejoined the treacherous main channel. It was like spending the day riding your bike down a nice trail, and suddenly turning into rush hour traffic. Bridge after bridge extended out in front of me, and a steady line of barges fought the heavy current and pushed up the river. The current was absolutely raging, and I shot ahead at breakneck speed without even paddling. If I saw an obstacle ahead, I would have to start turning nearly 100 yards early to miss it. I didn't have much control over my canoe.

The barges moving upstream threw some big waves, but it was the moored barges that were the real killers. They covered the majority of both shores, but when there was a gap between them they sucked thousands of gallons of water under the fronts, creating deadly whirlpools at the backs. Barges came by, and I was forced to go as close as possible to the moored barges. When the waves smacked them the water reverberated back and created huge areas of rough water within thirty feet of their sides. The waves had no shore to break on, so they rocked back and forth building energy and becoming more irritated with each passing towboat. The water on the river was turbulent and unpredictable, and although I knew getting sucked under a moored barge would mean death, the heavy boat traffic and wind forced me to cling to them.

The skyline was beautiful and the Arch was getting closer, but I couldn't afford to look up and admire them. I had fifteen miles of danger to get through, and it would get worse as I went. The Jefferson Barracks Bridge at the south end of town marked the end of the heavy traffic, but it seemed light years away.

After two very close calls in which I was rocked by waves and almost tipped, I had to take a break. I'd planned to go all the way through without stopping, but found a concrete slab at the big McDonald's near the Arch and pulled up for some much needed remorse from the perilous river.

Several tourists had watched my canoe nearly capsize on the rough water, and when they saw Lake Itasca-New Orleans on the side of my little green craft, I was approached by a hoard of people. A bunch of them started waiting in line to have their kids' pictures taken with me; one of them even asked how much it cost. It would have been fun, but the stupidity of what I was doing and the dangers that still lie ahead of me forced me to get back in the canoe. I accepted a free lunch and some contributions, and although I could have sat there all day milking the tourists, another bad storm was moving in, and I was on a mission to get to the Jefferson Bridge. Reluctantly, I waved goodbye and got back into my little death trap.

The next ten miles were spent zigzagging through heavy barge traffic. At one point I thought I was done. Pinned to the right side of two passing barges, I was forced to cling to the moored barges on my right. A moored barge ahead extended twice as far as the others, but I thought the passing pair would be by me before I closed in on the moored barge straight ahead. The current was too swift. I was forced to choose between being sucked under the stationary barge in front of me, or heading out to my left and being flipped by the monstrous waves from the passing barge which was clinging to the same side of the river as I was. An assist tow was traveling in front of me, and I looked up for a moment to see the workers staring at me through their binoculars, as if about to witness a car crash. Their expressionless faces were disturbing as they waited for the river to chalk up another victim. There was no escape, so I aimed for the left and put my life in the Lord's hands. The four-foot chop nearly claimed me, but the canoe stayed afloat, the moving barge missed me, and I narrowly avoided being spun around in the whirlpool that accompanied the irregularity of the steel shoreline to my right.

The next few miles were a blur of living hell that I was lucky to have survived. Several guys working on shore yelled obscenities at my recklessness or stared in disbelief. St. Louis was no place for a canoe, especially at flood stage.

The bridge was in sight, but before I could reach it, a doozy of a storm came out of nowhere. A wall of water raced across the water ahead and blanketed me. Lacerating winds held me in one place, even with the raging current. In the midst of it all, I couldn't help but laughing. I'd found the urgency I had been seeking. I was within a few hundred yards of the bridge that signified a major victory. Rain, wind, and waves were really pounding me, but I was too close to stop.

The rain was too strong to last more than ten minutes, but the wind refused to subside. After fighting my way to the first island on the south side of St. Louis, I couldn't take another second of fighting the elements. It was only 2:00, but I'd covered twenty-seven miles of torture. The Corps of Engineers guys hadn't been so far off on their warnings after all. After checking the island for murderous fugitives, I set up my piece of shit tent, took my soaking sleeping bag out, and tried to dry it in a tree.

I could care less if my tent was dirty and leaky and everything I owned smelled like an old basement. I could remember being very upset about a little ding on my car, or a stain on my favorite shirt. Everything I owned was in the canoe, and it was all ruined. I'd throw it away at New Orleans anyway. It was a great feeling. I belonged to nothing, was connected to everything, and nobody owned me. The simplicity of being alive had never felt so valuable. I was a young buck that had survived his first shotgun season.

St. Louis was behind me and I was entering the second half of my adventure. I was in the South. After spending the day napping, reading, playing solitaire, and listening to the Cards, I drifted off to sleep while it was still light out.

Rough Water

DAY 49

I slept like a log for twelve hours. The river rose another two feet overnight, but my tent and canoe were a safe distance from the water. The fast current helped me make excellent time, but I was constantly forced to scramble to the side because of steady barge traffic. I couldn't drift casually and read like I'd been doing in the previous weeks

The tows were much bigger. Up North, they were limited to pushing sixteen barges. There was no limit below St. Louis, and it was not uncommon to see forty-two or more barges in front of a single tow. The engines were much bigger, and the wake that shot out behind them was six feet high and lasted for over a mile. I called it the devil's spine. The majority of the danger was directly behind the engine, but much of it still found its way to shore, especially around corners.

The simple solution would have been to move to the side of the river, away from the main channel, but a new antagonist had been introduced to me. The river ran so swiftly, anytime there was a bend, wing dam, or island, the current spun into a gigantic whirlpool known as an eddy. They were as big as football fields, and had been known to grab large yachts, spinning them out of control for hours.

Wing dams were a series of rock dams under the water's surface built years ago to funnel the main channel and keep it at an adequate depth for the large commercial boats. They ran perpendicular from the channel to shore, and were visible on the surface because of the turbulent water they produced behind them. They were three times as deadly looking as the ones up north, and I didn't want to see what they'd do to a canoe.

Another major hazard that had come into play was driftwood, which had been set free from the flood. Some were nearly full size trees, and there were always several logs around the canoe. Floating logs may seem rather harmless, but since they were not held up by the wind, they drifted faster than my canoe and threatened to roll under me from behind and tip me if gone unnoticed.

I spent the day drifting down the middle of the river avoiding wing dams and eddies. When a towboat came into sight, I immediately paddled out of the channel to the other side of the buoys. Sometimes I got squeezed between the two dangers and was forced to pick my poison, usually opting to hug the edge of the buoys and ride out the barge wakes. I spent the day criss-crossing back and forth, constantly on the lookout for danger. Whenever an obstacle arose, I had to start moving well in advance. My paddle did little against the unpredictable water, and its main use had become that of a rudder.

After putting thirty miles between St. Louis and me, the barge traffic started to let up a bit, and I got into the pattern of riding the buoy line on the edge of the swift water. The river was devoid of pleasure boats due to the flooding and driftwood, and even the barges were having trouble. At a small marina near Kimmswick, I met a retired couple from La Crosse who lived in their boat, The Slo-Poke. Mike and her husband Wally filled me up full of stories of river lore. They told me about two Japanese Kayakers who had ran the river until getting their things stolen, and an eighty-five year old who turned his car into some sort of a paddleboat with a small motor. His only goal was to get to New Orleans before he died. They'd also spotted two guys in a crazy looking raft a few days earlier. These people had become a part of the River's personality, as I was hoping to become.

After waving goodbye, I was back alone. When I was young, I always imagined doing the river with my friends. After being alone on the river for seven weeks, I could not envision doing it any other way. The solitude had spoiled me. I couldn't imagine what it would have been like to confer with someone before making every little decision.

In Chrystal City, I stopped to dump garbage and got into a conversation with a man, his two teenage daughters, and his father. The old guy was the most interested in my trip, in fact he began a journey from Chrystal City to New Orleans once, but was forced to quit after two days because of brutal sunburn. Of all types of people I met on the river, old men were the ones I related to best. They realized the urgency I felt in going when it was still physically possible. With every summer that passed without me trying the adventure, I had an increasingly hard time living with myself. There was always something that prevented me from going, like jobs, college, or girls, but none of them ever panned out, and I was left sitting there every fall thinking to myself how that should have been my year. My youth was slipping away, and I was afraid not to go.

The most difficult people for me to talk to were young girls under twenty. They seemed so innocent, and I knew I wasn't. Engaging in any communication beyond small talk was to cross a line of sorts. As a result, I never connected with them, and missed out on a new, refreshing look at the world they could have shared. I always felt like they were laughing at the way I dressed or wore my hair anyway.

I drifted into St. Genevieve as the sun slowly set, covering forty miles without even paddling. For the first time in a long time, I was unable to fall asleep. My mind was flooded with millions of things I wanted to do. I wanted to call so and so and write to someone else. I wanted do the Missouri River, move to Alaska, become a whitewater rafting guide, become a fireman, buy a restaurant, travel the country in my car for a year, or just live in New Orleans once I got there. I loved the world again, and although I had no idea what I wanted to do, at least there were options. I looked forward to a million things. I wanted to get back home, but wished the trip could go on longer.

For some reason it felt like the trip was almost over. Maybe because I finally believed it was possible, and had proven my point. Maybe I'd do it again the next year, and take my time more. I was finally free. Could I take a job when I got back and risk getting reprogrammed? I would never be able to work for another person again.

After trying to answer non-urgent questions as well as possible, my mind drifted off to the spiritual side, as it often did before sleep. When my mind raced at night, sometimes I struck on something so profound, I wondered how it could have alluded me for so many years. After getting a glimpse, it somehow slithered away leaving me empty handed, trying to reopen the door that had just slammed shut. It was gone, but then something new came into my head, and I forgot what I was thinking about anyway. I felt the same way every night before leaving my body to travel to far away places that had answers to all questions. I'd wake up without the slightest inkling of where I'd gone, but I wanted to go back during the waking hours. I hadn't figured out the key yet.

Drugs gave me the same sensation of jumping from one profound undeveloped thought to the next with the guise of complete understanding. Thoughts stood alone, and without being classified into definitive clusters, they gave the impression of being a whole new way of looking at something as deductive reasoning capacity vanished. With the lack of compartmentalization skills, my senses couldn't just take something in and access the part of the brain I used to describe it in the past. My mind was forced to use the senses alone to find a new meaning for that stimulus, and as a result its importance was overestimated. After years of struggling with the pros and cons of smoking weed, it's the best explanation I could come up with.

DAY 50

I awoke, having all but forgotten the profound thoughts of the previous night. I'd never been a morning person, and usually lay there lamenting the hardships the reality of getting out of my sleeping bag would bring. I was out of water, and in need of propane.

Near St. Genevieve, I found a harbor up a crick a few hundred yards, and waited an hour for the place to open. While waiting, a group of beer drinking boaters pulled up. The river was too dangerous for pleasure boating, but they were camping just up the shoreline. They took me in and gave me Gatorade, water, and vegetables. They offered me beer, but it was too hot and too early, and I needed to stay focused and hydrated. It was already approaching 100 degrees. They left, and at 11:00, the marina restaurant finally opened. Everyone knew each other and looked at me funny. I had gone sixteen days without a shower and hadn't shaved in ten days. Their glances told me I was starting to look like a vagrant again.

Having my canoe to attract people's attention was one thing, but if I was on foot and all dirty, sunburned, and smelly, people kept their distance. Often I forgot my ragged appearance and started up a conversation, but was met with short answers and negative body language. After attempts to converse with a few gals were met with no response, I hunkered down in my chair, sipped my coke, and left. Darryl, the bartender, was a big guy with a huge heart. He watched quietly as everyone in the bar avoided me, and when I left he caught up to me outside with a huge container full of barbecued pork, chips, and two gallons water.

"Hey man, it's on me." That really made my day. Although it was hotter than hell, the river was still rising, and I was deathly afraid of whirlpools, I had water, a great meal, and was happy. I headed out of the crick, realizing chances were I would not see anyone else to talk to. The river south of St. Louis was very desolate, and although there were towns on the map, they were a few miles off shore due to flooding problems. It was very difficult to find places to get food and water, so I loaded up whenever possible.

The water particles in the river reminded me of people in a city. Put too many in one place and crazy, unpredictable things happened. If the banks of the river were straight and there was only one way to go, things flowed smoothly, but if the masses were given too many choices, they all sped off as fast as they could in different directions. Some moved straight and fast, but others stayed on the sides, spinning forever in circles.

There were more eddies and whirlpools to dodge, and more logs as well. Being Saturday, there were actually even a few brave pleasure boaters here and there. Boy, were they crazy. Even on the edges of the main channel I was finding cyclones of water all around me. I kept my eyes peeled and zigzagged around them. They reminded me of the previous winter when I hiked out a few miles to an island, camped four days, and ice fished. It was over forty degrees every day, and when I tried to hike back, a channel I had crossed before was open. It was getting dark fast, I had 150 pounds of gear, and no way back to the car. I walked down a half-mile or so, and found some ice, but there were springs bubbling up all over. I was forced to zigzag back and forth trying to avoid them, and at one point I looked around and was surrounded by bubbling springs for over 100 yards in every direction. I ended up falling through the ice three times. I made it back to the car, frozen solid, but still intact. Paddling through the minefields of whirlpools was similar to the helpless feelings of that cold day.

I stopped in Chester and had a Coke, but there wasn't much to see besides a big prison and a statue of Popeye. I shaved and washed up, and put on my new Keokuk shirt. I wanted to look presentable and find some people to spend the 4th of July with.

The whirlpools still scared me, but I was getting used to them and becoming more able to predict where they'd occur. Anytime the river turned I found a dangerous area, but on the straight-aways I was able to read and relax until a barge came.

Besides the perilous whirlpools, the fact I was low on food, there was no one to talk to, it was over 100 degrees, a heavy south wind held me up, the river was flooded, my tent was trashed, I was out of propane, and huge barge wakes kept trying to capsize me, I felt great. I was taking great pleasure in satisfying my own basic needs of food, water, and survival. I remembered how great it felt to be alive and how precious a gift life was.

Pondering the gifts of life all around me, I turned a corner near sunset, and was greeted by both the Mississippi Queen and the Delta Queen. I'd been looking forward to seeing them for a long time, and to see them silhouetted against the setting sun was really a moment. As I admired them, a couple of hillbilly catfishermen in flat bottoms motored up to me. They invited me to camp and drink beer with them, and despite my reluctance, they kept trying to talk me into it. One even started tying my canoe up to his boat. They seemed goofy, so I told them I needed to make it to Cape Girardeau by morning, and headed out. I watched carefully to make sure they didn't follow me, and didn't set up camp until well after dark. I slept much more soundly with a loaded gun near my pillow.

JULY 4TH 1999 DAY 51

The water was still rising. It was up another foot by morning. Every day I thought it would peak, but it kept going up. Within ten minutes of setting out, I had my closest call yet, with a barge that forced me into a whirlpool on a tight corner. The water spun violently, and waves from the devil's spine crashed into the eddy. A giant rock jetted out ahead of me, causing the river to do crazy things. I kept paddling, trying to keep the canoe balanced, and prayed out loud. "With God's help. With God's help." I had no control over my canoe. It was almost like a dream, but with God's help I somehow made it. It was such a close call that I was ready to quit for a few days and wait for the water to drop back below flood stage.

I was running into rough stretches, even inside the channel buoys. I'd be drifting along lazily reading, and become alarmed by the sound of rushing water. Scanning downstream, I looked for ripples on the surface, but it was difficult because the chop from the wind made everything very rough. I looked for points, curves, or other possible causes until bingo, I was close enough to see the bad spot. It may have been a ways off, but I was at the mercy of the current and had to start moving right away.

Sometimes I turned a corner in rough water and met a barge. He could be a mile off, but we closed together fast. I'd scan the shoreline for irregularities that could cause trouble, then choose left or right. Sometimes I saw a safe place to hide from the barge wake, but realized I couldn't get there, and had to brave the less favorable water.

That was the scenario I had encountered earlier, and it got my heart pumping so hard and fast I thought it was going to explode. There was no place to hide, and waves crashed against the eddy on the right side as I approached. I actually picked up my Bible, and read the first few words that I turned to, something about the eye of a needle, a camel, rich people, and the Kingdom of Heaven. It was sure to be a close call, and I wanted something pure in my mind, just in case they were my last thoughts.

After surviving the eddy, I pulled in below a campground. The place I had nearly capsized at was famed for a giant flat rock that stuck out above the water. It was called Grand Tower, and was also known as Devil's Rock. Its rough water had claimed the lives of many boaters throughout the years. The tow that had pinned me in had forty barges, and the people at the campground said they were some of the largest waves they had ever seen. Some had watched me struggle through the five-foot rollers, and were appalled at my presence on the flooded river in a canoe. They said it was a miracle I had survived the rough water of Devil's Rock.

My body still trembling a little, I took an hour off and made some calls. My buddies Dale and Bryan, who I introduced in La Crosse, had been hanging out non-stop for the last few weeks, and their stories of fishing and partying made me excited to hang out up there later in the summer. After talking to them, I got back into the water, vowing to be more careful. I felt very fortunate having survived the morning, but also felt an adrenaline rush to reenter the river, knowing it was unwise of me to do so.

Drifting along watching for more hazards, I thought back to the 4th of July in years past spent with friends. I thought of barbecuing, boating, fishing, partying, water-skiing, and other fun times. They were probably out doing all that stuff.

I wanted to cook something, but was still out of propane. I turned on the radio to hear the beginning of In a Gadda Davida. Drifting along eating cold beef stew, I spent seventeen minutes wondering what the song was about and where I'd stay that night.

Cape Girardeau was gaining a mystique in my mind. It was the first major river town south of St. Louis, and I was looking forward to getting there early and getting settled. I wanted a gal to spend the 4th with, and knew that if I was bold enough I might have the opportunity. All excited about the Cape, I arrived at 1:30. A giant wall blocked the town from the river and I started getting really bad vibes about the town. It was as if the town had severed all ties to the river and thought of it as a nuisance. Rather than set up camp below town and walk in like I did at Hannibal, I decided to keep moving, even though I needed water and propane.

Although I'd have to spend the 4th alone, it was the right move. I probably would've just gotten all crazy and hammered and regressed again. Besides, the 4th of July was just another day for me. I was free everyday, not just one, and didn't feel the need to pack everything in to one day before having to return to work on Monday.

I spent a good part of the next seven hours letting the current work for me. I cranked the tunes, ate the last of my snacks, smoked a cigar, drank some O.J., and had my own little 4th of July celebration.

The river was really trucking along, and by 8:30, I was already thirty-five miles south of the Cape, having covered over fifty-five miles on the day. Firecrackers popped, and party noises carried over the river from nearby. Getting a little lonely and restless, I walked up and investigated. After stashing my canoe, I worked my way through some thick brush, and wandered right into someone's yard. They were all sitting around the picnic table, and the kids were running around the yard carrying sparklers. It looked like a family picnic. I had my dirty old Led Zeppelin paddling shirt on, and popped out of the thick woods right in front of them carrying my plastic bag and three empty water containers. They looked like a nice group of folks, but weren't too sure about me. After trying to make conversation, I sensed I made them uncomfortable, and walked on down the road without asking for water. I was starting to feel like Frankenstein. It was getting dark, but for some reason I walked farther down the road, hoping to run into more people.

After strolling about half a mile, I was about to turn around when I saw a group of people sitting by an old shack with a couple of rusty camper trailers nearby. It was a secluded area, and they stopped eating and looked up toward me curiously. One of them waved me over. Down a little dirt road I walked to join the group.

The first guy I noticed looked exactly like Charlie Manson. He had wild eyes that were open so wide it looked like it hurt. The other guys in the group wore beards and old hats with steelworker logos, and there were a few women in the group as well. The severed head of a giant fish was stuck on a stick within a few feet of their table. Two big rotweilers lay on the ground near the old picnic table they sat at.

"Ya want some catfish?" The strong southern drawl came from a wiry man to my left. He had white hair, a white beard, and the same Manson eyes as the first guy. There were no plates, just a big greasy cardboard box filled with pieces of the fish that was still staring at me just a few yards away. It was thrust into my face and followed with so many eyes watching my reaction, that to refuse would be taken as an insult. "Don't worry, those rots won' bite ya. Although the fish was cold, it tasted pretty good. I was offered a beer, and made to feel right at home. The man to my left did all of the talking, and after getting my name, he introduced himself as Chet. Before I knew it, he pulled out his harmonica and started ad-libbing the blues.

"My name is Matt. I got them muddy water blues. Been on that river fifty-one days"... then he stopped, perhaps too drunk to come up with another line. Chet blew so hard on that harmonica and played with so much emotion that I thought his head would explode.

Chet went around the table and introduced everyone, except for the Manson guy. "He don't give out his name." he explained. People talked about the guy like he wasn't there, and judging from the fixed stare he held straight ahead at nothing, he wasn't.

"Shit, he's USDA approved crazy," the man in front of me explained. Manson turned to me for a second with those wide crazy eyes, but never spoke.

Another guy joined the table. He was only forty or so, but walked like his back was broken. They introduced him as Mason. He had just woken up and didn't say much, just sat there tonguing his false teeth between yawns while Chet continued to do all the talking. I tried to make conversation, but he wouldn't answer anything seriously.

"Are you from around here?" I asked him.

"Shit boy. We're all incested. She's my sister, he's my brother, and they're married." He proceeded to laugh hysterically and change the subject.

"Young white boy like you, traveling through the south alone, you must be brave." Boy's down in Cairo, they'll slit your throat for nothing." Chet told me stories about the South, mostly about Cairo. "Don't you go walking in them woods no more." You stumble onto one of them meth labs and they'll shoot ya, that is if the booby traps don't get ya first." "Shit, Yankee boy, you're in the South now."

They were real drinkers, and all had their own cooler behind them. After finishing my first beer, three others were put in

156

front of me. A Bud Light, an Old Style, and a Milwaukee's Best. I opted for the Bud Light. It was starting to get dark, and Chet insisted I pitch my tent in the yard and stay with them to party. I filled my water jugs with his hose and told them I'd be right back.

"No you wont." He paused for a moment. "Y'er scared." He'd read me perfectly. I'd fully intended on camping somewhere else. "I'm givin' ya my beer, feedin' ya my catfish, and offering ya a place to stay. It's your choice," Chet said.

I walked up to the picnic table, set down my plastic bag with my notes and cell phone, and took my wallet out of my back pocket and set it right on top of the pile.

"Feel free to look through my notes if any of you are curious. I'll be back in ten minutes." Chet's jaw dropped as he stared at me in amazement.

I ran most of the way back to the canoe, feeling a little anxious about leaving all of my money with a bunch of strange hillbillies. After dropping off my water and quickly grabbing my tent and sleeping bag, I hustled back and started setting up. Manson was walking toward me with a chainsaw. My heart jumped in my throat for a second, but he stopped short of my camp and started cutting up wood. I walked back up to the picnic table as he worked fast and furiously. Everyone else sat there drinking beer and yelling out stories over the loud humming of the chainsaw as Manson cut wood in the dark.

"Go give him a hand," Chet suggested, throwing me a pair of work gloves. "Go help him get us a big bonfire going." Manson was already starting to throw the logs and brush into a pile, so I walked over and started helping him. We worked together silently. I had never seen a man work so fast. He worked as if his entire life depended on getting as much brush on top of that pile as quickly as possible. It was still over ninety degrees, and he worked so hard and sweated so much I thought he was going to collapse. "Bigger." Chet yelled. We had a brush pile ten feet high, but apparently it wasn't enough. We added more and lit it. Flames towered thirty feet in the air.

The party had moved from the picnic table to the bonfire. As the fire quickly dwindled down, the night started to slowly evolve. Chet was acting very strange. He kept giving everybody at the table shit. He never stopped talking, always saying something rude followed by blasting on his harmonica and laughing hysterically.

I was getting along pretty good with Mason, and he was making me some stiff drinks, making sure I had one every time that he did. After drinking together most of the night we got to be buddies. He went to his trailer and came back with an entire cardboard box full of Playboy magazines from the eighties. They were very special to him, but he wanted me to have them for my trip. Having to keep my supplies to a minimum, I had to hurt his feelings and turn down the gift.

Looking across the fire, I noticed something very peculiar. The lady across the fire from me was sitting in a revealing manner, and she wore extremely short shorts. My eyes met hers accidentally, and she began winking furiously at me. Every time I looked up, she was still trying to get my attention. Frustrated, she went over to the pile of wood next to my chair and bent over for a lot longer than it took to pick up a piece of wood. Nearly all of her butt was exposed, and she slapped it and said, "How do you like that ass?" Everyone was drinking, laughing and carrying on. No one else had noticed.

Chet had six harmonicas on his lap. He kept playing his songs all night, taking a break every once in awhile to shout insults at everyone. Once, when he couldn't get the right note out of one after several attempts, he got up and cursed, threw his hat as far he could, and launched the guilty harmonica into the thick forest behind us.

"You ain't my friends, you're just my kinfolk," he yelled at everyone, "and I don't know who this bum of a Yankee is goin' down the river takin' all of my food and beer." Without further comment, he picked up another harmonica and started blasting away again, starting a song but never finishing it. All night long he tried provoking me into an argument. He dared me to offend him, but I kept my mouth shut, and watched everyone. The night went on and the theme became more and more racially motivated.

"You see how we all look at you in your eyes when we talk to you boy? We're reading you son. Seeing if we can trust you or not, and seeing if you get scared off or not." Chet tested me constantly. It was like he was checking out my character or something. He stood up and put his finger on Manson's hat. It read Good Old Boys, Anna, Illinois. "Anna, Illinois" he said. "That stands for ain't no niggers allowed. You figurin' shit out yet boy? Do you know who we are yet? You're gonna hear some shit tonight boy, and you're gonna see some shit tonight. Don't you say a fucking word." Chet laughed wildly, sat down, and went on playing his harmonica.

The fire died down and we were out of wood, so I walked toward the woods to get more. Manson met me halfway back. He spoke for the first time.

"What you hear or see tonight stays here, and if I tell you to git boy, you git, and I mean now boy." Averting my glance from his deathly Rasputin stare, I nodded affirmatively, and headed back toward the fire. He was not the type of guy you wanted to spend much time alone with in the dark. As the fire flamed back up, I noticed and understood the hooded wizard tattoos on both forearms.

Chet was really peeled. He took the fish head off the stick and shoved it near the crotch of the seducer woman. Getting bored with that, he threw it at Mason. Mason caught it and threw it back to Chet. A crazy game of hot potato ensued.

I stayed up all night with them, listening to appalling stories, and keeping my mouth shut. By the time the last of them passed out, it was already getting light out. I packed up my tent, walked back to the canoe, and reentered the turbulent water. The first island I found would have my name on it. It felt good to be on my own again.

Chapter 11: Wickliffe, Kentucky

Day 52

After setting up my tent on a sandbar and grabbing a few hours of sleep, the sun was too hot to bear. I felt like crap, and it was hard to concentrate. The day was spent in surreal drift. It reminded me of the morning after Hannibal. I thought about how naïve I was. I'd been way too trusting, and the last night was a good wake up call. I'd been in the South before, but only in the touristy areas.

The people I'd been running into lately were not like the ones from Minnesota I grew up with. Combined with the dangerous water, I wished I had someone to travel with. I had covered 1,350 miles, but wasn't sure if I had another 1,000 in me.

After choosing not to stop in Cairo, I hit the confluence with the Ohio River. It was a major milestone for me. The cleaner Ohio refused to mingle for the first mile or so. Although I didn't have any maps of the lower river, I guessed the trees ahead of me were in Kentucky. After paddling across a huge bay, I paddled up a little slough to where the town of Wickliffe was supposed to be.

After crossing some tracks and cutting through a field, I found the town. I had to look at all of the license plates to make sure I was in Kentucky. My shoes were gone downriver, and I was forced to wear my little nylon river shoes at all times. It really hurt my feet to walk. I was too dazed to really care where I was.

My parents had been in contact with the parents of the canoeists behind me, and apparently Geoff and Chris had been laid up for a few days back in Iowa. They were headed to Antarctica after the trip, were forced to get physicals, and one of them had to get his wisdom teeth out before they could go on. They had expected to catch me by then, so I'd been taking my time. I was in Kentucky, and they were getting out of Iowa.

I was feeling very down. Examining my motives, I discovered I was taking the trip for egotistical reasons. I had been strutting into towns looking for attention as if I deserved a medal or something. I was a little ashamed of myself. I decided to play it low profile and stop trying to get free meals and stuff. I was a little afraid of the South, and wasn't looking forward to spending the next month alone. After spending fifty-two days by myself, I was beginning to see my own weaknesses magnified. I'd lived my whole life with the illusion that I was my own island, but the loneliness was starting to get to me. I knew I couldn't lead my entire life drifting into town for a day and then paddling downstream like nothing happened. For the first time in my life I realized that someday I'd need to find a place to tie my canoe. I watched the people of Wickliffe go through their every day lives and wondered what it might be like to live there.

While looking for some propane at a gas station, I met a lady named Mary. She noticed I felt a little down, and offered to give me a ride back to my canoe. I needed maps and propane, and she got on the phone and found a boat store that could accommodate me. Mary was older, but she was still an attractive lady. She had a sadness and real-world knowledge to her that helped us connect. She could see I was just learning things she had learned long ago and thought of it as her duty to give me some advice. She drove her car down an old farmer's trail and brought me right up to the dark finger of water where my canoe was hidden in the shade.

"My daddy used to take me fishing for catfish here when I was a girl," she revealed, almost with tears in her eyes. We lingered there for a few minutes, and even though we had only known each other for less than an hour, it was a difficult goodbye. "Promise me you'll be careful," she insisted. "Remember sometimes you only get one chance at things. Make sure you make the right decisions when you're young." Her eyes pleaded her case. By the way she said it, I had the feeling she was really afraid for me, and hoped I would make it through. We said goodbye and I left our little Kentucky magical place, ready to spend the next month alone.

The Boat Store was only a few hundred yards downstream, but I didn't see anyone around at first. Walking around the corner on the docks, two guys my age were working on something. I was about to ask them for some propane when I noticed their bicycles, hooked up to a homemade raft of sorts. It was the guys from Tennessee! I hadn't heard much about them since Iowa and was under the impression I'd passed them in St. Louis. They offered me a milk. I'd been on the river for almost two months and couldn't remember the last time I'd enjoyed a glass of milk. I'd have traded an entire case of beer for one glass of milk. Hour after hour flew by as we talked about our trips and the different places we had stopped. We were part of a handful of people, who had experienced the river in a special way. Like three Martians meeting coincidentally in the middle of an Oklahoma cornfield, we got along instantly.

Ben and Jason were laid back; real laid back. I felt very high strung around them, and was eager to talk to someone who had shared my trials and tribulations. It was obvious they had been on the river too long to be in a hurry. They were taking their time and enjoying every minute. The too were sharp, athletic, bright eyed, alert, and very likable, but they were almost as disheveled as I was. They both had long hair in their eyes and unshaven faces, but their spirits were both shining so brightly that no matter how dirty they were, it was impossible to cover their happiness.

Ben did most of the talking. He had the born leader look, like you'd expect out of a college quarterback. Jason was reserved, and his mind was constantly churning about something. He had the philosopher's look of constant contemplation. They complimented one another perfectly. As for their raft, it was a hodge-podge of Americana itself. Adorned with big flapping flags of The University of Tennessee, and the U.S.A., it was a tree fort on oil drums floating down the river. It was propelled by two bicycles that turned a paddlewheel and adorned with two big tree limbs sticking out of the sides that had been turned into homemade oars. The raft was every young boy's dream, and would have made Mark Twain himself proud. It represented perfection.

After talking to them and seeing their healthy laid back approach to the river, I decided to make some changes. It was time to throw away the book, stop tracking miles, and just let the river carry me away. I wanted to enjoy the rest of the trip with the same Huck Finnish carefree aura those two adventurers carried with them.

They were doing a TBS television program and a local interview during the next few days. The two had permission from the Boat Store to sleep on the docks, and invited me to hang out with them as long as I wanted. Up to that point, the thought of paddling less than twenty miles in a day was unheard of as I constantly pushed myself. I looked forward to a few days off to regroup and let the floodwaters subside.

We spent a good part of the night hanging out with the barge guys. Their pecking order was so well defined they reminded me of a pack of wolves. One guy was always in control, one guy was always picked on, and the others were at various points in between. They seemed to be aware of our presence, and the aggressive wolves were even nastier to the little ones then they may have been on a different night.

I slept on top of the raft under a brilliant display of stars.

Freedom

DAY 53

Waking up in a strange or unfamiliar place always filled me with panic until I became re-acclimated to my surroundings. Waking up in the middle of the night, the only things I saw were the stars above me. The sky was my home. I drifted back to sleep feeling happy and free. By 7:00 the sun was too hot to sleep. I spent the early morning hours rearranging everything and getting it out of the way for the TV cameras.

Ben borrowed me his bike and I rode it into town to do some exploring. I was in an excellent mood, and stopped into nearly every business in town to meet people. Never had I seen such a friendly little town. Everyone waved and smiled and was eager to have a conversation. Robert, a guy who had been working at the Boat Store the night before, saw me in town and invited me to go out fishing with him. He said to meet him at the docks at noon. I hoped to meet a nice Kentucky gal, but had no such luck.

Robert showed up at noon with a twelve-pack. We drove around in his old pickup truck on little dirt roads. I wasn't eager to drink, but he really wanted a drinking buddy for his day off so I swilled a few with him. It was so hot we spent more time driving around then fishing. The bass weren't biting anyway. Robert showed me another side of Kentucky. The plush green rolling hills and tobacco fields were beautiful, and we saw several deer as we drove around. I was really starting to like Kentucky.

Robert was a little different than the other wolves at the docks. His dream was to be a riverboat pilot someday, and he was ready to do whatever it took to achieve that goal. It was a great break from the river for me, but I was feeling really drained. It was over 100, and I still hadn't caught up from staying up all night on the 4th. I needed to sleep, but there was nowhere to go except back to the docks.

The rafters were finishing up their second interview, so I made myself as invisible as possible. I had absolutely no desire to be on television. After the crews left I tried to make myself comfortable on the docks, but it was too hot. I jumped into the water every half an hour to cool off and rejuvenate, but heat and lack of sleep were taking a toll on me. Although a part of me wanted to get back down the river, I was looking forward to traveling with Ben and Jason and decided to wait for them to leave the next day. Still, it was hard for me to remain inactive all day, so I walked back into town. The people were just so friendly. I was offered three rides, and by the end of the day I must have met half of the town of Wickliffe. Gosh, I loved Kentucky. The South wasn't so bad after all.

Although my feet were hurting pretty badly, I milked the town for all it was worth and killed the whole day there. As I was making a phone call, Mary pulled in. She recognized me from the road and was wondering what I was still doing in town. She gave me some ancient Indian beads, promising they would keep me safe for the rest of my trip. After finishing up my calls, I began walking back to the docks but was lucky enough to catch a ride with an old guy named Ted.

Everyone kept asking me what I was going to do after I got to New Orleans, and how I was going to get back home. I really didn't know. I didn't even have a clue. I didn't want to think about it, but had a strong feeling it would all work out somehow.

It was after 6:00, but it still felt like it was over 150 degrees on the docks. I worried my canoe and gear would melt. I was sick of killing time without moving downstream. I tried reading, but whenever I got started, someone came up and started talking to me. It was very frustrating at first, but I realized my selfishness, and tried my hardest to listen to everyone better and gain some insight into what made them who they were. I was such a terrible listener and probably missed a lot of important things. We were becoming celebrities in the town, and everyone wanted to come down and say hello.

The significance of my trip was completely overshadowed by the glamour of the raft, and although it made me feel a little left out at first, it ended up being a worthwhile humbling experience. I'd only known Ben and Jason for one day, but it felt like I'd known them my whole life. I was happy to let them receive the accolades.

I spent the early evening with Jason, Ben, and Robert, sitting on the docks drinking beer and catching catfish. It was still hotter than hell, and when the sun went down, the mosquitoes really came out. It was the worst they had been so far. They were too thick to stay out long after dark and I needed a good night's sleep, so I found a little patch of trees on shore, and set up my tent for the night.

DAY 54

At some point every winter in Minnesota, I got tired of looking at the barrenness of everything and regretted the fact that I didn't appreciate more the green beauty of summer. Unzipping my tent and looking out at the Kentucky shoreline, I was finding that appreciation. Ben's parents were visiting the rafters. The two had to do some repairs on the raft and were scheduled to do another interview. We weren't planning on leaving until after noon, so I walked back into town to kill some time. Everyone in town was still talking about the railroad serial killer. Apparently they had found his car in Cairo, which was only four miles away. Every town I stopped in claimed he was in the area.

At the Indian Mounds, I met Chris, and he traded me a free tour of the historical site for a free tour of my canoe and the raft. Chris was a writer who wanted to show his son Zed that there was more to life than MTV and Nintendo. After checking out an ancient Indian dig site, they drove me back to the docks and I showed them our crafts. Of course they were much more interested in the raft.

Ben's parents were very nice, and they got me some things in Paducah. By 1:00, the raft was not quite ready to leave yet, so I paddled down eleven miles to the next boat ramp and waited for them. I was armed with a full canoe of supplies and a map of the lower Mississippi. It was two feet long, and nearly sunk my canoe.

The river had dropped considerably over the last few days. After parts of three days in Wickliffe it felt like I was starting out for the first time again. Everything was awkward for a mile or so until I got back in the groove. It took three hours to get to the landing. There was a town nearby, so I walked up the road to see how close it was. After a few hundred yards, I ran into three black guys about my age walking toward the river.

The seed planted by the hillbillies the other night began to sprout, but the three young men smiled and were very cordial. They took me down to the river and showed me how to catch crayfish, we had a big rock-skipping competition, and they invited me to go fishing with them later. The way they killed time and enjoyed the river reminded me of myself growing up on the Zumbro River. I told them about the raft, and they figured it was worthwhile to wait around and see it. After killing about an hour with my new friends, something strange appeared on the water's horizon on the north. The raft was on its way.

After waving goodbye to the three guys, we set out down the river again. The raft was held up by the wind and moved much slower than my canoe. I tied up to it and we drifted down the river together. They both took a spin in my canoe to see what my mode of travel was like, and I pedaled their bicycles and manned their oars in order to gain an appreciation of what they were going through.

Not until I climbed on the roof did I fully realize the majestic nature of the raft. It was a different world from the top of the raft. I was accustomed to sitting a few inches off the water, and everything looked the same after awhile. Up there, I was above the trees and could see everything. I stood on top of that raft for timeless moments watching the world slowly unfold. Kentucky was to my left and the boot of Missouri to my right. An endless array of forests and sloughs stretched out on all sides. I could reach out and touch the clouds. I stood on the pinnacle of life watching the future ahead of me.

For the first time on my trip I didn't know what mile marker I was on. It was day one again. The sun was beginning to set, and the river was more beautiful and limitless than it ever was. I wished that every man who ever lived could spend a few hours of his life standing on top of a raft, heading down the river with no schedule.

After anchoring, we went under the mosquito flaps and talked about life's questions. Although I needed sleep, Ben and Jason were rational yet open-minded thinkers, and I savored the moments of debate with them. We left no topic untouched, but ended up discarding those with which we crashed into the giant brick wall of relativity.

That night I slept under the stars again on top of the raft. There was no sign of any artificial light, and it was without a doubt the most brilliant display of stars I had ever seen. I invented my own constellations, and counted several shooting stars. I woke up a few times to a brilliant sky, which I visited during my cosmic dreams.

DAY 55

My spirit returned to my body on the raft at 6:30. It was already too hot to fall back asleep. I left a note for the slumbering rafters and paddled ahead five miles and up a little slough to Hickman, Kentucky. It was fun walking around town and talking to the friendly locals. After a brief stint in town I paddled back down the slough, and was promptly greeted by the high flying flags of the raft. My note had blown away and they were quite confounded as to where I had disappeared.

It was time, they explained, for me to be initiated into the raft. The first thing I had to do was the Huckleberry flop. It consisted of a dangerous leap off the roof over the front of the raft which extended several feet out. I completed the jump with ease, and after the first scary bound, did it several more times.

The rest of the day was spent in the kayak. I had never been in one before. It was very tippy at first, but by the end of the day they had taught me how to roll upside down and come back up. As if that wasn't difficult enough, Ben came up with a kamikaze idea. He brought the kayak up to the roof of the raft, which was about ten feet off the water, and insisted that I shoved him off into the river below. I was sure he would kill himself, but somehow he made it, and Jason volunteered to match the feat. There was no other option for me than to do the same. It was scary as hell, but the rush that came with hitting the water, diving under with the nose, and coming back out more than made up for the fear. Sometime during the day, I hit my 1,400th mile.

At New Madrid, the river made a twenty-six mile loop in order to gain less than half a mile on the Gulf of Mexico. At the top of the loop was the town of New Madrid, and we watched the most spectacular sunset over the town water tower. Having been appointed the advanced scout for our mission, I paddled into town with a cooler and got beer and ice cream. There were kids cruising all over town, and although I had the opportunity to talk to several girls, I was far too grubby to make much of an impression.

It was pitch black when I got back to the river, and I had no idea where the raft was. I let out a few howls to get their attention, and they flashed their lights at me to reveal their location. We feasted on T-bones they'd saved for a special occasion and deserted on ice cream and beer. Already, the rafters had nearly converted me to country music. Although the mosquitoes were real pests, I slept out on the roof of the raft again.

DAY 56

We were all tired and dull in the morning and no one did much talking. The two had actually whittled their own chessboard, complete with all of the pieces, and both proceeded to pummel me on it. It was a tough morning of maneuvering the wind and turns, was unbearably hot, and none of us was in an excessively good mood. Not wanting to wear out my welcome, I headed back out on my own for awhile.

Solitude was new and fresh again, and I spent most of the day reading the Book of Mormon I'd received back in Nauvoo. Although it was more fun being on the raft, I figured we would keep crossing paths all the way down to New Orleans. I could make much better time in my canoe, and could run into towns and explore. It was kind of neat knowing they were just a few miles back, and Chris and Geoff would catch up within a week or so. There were a lot of things to look forward to.

The day included one close call with two passing towboats. A forty-eight and a forty two-barge tow were passing on a tight corner, and I was forced into a whirlpool on the left shore. It was so tight I thought they were going to collide, and I watched one of the tows roll over several buoys trying to slide out of the way. Close calls were getting rarer as the floodwater subsided.

Near Carruthersville, I found a nice sandbar with two boys fishing on it asked if they minded if I camped there. They were the kings of the place and didn't have to worry about parents, other kids, teachers, or authority. It was theirs. After dropping out of high school, they spent every day on the sandbar. Although only sixteen, one was engaged to the other's sister, and the other had a crush on his buddy's sister. The mother of one was about to marry the father of the other. I was pretty sure if I came back to the spot in fifty years they'd both be sitting there.

They offered me some worms, we built a big fire, and sat around fishing together well after dark. Gary caught a nice cat, and imagining I was hungry, he cleaned it up and cooked it over the fire. They were very resourceful, and went on and on about all of the things I could eat out of the river. Steve gave me his lucky penny and promised that if I treated it right, it would treat me right also.

JULY 10TH, 1999 DAY 57

I was startled at dawn by an early morning fisherman. He was a nice black man from the South, and volunteered to watch my things while I walked into town. I took my time in town, hoping to let the raft catch back up to me. After getting groceries and water, I hid them in a culvert and continued on down the road to a restaurant where I feasted on a huge mess of pancakes. Upon arriving back at camp, the fisherman informed me that the raft had still not been by. It was odd that the raft hadn't caught up to me yet, so after a few lazy miles, I pulled in at a boat ramp on the south end of town.

As I pulled the canoe on shore and walked up the concrete landing, a black man pulled up in a Cadillac to see what I was up to. His front tooth was golden, and he held a forty-ouncer of malt liquor in his left fist. It was only 9:30. When he discovered I'd paddled from Minnesota and was on my way to New Orleans, he laughed so hard he shot beer out of his nose, and had to walk down to the landing with me to see the Minnesota license on my canoe before he would believe me.

A few old guys shot the breeze around the town fruit stand. A little red-haired freckled kid found an old broken whiskey bottle and ran up to show his grandpa, but his grandpa made him throw it out and help me carry my cantaloupe to the canoe. He was a bit upset, but soon forgot as he struggled to carry the big melon. There was no sign of the raft, so I walked up to the payphone. An old pickup pulled up at the same time I did.

"You need to use that phone?" I asked the old man in the truck.

"Nope. I'm just watching the river flow. I'm eighty years old, and I've been coming down to this spot every day for the last twenty years to see that river." I imagined his wife had died twenty years ago, or she was alive, and he came out there to get away from her. I mistakenly referred to the trees across the river as Kentucky, but he corrected me by letting me know that it was Tennessee. We sat there a few moments appreciating the morning, when his eyes got big and he pointed upstream. "What in the heck is that?" Before I even turned to look, I knew it was the raft he was referring to.

They showed no signs of pulling into town, so I paddled out to the middle of the channel to greet them. The river was dropping so fast that they had woken up that morning and discovered their raft was completely beached. It took them all morning to dig it out. They were doing another interview that day and were running late, but invited me to join them at a bridge a few miles downstream where we met the Dyersville paper.

The folks from Dyersville were a husband and wife tandem. I wasn't keen on the idea of doing any more interviews, but the guys in the raft were practically national celebrities, and with them it was hard to avoid. The interviewers were very fired up about our forms of transportation and made me feel very at ease.

We had another fun day swimming and kayaking, and I avenged my earlier losses by beating them both at chess. We enjoyed the fruit from the stand and traded some food. While I subsisted almost entirely on Hormel brand canned food, they usually dined on macaroni and cheese, soup, and ramen noodles. It was nice to add some variety, and they were willing to give up two cans of generic soup for each one of my Hormel cans.

After spending the majority of the day together, I went off on my own at 6:00 for some reading and reflection. Shortly after departing, I hit two major milestones. The first was the state of Arkansas, and the second was my 1,500th mile. It was great to be out of Missouri, and I was excited about being only a few days from Memphis.

I was into a nice rhythm of spending the days with the raft and going off on my own for nights and mornings. It kept me from getting lonely, helped me appreciate my solitude, and made running into the raft exciting. It was a thrill to look around the corner and see it on the horizon or pass some people on shore and find I was within a few miles. We always had a lot to share when we saw each other. It was like we were neighbors from friendly Indian tribes and got together every few days to trade and converse.

Hitting my two milestones put me in a great mood. I called my friend Jodie in Minneapolis and wished her a happy birthday. They were having a keg at her house and several of my friends from college got on the phone to say hello. It was neat to be out in the middle of nowhere and hear their party going on. I wished I were there, yet I was pretty glad to be where I was on the river.

After covering forty-six miles on the day, it started sprinkling and the wind came up. I found a huge sandbar to camp on. It was bigger than a small golf course and didn't offer much protection from the wind.

DAY 58

Near morning, a thunderstorm moved in, and my patchwork tent couldn't take the heavy winds from the storm. It collapsed on top of me and a drenching rain soaked all of my things. I spent the day's dawning moments outside in the rain trying to keep my tent standing up. My poles were all tattered, and I was forced to improvise with some long sticks. Luckily, the storm blew over, the wind died, and I was afforded a few hours of sleep in the damp, lopsided shelter.

It was the coolest day in weeks. I took my time getting going in the morning and did my best to dry my rain-soaked possessions. Near Osceola, Arkansas, a Cajun pulled up in a big boat and informed me I was still ten miles ahead of the raft. I wanted them to catch me before Memphis.

At Osceola, I stopped at a boat ramp to dump garbage and get water. It was empty except for a great big black man named Roosevelt. He sat on a picnic table next to his van watching the river and enjoying his day off. He told me about his grandchildren who lived in St. Paul. They meant a lot to him, and whenever he had some vacation time he drove his van all the way up to see them, picked them up, brought them back to Arkansas for a few days, and then drove them back to Minnesota and returned home. It seemed like a lot of driving to me, but that, he explained was the fun part.

A few miles south of town as the sun was setting, I came across one of the prettiest scenes yet. It was the calmest I'd seen the big river during the whole trip. Not one ripple appeared on the placid water. Trees on the Tennessee side clung to the edges of sandy cliffs. The sunset turned the sky different shades of pink, red, yellow, and purple, and the water provided a perfect reflection of the Tennessee shoreline. I couldn't tell what was real and what was reflection. There wasn't a barge within earshot, and whistles of songbirds filled the air. I was probably the only sign of any human existence for five miles in every direction. Everything was so peaceful and undisturbed.

Finding a beautiful sandbar on the Arkansas side, I spent a few moments before dark walking the beach and exploring the hills. Everything seemed so natural until I found an area littered with garbage. It ruined the moment.

The mosquitoes were getting bigger and more vicious every night, and I was forced inside the tent before they annihilated me. I fell asleep listening to Art Bell talk about Armageddon, and it caused me some very strange dreams.

Hygiene

CHAPTER 12: MEMPHIS

JULY 12TH, 1999 DAY 59

I spent the morning fishing and exploring, hoping to see the raft so I could drift into Memphis with them. Finally they came around the corner, but had a third person with them. The guy had long blonde hair, and reminded me of Spiccoli on Fast Times at Ridgemont High. They tried convincing me he was a stoner they'd picked up along the way, but soon revealed he was their friend Dave who'd met them for a day on the raft.

We spent all day playing spades, doing flips, and swimming. They taught Dave how to roll a kayak, and we all launched it off the top to show him how brave we were. With a fresh person on board, the river seemed new again. It was a fun day spent acting like little boys. We were sitting on top of the raft, drifting along lazily, when we turned a corner and Jason yelled out excitedly that he could see the skyline of Memphis in the distance. Especially prominent were the silver sides of The Pyramid. I could see the reflection of the sun off it for nearly ten miles. It was like being in the Wizard of Oz and seeing the Emerald City way out ahead over a giant field of poppies.

We were giddy the whole way into Memphis. Everyone on shore waved at us and stared in wonder. After getting permission from the Memphis Yacht Club to dock there for free, we went out for pizza with Dave's dad, Norb. We ate at some fancy place on Mud Island and watched the Home run derby from the All-Star Game. It was like being back to the mainland after being stranded on a deserted island for months. We admired the girls in the place, but they were Beverly Hills 90210 wannabes and had the same hairdos and phony smiles. I had no desire to talk to any of them.

Norb took us to see Beale Street, and the five of us all walked around. The Jazz, sounds, girls, beggars, street musicians, and crazy outfits were complete craziness. It was getting late and everyone was tired, so we didn't stay long. Back at the Yacht Club I was ready to call it a night, but as I laid there on top of the raft trying to fall asleep, something told me to go back to Beale Street and experience it in my own way. It was just too crazy not to spend some more time at, and I hadn't had a beer in quite awhile.

The Club office was open all night, and I went to talk to the guy working there to ask if it was safe to walk to town at night by myself. Robby warned me against it, but volunteered to give me a ride, and even said he would come and get me when I needed to come home. It was too easy to pass up, so I waited for him to complete his rounds, and jumped into his old car with him.

It was a short drive to Beale Street in Robby's 1984 Caprice Classic. The car was loud and rusty, contrasted by Robby, who was quiet and sharp. Robby had turned out like every mother hoped her son would be someday. He was a member of the church choir, took part in the Distinguished Gentlemen's Club for young black men, and was involved in programs to help inner city kids. Hearing the door of his old car slam shut behind me, I knew I was walking away from something good and prowling toward the crazy streets of Memphis, where only evil could await me at this time of night.

Beale Street had only gotten wilder in the time since I had left it. It still had the same cast of characters, but the casual tourists had gone home, and those who remained were really drunk. Going bar to bar and having a beer at each, I was hoped to meet some women but ended up spending more time talking to street beggars than good looking girls. The place was crazy, but I was still pretty sober, and I felt like I didn't fit in.

After boosting my courage to approach a few girls and being soundly rejected, I was about to call Robby when a homeless crackhead cornered me into a conversation.

"Hey man, you got a smoke?"

"Sorry."

"How about a few bucks?" His entire body shook when he talked, and he followed me down the street tapping my shoulder.

"Sorry man, I'm out of luck myself."

"You on the streets too?" I looked like it. There wasn't much difference between the rags he wore and those I had on, and he'd probably had the most recent shower.

"I got to find a way back to Minnesota," he explained, not waiting for me to answer his previous question. I hadn't had a good talk with anyone all night, and made the mistake of revealing that I too was a Minnesotan. The guy was on me like a fly on shit, and I couldn't get out of the conversation. He put his face real close to me when he talked and kept grabbing my shoulder. He yelled for money to everyone walking by, asking for money for the two of us to get back to Minnesota.

I looked for a way to get away from him. Two nice looking girls walked by us on the sidewalk. I made some eye contact with the tall blonde, but she quickly looked away.

"Hey sexy, how about some change. We need to get to Minnesota." Neither gal looked up. "Bitches," he muttered under his breath, but loud enough for them to hear.

The girls quickened their pace and walked into a nearby bar. One was tall and blonde, while the other was short, brunette, and had dark features. They looked nothing like the rich, suburban type girls I had no interest in, but gave out an aura of light-hearted free spirits. They looked like the kind of girls I'd get along with, so I followed them into the bar. Luckily for me, the bouncer at the door let me in, but refused my new friend who was tagging along. He looked at me from outside the window like a housedog that had been left home from the family trip. I was happy to have gotten rid of him. The two girls saw me heading through the door and made tracks to the opposite end of the room. After grabbing a beer, I waited for them to get settled in, and walked over to say hello.

"Sorry about that guy outside."

"Oh, you mean your asshole friend?" the blonde exclaimed, while the brunette just looked away, obviously uninterested.

"I have no idea who that guy was, I'm glad the bouncer didn't let him in here."

"What are you doing in Memphis?" the tall girl asked, as the other seemed frustrated her friend was letting the conversation continue. When I told her I was paddling a canoe the length of the river, she told me to go to hell, but after we talked for a few more minutes, she started to believe me. The two of them were from California, and were taking some kind of Thelma and Louise road trip around the nation.

The tall blonde did all of the talking while the brunette did her best to ignore me, occasionally tossing hostile glances in my direction. Meanwhile, I was starting to hit it off with her friend. She invited me to sit down with them, bought me a drink, and after twenty minutes, our feet were starting to accidentally touch under the table. Stacy and I were both leaning over the table, locking eyes, and occasionally touching hands together, while Jenny was getting mad at me for ruining their time together. Every time I looked up at her, she was giving me the evil eye. Jenny tried dragging Stacy to the dance floor, but Stacy was too busy talking. Stacy ordered the three of us a round of tequila shots, and Jenny made sure she didn't touch my glass when we all clanged them together. She kept looking at Stacy like she was trying to tell her some secret message without me finding out, but Stacy was getting too drunk to notice. We were all getting a little peeled.

The two were like night and day. Stacy was the radiance of the sun, while Jenny was pitch black. She was a good-looking gal, but looked like a pissed off version of Sandra Bullock. I wasn't a big fan of Sandra Bullock, especially one who hated me. Jenny got up to use the bathroom, and Stacy and I agreed we needed to find a guy for her.

We were getting more and more juiced, and after another round of tequila, the two girls got their courage up enough to get on stage and sing karaoke. I guarded their purses while the drunken crowd cheered. As they exited the stage, some studly, model looking guy grabbed Stacy by the wrist as a slow song came on. She looked over at me as if to say sorry, and proceeded to dance with him. It wasn't that big of a deal to me at first, but by midway through the song, the two were starting to get along well, really well.

Although I'd just met her, rivers of jealous adrenaline filled me. To make matters worse, I was forced to sit at the table alone with Jenny, and the two of us sat there in a silent grudge match. We both looked up at Stacy and her new catch, but the funny part of it was that Jenny looked more pissed off then I did. I began to believe the three of us were all fighting over the same girl.

It was an awkward moment. I wished the song would hurry up and get over and Stacy would choose to come back to our table. Instead, another slow song followed, and the two of us were sentenced to another five minutes together. Maybe that's how hell would be. They'd take the person who you hated more than anyone in the world, turn the two of you into trees, and make you stand next to each other for eternity. That was about how I felt sitting across from the devil-woman. I couldn't take the silence any longer.

"Do you want to dance?" I had no idea why I asked and even less comprehension of why in the world she said yes. We both felt like third wheels, and decided to go make a bicycle of our own. Like a fullback and tailback, we busted through the perimeter of happy couples, our hands clenched together in a hateful grip.

Our replacement bodies met and we both closed our eyes and swayed together to the music. I wasn't sure if it was the irony of the situation, the Tequila, or when I discovered she had breasts like Dolly Parton, but somehow, something happened. Her hands began to roam my back, her face nuzzled itself closer to my neck, and I felt her hot breath on my throat. I was dancing with the most beautiful woman in the world.

The song was over, but the two of us kept dancing. It didn't matter if the song was fast or slow, we were glued together. I was a pawn, but could care less.

I wasn't sure how long we stayed at the bar, but I'm pretty sure it closed at 4:00 in the morning. The three of us staggered through the streets of Memphis looking for a taxi, but there seemed to be none in the entire town, until one finally pulled up. I had no idea where the driver was taking us, but after winding through empty street after empty street, he finally pulled up somewhere near the interstate.

The two girls snuck me into an all womens' Hostel. After climbing an eternity of stairs and trying our hardest to be quiet, we reached their room. It was already after 5:30, but they insisted on getting out some highly touted California bud and partying until sunrise. The girls were wild. It was hotter than hell in the non-air conditioned room, and the two proceeded to get comfortable, sometimes forgetting I was even there, but at other times being quite aware of the fact. We spent most of the time partying out on the balcony. It overlooked I-55, and while people traveled their Monday morning commute, we were still going strong as the sun rose. I wasn't sure if they didn't notice the loud roar of interstate traffic or didn't care. They put on quite a show.

Although there were only three of us, we did enough damage that night to make a group of twenty Animal House residents proud. Horns honked, brakes slammed, wheels skidded, and cars swerved on the interstate below. People have a tendency to mess up traffic to watch accidents and other things. The Monday morning Memphis commute was a disaster that steamy July morning.

It must have been 8:00 when I collapsed. I had a graphic dream of hanging off the side of a steep hill clutching at roots on the side, but they kept breaking off and I fell, only to catch more roots and have them break too. I was tumbling off the side of that big cliff quicker and quicker, and knew that sooner or later I was bound to run out of roots.

I awoke in a tangled mass that wasn't blankets. My first instinct was to unzip my tent and check on the canoe, but I soon realized I was far from the river. It took a few moments to piece together the carnage, and I wondered how much of it was real. Based upon the occupants with whom I shared the room, I knew that part of it was a reality, but I was more concerned with finding out where I was and getting back to the Yacht Club.

I'd been reading the Bible regularly, and had spent hour after hour alone in the canoe trying to have more faith. That stuff was easy to think about in the canoe, but after ten drinks on Beale Street it became easy to forget. It had been the same old story for me as long as I could remember. I sat around by myself feeling religious, only to forget everything at the first moment I was tested. I wasn't sure at what point it happened, but it's almost as if I'd see an opportunity arise and put God on hold until later. It just seemed too easy, and I figured I could always join the church council or something when I got older. How many chances was God going to give me? When would I reach up for a root and find nothing? I was almost to New Orleans, and still didn't have a clue.

Memphis

DAY 60

While the girls showered, I walked downstairs to check the place out. It was like an old haunted house. Before I had explored very far, I turned a corner and ran right into an old white haired man with a cane. He bombarded me with questions and accusations.

"Who in blazes are you? Who let you in this place? Where did you come from? How did you get through the door? Who are you with?" His scowling face flushed bright red as he cornered me in the living room and shook his cane in my face. I had only been awake for ten minutes, and was still very disoriented. Then I remembered it was an all girls' place, and they had snuck me in the night before. I didn't know what to say, so I just stood there looking dumb, and tried to do my best Opie Taylor face.

"Get out of here right now before I call the police. And never come back." He forced me out the back door, and I was out on the streets of Memphis with no clue how to get back to Mud Island.

The gardener was tending to some shrubs out by the fence, and when he saw the old guy push me out, he started up a conversation with me as I walked by.

"I see you've found the Colonel's bad side."

"Yea, I guess I wasn't supposed to be in there." He was a rough looking guy with long hair and several tattoos. He lived in the men's quarters for free in exchange for doing all of the yard work. He was about to head downtown, and was cool enough to offer a ride back to Mud Island. I wanted to wait for Stacy and Jenny, but they had no idea where I was at, and probably figured I'd already split anyway.

The guys in the raft were nowhere to be found, so I crawled in and tried to sleep. It was already very hot, and I sweated like a pig, but was at least able to salvage a few hours of recovery before the afternoon sun made it unbearable. By 1:00 it was too hot too sleep, but I still tried. Instead of falling asleep, I laid there wondering if I was glad to have made the trip back to Beale Street. I felt like a piece of shit.

Had I lost my peace again? What about all of those moments out on the river when I felt so pure and close to God? Was that all a bunch of talk? How could I feel like such a good person one moment and turn into a savage the next? I just couldn't do anything in moderation. I had to party the hardest, stay up the longest, and drink the most. I needed to always be the last man standing, but was afraid to wake up one day and realize I'd gotten my wish, and was standing all alone.

The rafters returned, and we checked out a model of the Mississippi River on Mud Island nearby. We walked along, admiring how far we had come, and checking out towns we would soon paddle into. Surprisingly, there were very few.

With an average gap of one hundred miles between towns, all we had left were Helena, Greenville, Vicksburgh, Natchez, Baton Rouge, and then we'd be there, New Orleans. The words were sacred to us. The closer we got to the Gulf, the more flooded the river became. It was supposed to accurately show the level of the river, but by Baton Rouge there was water running out over the sides, flooding the concrete in all directions. Little kids tiptoed through puddles asking their parents questions about the river, and I felt like proudly announcing to everyone around that we'd come down every little bend they saw.

The Gulf of Mexico was represented by a giant swimming pool, and by the time we arrived, we discovered what was causing the flooding. They had a fishing tournament over the weekend for kids and had filled the entire Gulf of Mexico with catfish. The drains had gotten plugged and the entire model of the Mississippi was flooded.

The supervisor had short blonde hair, a tremendous body, and was just a little older than me. She had just started her new job, and was eager to appease her vacationing boss who had sent her an email to do whatever it took to get the fish out by the end of the day. She was swimming in the pool with six teenage black boys trying to trap the fish with volleyball nets. It was very hot, and her young male assistants were all shirtless, while she ran around the chest-high, cool water in a white tee shirt and shorts.

They baited the fish into a corner by throwing breadcrumbs into the pool. They surrounded them with the nets. They tried scaring the fish all to one side. It was frustrating for the lady, but she kept trying. They'd worked at it for two hours without catching a single catfish with those volleyball nets, but someone always had a new idea.

Since they were having no luck, she had no objection to Ben and I jumping into the Gulf of Mexico and trying to help. The water was cold. Everyone was screaming at once, and every few minutes, someone yelled they had caught one, only to lift an empty volleyball net. The eight of us guys in the pool encouraged the lady to keep trying.

She wanted to give up, but we'd come up with another strategy to keep going, and she was so worried about pleasing her boss that she'd agree. The irony of it all, was that of us eight guys, none of us really cared about catching any of those fish, we just wanted to keep the pretty lady in the white tee shirt in the cold water as long as possible. As if I hadn't seen enough boobs in the last day to last me a lifetime.

After spending over an hour in the pool without catching a single fish, we finally gave up. After I'd had my first shower in nearly a month, we drank a few beers and shared riddles at the raft. An obnoxious guy who looked like Sammy Hagar ran around the docks talking about all kinds of crazy things that didn't make any sense to else, but they made perfect sense to him. To him the world was simple; to everyone else he was insane. I related quite well.

Music started coming out of the speaker in a certain way, like a voice hanging alone over my head. People's words were insignificant, but I could read exactly what they felt on their faces. I could read their fears and insecurities, and could always tell if they were lying. I picked apart everything into simple black and white. The differences between the rich and the poor became obvious. I felt love and sensed attraction. My eyes met those of others, and I felt the link between us as we telepathed information to one another. There was nothing to get hung up on. Everything was wide open and limitless. Stubborn, narrow-minded people were buzz kill and needed to be avoided. To think in such a way, and to walk into a room with ten people, it took less than one minute to discover if one other person in that room was following the same train of thought. It was magical, as if all the answers were right in front of me, and they were there the whole time. All I had to do was open my eyes to see it. It was so plain and simple. It was so easy to see, yet impossible to explain. It was tragic, forbidden knowledge, but was impossible to express.

A girl working at the office of the Club introduced us to her brother, Marshall. He was a student from the University of Tennessee, and lived on a boat in the marina for the summer. His sister had just gotten him a job working at the Yacht Club, and he was supposed to start the next morning. Marshall's life was drinking. It was all he talked about, and it was all he liked to do. Marshall had invented his own expression to be used as an emphasis on any statement. "That's bad ass," he would say, and the more he drank, the more he emphasized. After telling us story after story about his college drinking adventures, he invited us onto his dad's yacht for a night of drinking.

At the yacht, Marshall fed us beer after beer after beer. We played spades, smoked cigars, listened to tunes, and got shit faced. The last two nights of non-stop partying were taking their toll, but Marshall was a fun guy, so we kept partying. The three of them were big Tennessee fans, so they kept playing the song Rocky Top, over and over. I was even starting to learn the words and sing along. By 6:00 in the morning, we all finally passed out. Marshall's first day on the new job was to begin in two hours.

DAY 61

It was after 10:00 before any of us stirred. A ringing phone was followed by Marshall swearing. It was his first day of work and he was already two hours late. After scrambling around to get ready, we left the comforts of the air-conditioned yacht for the hot Memphis morning on the dock. I was extremely drained. When the raft left at 11:00, I decided to charge my cell phone battery, run to the post office, and take another shower.

While my cell phone battery was charging, I walked up to the Mississippi Model to see how it was coming. They were draining the pool to get the catfish out. Near the confluence with the Ohio, I met a beautiful country singer named Janet from Okechobee, Florida. She was about forty-five, but looked like a Playboy model.

Most people at the River Museum were dressed in tourist garb, but I was under the habit of going shirtless wherever I went. My body had never been more tan and muscular, and to confine it to clothing seemed so restrictive. One of the workers came up and told me I had to put a shirt on or I couldn't be in the museum. What a stupid rule.

After giving the raft a three-hour head start, I finally left Memphis. I hadn't had any sleep in the last few days, and was feeling extremely tired. I was done partying for awhile. Being dead-tired always threw everything into focus for me. The feeling was similar to the one I had leaving Hannibal, Grand Rapids, Prairie Du Chien, and Alma. I saw exactly where I stood at that point in my life. I was crossing the line I'd been looking across for my whole life and was out there in no-man's land.

The river after Memphis was desolate. I wasn't sure what day it was or how long ago stuff happened. When was I in

Iowa? Was it a few days ago, a few weeks ago, a few months ago? Was I ever in Iowa? I couldn't really tell. My ass was dragging. I entered the state of Mississippi, and looked to camp on the first Mississippi sandbar I saw.

The barges reminded me of the big steel monsters in The Empire Strikes Back. They were unfeeling robots, and I was sure they wouldn't think twice about running me over. I didn't think of them as having a captain, but as metal zombies acting on their own accord. They represented the only regular interaction I'd have for the next several weeks.

When I was a little kid, I used to imagine what it might be like to be older. I envisioned a nice fun job, a big happy family, a house on a lake full of fish, and lots of money. No one told me how it would really be. No matter how hard I tried, it turned into shit somehow. Maybe the dream was just an illusion. It seemed possible, but why didn't it work? Why couldn't I just be happy and content about things? Like everyone else, I strove toward the American dream, until one day I realized I was working jobs I hated in order to make money to buy things to impress people I didn't like anyway. That's why I was out on the river. There was no one to impress, nothing to lie about, and everyone was on the same playing field. There were no false hopes to depend on, just keeping my canoe from tipping, finding a safe place to sleep at night, and getting enough food to stay healthy. People said I was running away from reality, but I was finding it.

Good bye Tennessee. Hello Mississippi. Every time I turned on the radio station I heard a country song about Memphis. Maybe it was Memphis. I've Been Living on the Wrong Side of Memphis. I go Walking in Memphis. The Night I Fell in Love with the Queen of Memphis. Every one I heard had a new significance for me.

Although I didn't catch up to the raft, I ran into two rich guys in a bright yellow boat who told me I was within two miles of them. They both had gaudy gold chains on and were drinking beer. They told me a story about some guy in a flat bottom who had discovered a dead body floating near there just two days earlier. I was glad that I didn't have to find it and also glad it wasn't me.

I pulled up at a sand bar on the Mississippi side at dusk, but had waited too long. The sun had set, and the mosquitoes were out in full force. They nearly carried me away as I struggled to put up my old dilapidated tent, slapping my face, neck and arms with my hat as I went. In the two seconds it took for me to unzip the tent, throw my sleeping bag in, and get inside, thirty mosquitoes invaded. I spent the next hour slapping at them in the dark, losing a quart of blood in the process. Hundreds waited outside, covering the entire screen flap of my tent. I sprayed every hole in the seam with repellent and stuffed them with pieces of clothing to keep them away. Although it was hot, I was forced to sleep with my face inside the sleeping bag to keep them from biting me.

DAY 62

It was scorching hot in the tent, but I lay there frying until 10:30. Besides Memphis, there was absolutely no shoreline development on the river since Kentucky, and the sameness of everything lulled me to sleep. Every time I turned a corner, it felt like I had already been there before. It was green and blue for as long far as I could see. Besides the two guys in the fancy boat, I hadn't seen any signs of life since Memphis.

I turned a sharp bend, and was greeted by some sort of futuristic temple. It felt like I was on a different planet. It looked like something out of some new-age science fiction movie, and covered the entire Mississippi shoreline with neon flashing lights and huge pillars and domes. My first reaction was to hide. The thing was so majestic I was sure they'd have armed guards ready to shoot down any invaders. The stark contrast to the rugged landscape was unbelievable. What did casinos look like to God?

I weaved through scores of wide-eyed people praying to little metal, bell-ringing Buddhas. I could care less about getting rich on my nickel machine. I was after free pop, air-conditioning, and cocktail dresses. After walking away a few cents ahead, it was back to my canoe and the never-ending nothingness.

After a slow start, I lulled my way through forty miles, and had covered 1,632 on the trip. The day was spent in constant daydream. I was almost done reading the Book of Mormon, and it made me feel very spiritual. Every time I turned the radio dial, I found a religious station and was forced to make a decision. To turn the knob to something worldly was to turn my back on the voice of the Lord, so I soaked up every bit of religion I could. My numb brain was confused, but every time I banged my head against the wall trying to come up with answers, I came up with a solution by classifying everything as either good or evil. I looked at everything around me and called it good or evil. Trees were good, barges were evil, water was good, music was evil, clouds were good, airplanes were evil. I wanted to be good, but was always evil.

I was struggling with the concept of Christ dying for me. It was one thing to believe in Jesus, but it was another to really see how the whole thing worked. I tried to visualize the big picture, but it was unfathomable. I always tried my hardest to do the right thing, but it was impossible for me, and I ended up doing the exact opposite. The radio told me he redeemed me, justified my life, and had forgiven me. What did I have to do? Sometimes it seemed so simple, but then I lost it, and couldn't find it again. Every day I tried to start new again and be pure, but without even thinking, I fell away again.

I dreamt that I lived my life in a beautiful mansion on the ocean, but as the years went by, I realized that although beautiful on the outside, the inside walls were made of sand and were starting to crumble. Rats were coming inside, and water from the ocean was working its way through the cracks. My broke down palace was about to collapse.

CHAPTER 13:HELENA, ARKANSAS

DAY 63

At Helena, Arkansas, I put on my jean shorts, washed my face, and put on my cleanest shirt. I had been on the river for over two months and hadn't done any laundry. After stashing my canoe in the woods near town, I walked up to a park but hit a dead-end slough between the city and me. I wanted to give up, but needed water and felt like talking to someone. After paddling around a big peninsula, I entered the slough and tucked my canoe away in the bushes near a boat ramp.

A friendly black woman at the Visitor Center recommended I eat at Bullock's. Some painters stopped me as I entered the place.

"You don't want to go in there, boy. White folks don't go in that place." I went in anyway. An old black man sat in the doorway under a big sign that said Soul Food. Deafening jazz music played. An old-school black man thumped his thumbs against the table to the music, and a Bob Marley-looking guy mowed down a plate of food at the bar and grooved to the loud tunes. I couldn't see his face through the dread locks, but he looked about my age. They were the only other patrons in the dark restaurant.

The inside reminded me of some of the houses I lived at in college. The kitchen was on the other side of the bar. A broken two by four held the right side of the bar up, creating a two-inch slant to the left. It looked like my grandpa's old kitchen. There was no menu. Six steel pots simmered on the stove containing whatever Cora happened to be cooking that day. I tried to get her attention over the loud music, but the large black woman in the flowered apron was content on stirring the pots and didn't notice me.

I sat at a table alone, and was about to leave when she walked over to me with a fan in one hand and an overflowing plate of food in the other. I don't know what I ate, but I eagerly devoured every last scrap. It was a mess of different flavors and textures, all new and delicious. The loud music was really taking me away. I found myself jamming along with the old-school guy and the Bob Marley-guy. Between songs, I looked across the dark room at the old man. He wore an old tattered suit he'd probably owned his whole life, but carried a youthful expression on his face. I tried to ask him what kind of music it was, but it was too loud too talk. He looked over at me and broke out laughing as he fed more quarters into the jukebox. The loud music went on.

"About five dollars," Cora explained as she came up to my table. I gave her six and thanked her. She took my picture for the "wall of fame," and I left feeling like I'd been invited to a secret clubhouse and had just walked out of a time warp.

The sunlight blinded me for a few moments as the sounds of the loud music still rang in my ears. The painters across the street looked at me like a traitor as I walked out.

By the time I'd gotten a few groceries, a birthday card for my mother, and found a post office, my feet ached. The loss of my shoes at the Missouri River was a big mistake. My rubber river shoes were not made for long walks and were ripping out. Still, I refused to replace anything I could live without. Heading out of Helena, it was hard to fathom I was riding the same water that flowed by my old stomping grounds in Winona.

The bigness of everything around was taking a toll on my mind. I wanted to hang around Helena longer, but needed to keep going. There wouldn't be many chances to converse with people, so I imagined I was no longer alone, but was with myself at age seventeen. I'd done this before when I was lonely and bored. I looked at my younger self and asked him what he wanted to do. He usually wanted to get messed up or chase women. So we went at it together, him with his energy, and me with my knowledge.

Ten miles south of Helena, we came across a sandbar on the Arkansas side that was so big it looked like it's own country. I wanted to keep going and make some more miles, but my younger self insisted we explore it.

It was our island, and we explored it and ourselves with help from a little Californian care package. We walked around the entire thing as if we were the first men on the moon. The textures of the sand were crazy. We toured craters, crevices, and other interesting things and places. The island became our entire existence. Earth no longer lived, and we would have to salvage a new life out of whatever we found there. The scope of the universe had shrunken down on me, and the only things that existed were those in my immediate vision, the sounds of the birds overhead, the smell of the river, and the feel of the moon under my toes.

> *I walk along an endless plain of sand.*
> *Little green bugs seek shelter under my feet.*
> *Trying to keep up,*
> *Half are crushed.*
> *I barely notice.*
> *Am I their God?*

As my feet carried us further into the unknown, my brain swam further away. I was completely letting go. At times I'd reached that place before, but had always turned back when it started to get scary. It was a place we were not allowed to go. It was the place of instant understanding. To even think of entering could be deadly, because every time I went, there was a good chance I might not come back.

> *I am,*
> *But I don't know where I am.*
> *I can't communicate it to anyone.*
> *It's that place, that other side.*
> *Where we dream.*
> *The trance,*
> *The meditation location.*
> *Where all questions are answered.*

I had arrived at the door and my hand was at the knob. I'd reached it before, but had been too afraid to go on. I had peered through the cracks, gotten scared, and run away. My hand turned the knob. Slowly, the door was starting to open.

> *I have to make the Choice.*
> *The decision awaits.*
> *Instant understanding,*
> *Or confusion forever.*
> *With this knowledge comes severance,*
> *And I will not return.*
> *No, this is not death,*
> *But it is an unknown place,*
> *Where the mind goes,*
> *Never to return.*
> *One choice... for an eternity.*
> *But, is it good or bad?*
> *Is it evil?*
> *Is it a taste of heaven I am seeing?*
> *Or a trap... to steal my soul?*

I was sure it was good when I was there, but coming out, I condemned it to be false. Several times I'd arrived at the door, became frightened and walked away without opening it. I'd never walked through. If only I could translate that silent knowledge into my language, but my reason hid the meaning. I needed to throw away reason to comprehend it, but was afraid, and again walked away at the brink of decision.

At the moment I decided to walk away from the door, everything changed. It was as if my alarm clock was going off, and I was pulled out from a wild dream. I was no longer on the moon. I was no longer the only inhabitant on a new planet. It was just a big stupid island. My feet were hurting me, and I had a half-mile walk to get back to the canoe. What was I doing wasting good paddling time anyway?

As I walked back to my canoe, the raft appeared on the northern horizon. I thought they were out in front of me, but I'd passed them in Helena. It was only 7:00, but a storm was moving in, and they decided to camp on my island for the night. They anchored near shore, I set up my tent, and we went into the raft to play cards. Although the rain never came, by dusk it was started getting windy. As we sat in the raft, an especially big gust came up. I heard a strange sound outside, like something rolling across the beach. It was my tent blowing away. I chased the damn thing at a dead sprint for 500 yards until I caught up to it and brought it back. Two of the poles were lost, so I stuffed it into my canoe and decided to try to find them in the morning. After finishing out a few games of cards and sharing our experiences in Helena, we called it a night.

It was too windy for mosquitoes so I slept right on the beach in my sleeping bag. Although exhausted, it was hard for me to fall asleep. I wasn't sure how much more life on the river I could take. My thoughts were getting stranger and stranger, and I knew that I was on the edge. It was one thing to stay away from the mainstream, but I was hanging off the edge of the waterfall. Looking out at endless stars, sand, moon, and fog, I imagined the vastness of the universe and my own frail, feeble existence in it. There were so many mysteries, but I would be much happier not trying to figure them all out. I wished I could be happy to be, and not ask questions that were impossible to answer. I would still go out and have my fun, but would have to stop searching for forbidden doors.

DAY 64

Near dawn, the wind died and the mosquitoes showed up. I mummified myself in the sleeping bag and kept my face covered. They found a way to bite me anyway.

If alone, I would've hurried right off in the morning, but the two rafters were in the mood for fishing. We had no bait, so we tried using bread. At first it kept falling off, but we perfected it with some strips of red licorice and caught several nice catfish. While we were fishing, I took a break and scanned the beach for my lost tent poles. I was lucky enough to find one, and salvaged the other out of a piece of wood.

It was a Saturday. It seemed like it was Saturday the day before. Every day was a Saturday. Ben and Jason decided to head out later that morning, but I was enjoying the fishing and decided to stay longer. I also wanted to be alone in order to sort through some of the thoughts I was having the day before. It was peaceful just sitting there and fishing, but the fish were not biting anymore. I tried to retrace my steps from the previous day and see if it triggered any memories, but nothing significant occurred.

I was about to leave, when I thought of the two canoeists behind me. I hadn't talked to Chris's mom since Wickliffe, Kentucky, and I was curious to find out where they were. I had been moving slow in the last week, and figured they must have been close to catching me. Chris's mom was very surprised to hear from me. She had gotten off the phone with Chris less than an hour earlier, and they were just leaving Helena. What a coincidence. The river was 2,300 miles long and they were only five miles behind me. Eager to meet them, I waited on the island for them to turn the corner.

An hour had not yet passed when an aberration appeared on the smooth surface of the water to the north. I noticed two heads, one in the front and one in the back. It was a red canoe! They were hugging the far shoreline, and I made a flag out of my orange vest and a big stick in order to attract their attention. I ran along the beach waving my flag before they finally looked over and realized I was trying to get their attention. They tried pulling in toward me, but the current was too strong. The best they could do was the tail end of the island, so I ran back to my canoe, pulled my fishing lines, and paddled to them.

Chris and Geoff looked how you'd imagine two guys to look who'd been living on the river for two months. They were tan and muscular and had thick burly beards. The expressions on their faces told they had seen many things. I felt like the big foot monster having just discovered that there were others of my same species on the planet.

It didn't take me long to realize that the two sturdy young men were hardcore adventurers. They were killing time before spending the winter in Antarctica, and had decided to paddle the length of the Mississippi River in order to pass the summer months. Chris looked like a combination of Jesus and Brad Pitt, while Geoff gave the appearance of a charismatic business executive turned mountain man or island native. They'd averaged nearly forty miles per day and were intent on finishing as quickly as possible. I had done the northern part of the country like that and was originally hoping to paddle the rest of the way with them, but since St. Louis, my outlook had changed. I'd gotten accustomed to my lazy lifestyle of reading, allowing my mind to wander aimlessly, and letting the current take me away. Looking at their strong, rugged appearances, I knew I wouldn't be able to keep up with them, but wanted to at least try for a few days. With no structure in my days, my mind was teetering on the edge of reality. Having a day to day mileage goal to focus on and someone to converse with seemed to be a pretty good idea.

We spent the rest of the day sharing stories and basking in our freedom. They had another guy with them earlier. They described him as a reckless wanderer of sorts. He had never been in a kayak in his life, and after hearing of their canoe trip had decided to kayak the entire length of the Mississippi with them. He bought the kayak up in northern Minnesota, and as they sat at the campground of Lake Itasca State Park the night before they began, Chris had to convince him to at least try it out before attempting to go down the third largest river in the world. He spent the last ten minutes before sunset zig-zagging around Lake Itasca. Needless to say, the trip didn't work out so well for him.

While I had been fortunate enough to miss the mosquitoes of the north, their expedition had not been as lucky. They had been bombarded twenty-four hours a day, and were forced to wear head nets for the entire duration of northern Minnesota. The mosquitoes were so bad that they had a serious talk about aborting their trip, but decided after two weeks that they had come too far to quit. They also had a problem in the swamps before Bemidji, and had spent an entire day traveling twenty miles up a stagnant crick only to reach a dead end and discover they had wasted an entire day.

As we found a sandbar to set up camp, the mosquitoes we encountered were the worst I had seen. They rated them a five on a scale of one to ten, and casually enjoyed their dinner outside with no repellent, while I sought refuge inside my tattered tent.

Huckleberry Flop

DAY 65

Lewis and Clark woke me up before the crack of dawn, and we were paddling in minutes. Although I wasn't used to getting up so early, I was lucky enough to witness a fantastic panoramic sunrise. I imagined that ninety-nine percent of Americans who were seeing it were probably stuck in traffic somewhere.

We had gone about ten miles when we caught up to the anchored raft. They were soundly sleeping on the side of the channel, and we nearly scared the daylights out of them when we woke them up. It was an unprecedented day in Mississippi River lore. It was the meeting of three expeditions in the middle of nowhere out in the boondocks of Mississippi, and we were determined to make the most of it.

The five of us had a blast sharing our stories and motivations for taking the trip. Ben and Jason volunteered to make us a special meal of blueberry pancakes, and we were just starting to eat when a big pontoon pulled up. Three drunken hillbillies chugged beer and passed around a big jug of homemade wine. It was only 9:00 in the morning. The guys in the pontoon had enough beer to support a small trailer park, and kept throwing us beers left and right. We feasted on beer and blueberry pancakes as the eight of us drifted down the river together. We showed them the huckleberry flop and other daring raft and kayak tricks, and they boarded the raft and checked it out. One of the guys needed some d-cell batteries, and we traded him some of ours for a case of beer.

The five of us spent the day engaged in non-linear discussions about doing anything possible. We talked about walking the Appalachian Trail, climbing mountains, biking across the country, Alaska, whitewater rafting, beer, football, and women. We shared our stories of people along the way, favorite towns, places, highlights, scary moments, places we had all camped, and times we felt like quitting. It was like when you told someone you had to be there. Well, we had all been there. We all had a common focus and spent the day talking about it.

We spent the scorching afternoon having diving and flipping contests and doing tricks on the kayak. Both Geoff and Chris learned how to roll it and did the kamikaze launch off the top of the raft. We spent the day like a bunch of ten-year olds, and I didn't pay any attention to the mile markers. For the hardcore canoeists, it was the only day they'd spent without pushing themselves. For me, it was the only day in awhile I didn't sit all day alone asking myself questions pertaining to my existence. I knew it was a one-time thing and would be the last day we would all travel together.

As the sun drifted lazily across the sky, I found myself feeling more and more distant and aloof from the other four. I'd been alone for sixty-five days, and it was my first experience as a part of any kind of group in a long time. It was hard for me to remember how to function with others. I was silent for the most part, but then shared any random thought that came into my head at other times. Although we were all together on the raft, I still felt like I was alone in my canoe. From the reactions of the others toward me, I felt like I was coming off as weird or eccentric. They wondered how I spent twelve hours each day in my canoe, and why I'd rather be alone all the time.

Even though they were four of the coolest guys I'd ever met, I found myself yearning for solitude once again. I had a lot of things left to figure out and not much time left. I felt like I was going backwards again. My ultimate peace just a few days back was completely gone. I closed my eyes and opened them, and had no idea if I was going upstream or downstream. Things were getting confusing. I gazed off at an indefinite spot on the horizon and blanked off for a few moments, thinking about nothing, yet thinking about everything. Why was I there? Branches on trees moved and seemed to be communicating something to me. Bits of cotton floated in the air and I switched places with one to see what it was like to fly for five minutes only to hit the water and die.

The conversation went on around me but I was oblivious to its content. I tried my best to listen to the context of the conversation, then lost myself again to the ripples on the surface of the water. I was always so lost in a crowd. It's as if I went on autopilot or something. My ears heard but I paid no attention. My mouth spoke, but I had no idea what it was talking about. I must have been very hard to get along with since I was always at a different place. My goal was to try to stay away from that place, to stay in the moment. I wanted to learn how to listen and stay focused on the conversation at hand. Still, I'd gotten so close to that door, and I was still dying to find out what was behind it.

We anchored at dusk. I focused very hard on keeping track of what was happening around me and practiced my listening and awareness skills as Geoff and Chris told stories of scuba diving and mountain climbing. We stayed on the raft until 10:00 and had to swim back to our tents in the dark as mosquitoes attacked.

Kamikaze Kayaking

DAY 66

We woke up at 6:30, said our good byes, exchanged addresses, and left at our own speeds. Chris and Geoff quickly moved ahead at a little over five miles per hour, I was doing just over four, and the raft drifted along at about three and a half. I watched the canoe disappear ahead while the raft disappeared behind. I knew there was a good chance we may not see each other again, but we had all taken the trip for different reasons, and were going about it in our own separate ways.

Back on the river alone, my head was starting to clear again. I'd get so wrapped up in trying to find answers for everything, and end up all confused. After paddling for a few hours, I ran into an old river rat in a flat bottom fishing for catfish. He was a gray old man with a white beard and dirty overalls, and looked like Uncle Jesse from the Dukes of Hazzard. He asked why I canoed alone, so I asked him why he fished alone.

"I got some friends who come with me some days, but I hate waiting around for other people. I go fishing whenever I want, and if I don't feel like it someday, well then I just stay home and watch television." He also told me he had seen a big black bear that morning, but I told him he was full of it. "No shit," he explained, "them bears are all over the Arkansas side. They released a big herd of them in Mississippi, and they all swam over to Arkansas because they like it better here. You just watch that Arkansas shoreline, and I guarantee you that you'll see a bear before you hit Louisiana."

I left the friendly bear-watcher behind, and although I figured he was just telling stories, I couldn't help but keep my eyes fixed on the Arkansas shoreline. Every time I saw a stump, I was sure it was a bear. I must have seen thirty bears that day.

It was another long and lonely day, but eventually the minutes turned to hours and the inches turned to miles. Inevitably, I started thinking about the purpose of life again. It was just a gift, and we needed to enjoy the short amount of time we had, treat each other nice, try to live up to God's expectations, be sorry when we couldn't, and realize that there was one who did, and he died so we could live. But, what was the earth, and what was my body, and what was a soul, and who was I? The questions made me very confused, so I tried one last time to look around at the beauty all around me, and enjoy the sights, sounds, smells, tastes, and feelings, and savor getting to know others and sharing in their company. Maybe that was what it was all about. Maybe I needed to stop asking so many unanswerable questions and just trust in God's plan. Sometimes I felt like I'd glimpsed the other dimension from some deep meditation, drug induced trance, or crazy dream, but that might have just been the devil trying to trap me.

Down the river I drifted, trying to enjoy a beautiful July day, and hoping to make it to Greenville by dark to find water. I was starting to look forward to New Orleans, but the idea of being done scared me. There were no towns down anymore and very few people on the river. It wound back and forth like a snake and it was unbearably hot. I couldn't believe it was my sixty-sixth day on the river. I couldn't hold out for more than a few more weeks, but I'd try to savor the last few days. Everything looked the same, like one constant déjà vu. I tried to convince myself that I hadn't been there before and constantly scanned the shoreline looking for something new. I had already dreamt every moment of the river before, and was just reliving it.

Out of nowhere, the thunder rolled. I was very glad; it broke up the monotony of the day. There was no escaping the draining heat of the sun. The weather had been exactly the same nearly every day since St. Louis, and the cool rain that was beginning to fall soothed and rejuvenated me. The storm was quickly on me, but I made no effort to escape it. After putting plastic bags over everything, I was prepared to be drenched. Although I had several possible spots to pull over and escape the deluge, I wanted to suffer through it. It was the worst downpour I'd seen on the entire trip, even worse than St. Louis. I paddled harder during the rain then I had in a long time. Sideways rain stung my face and eyes, and I couldn't see the front of my canoe, but it was a big adrenaline rush and made me feel very alive. After ten minutes a pleasant mist filled the air.

I cooked up some Hot Tamale sandwiches, eating the last of my bread and licorice, but leaving a small piece of each to use for emergency bait. My licorice was covered in sand, as was my lemonade glass, but I was so used to being covered in sand, it didn't matter if I digested some occasionally.

My mood had gone way up, partly because I was out of water and all of my stuff was soaked. Three straight weeks of ninety-five degrees got really old, and I had something new to contend with. The cool wet day also gave my weathered face and lips a break from the scorching sun. Having little problems like not having any water and being soaked were fun, because when I finally dried my things and got a drink, I learned to appreciate them more. I was so sick of canned food I had to starve myself until about 2:00 in the afternoon, and then I was hungry enough to eat anything.

Near dark, I finally ran into Greenville. I had traveled fifty-one miles, and had set my record for longest amount of time without getting out of the canoe. I was really pumped up about hitting the town. Unfortunately, the actual town of Greenville was several miles away from the river, and all I found was a park. Chris and Geoff were at the same place and we all camped together. Geoff went to bed early, but Chris and I stayed up awhile and he told me wild stories about surfing and living on the islands.

DAY 67

I got up early in the morning and decided to try to get a head start on Chris and Geoff. I had hastily pulled my canoe onto a beach and tipped it over. Unfortunately, I had dragged it nose first through a giant anthill. My things were completely covered in fire ants. Thousands crawled inside my food bag, and they covered the bottom of my canoe. Most of my food was ruined, and I had to throw away two bags and combine everything that was salvageable into a third. I spent two hours dragging everything behind me in the water trying to drown the ants, but the things wouldn't die. My ankles were getting bit like crazy and I already had little welts all over my legs. Every few minutes I jumped out of the canoe to try to get them off of me, and several times I pulled over to a beach, took everything out and soaked it, and filled my canoe full of water. They would not die, and more kept biting me.

Chris and Geoff caught me at 10:00. They were such strong paddlers that it was very hard for me to keep up with them. I was always just a few yards behind them trying to keep up, and it was starting to feel too much like work. Besides, I hated following the leads of others. It didn't take me long to realize I wouldn't be able to keep up on their fifty mile a day pace. I was still busy picking fire ants off my ankles and felt like I wanted to just sit back, drift, daydream and read. After hanging with them for twenty miles, I wished them luck, and told them I would write to them when we all got home.

Floating on my own, I wondered how I'd handle New Orleans. If the trip was like life, I couldn't get attached too much to anything. I couldn't bring it with me anyway. When I got to the end I would get rid of my canoe, throw away all my stuff, and only bring with me what I could carry in my backpack. I envisioned living in New Orleans for a few months, getting a job at some bar or restaurant on Bourbon Street, and finding some cheap rundown apartment to live in.

It was another scorcher of a day, and the radio claimed it was over 100 degrees. I'd perfected diving out the side of the canoe, and it was necessary to do so every half-hour or so in order to avoid heat stroke. Unfortunately, the first time I tried I forgot to take off my sunglasses and lost them to the bottom of the river. Every time I jumped in the water, I saw how far I could swim along the side of the canoe without touching it. My record was forty-five minutes, covering almost three miles. It was kind of scary swimming in the river that far south. It was getting really dirty, and I kept thinking about alligators, even though I knew they stayed away from the main channel.

In the early evening I hit two major milestones. I finally entered the state of Louisiana and covered my 1,800th mile. I was so excited to reach the sportsman's paradise, that I raced the Robert A. Kyle, hanging with it neck for neck for three miles. Although I expected a bunch of gators or something to welcome me, Louisiana looked absolutely no different than Arkansas or Mississippi.

I still had fire ants in my canoe but rigged up a trap to try to kill them. I soaked my towel in Kool-Aid, tied it to the inside of the canoe, and when all of the ants swarmed on it, I flipped it over into the water and drowned them. It took a long time to kill them off, but my method was working quite well until somehow the towel came untied and sunk. I had been wearing a camouflage boonie hat to block the sunlight from my face, and while maneuvering around a dyke, a gust of wind came up and blew it off my head, and it sunk before I could grab it. I wasn't having very much luck on the day.

The little town of Mayersville was just a few miles off the river, and Chris and Geoff's red canoe sat on shore at the boat landing near town. They'd hitchhiked into town for supplies. I decided to paddle right past and let them catch up to me later.

The forecast called for strong storms, so after paddling a few more miles I found a sandbar on the Mississippi side and set up camp. It took me nearly an hour to get everything ready as I picked fire ants off my sleeping bag and tent and submerged my canoe to kill any remaining survivors. While setting up my tent, Chris and Geoff came around the corner, and the three of us camped together again. Funky clouds formed, and lightning flashed in the distance. My tent had several holes, and two poles were made of driftwood. I wasn't sure how it would handle another storm, but it missed us to the north.

Sleep that night was terrible. There were only a few fire ants that alluded inspection, but I had so many crawling on me all day that it still felt like they were all over my body. I scratched at my back and torso thinking I felt them on me, but they weren't there. I had been sleeping without a pad for over nine weeks, and it felt like the ground was getting harder every night. I had broken a rib several months before the trip, and it was really starting to hurt again from sleeping on the solid earth every night. I wanted to bring a sleeping pad, but it was just one more thing to lug around.

DAY 68

By 5:30 in the morning, my traveling companions had already hit the river. I was pretty sure I would not run into them again. I woke up long enough to wish them well, but went back to sleep and didn't get up until after 9:00. Their plan was to cover fifty-four miles and make it to Vicksburgh that night. That was too ambitious for me. I dreaded the idea of even spending another twelve hours in my canoe. It had been a long time since I had made any new friends and I yearned to find a town. Lake Providence, Louisiana was just a few miles off the river, so I paddled into the backwaters to the spot I guessed it to be, and decided to try to walk toward the town cross-country.

The thick, impenetrable brush was covering me in scratches, so I got back in the canoe and paddled farther down the slough until I found a patch of woods that wasn't so brushy. After walking a few hundred yards the noon whistle blew, and I knew I wasn't far away. Unfortunately, the woods between the whistle and myself were way too thick to travel through, and I was forced to back track to the south. I had been warned about wandering around in the woods, but I really wanted to find the town. I hit an old trail, and although it wasn't heading toward town, I figured it had to go somewhere and I followed it. My ankles were itchy from all of the fire ant bites, and my legs had gotten scratched up from the woods and stinging nettles. They itched so badly that I used my hands to scratch them as I walked around the woods like a monkey. Finding a mud

205

puddle, I covered my legs completely in order to soothe them. I was able to stop scratching but had to stop and replenish my mud supply every few hundred yards.

After walking the trail for almost a mile, the forest opened up into a small swampy area with a hill on the other side of the valley. The water in the swamp wasn't deep, but I sunk in the mud as I walked. It felt good on my irritated legs but my shoes kept popping off. A small finger of deep water divided me from solid ground again. Luckily, there were some logs lying across the water to cross. I did my best balancing act across the body of a fallen tree to get to safe ground. Water splashed a few feet away as a small alligator jumped off the log into the water. We must have been mutually afraid of one another, because he slid off the right side of the log, and I got so excited that I jumped back and stepped off the left side of the log into the muddy water. The moment I hit the water, I was sure a big gator was going to grab hold of my leg and take me under, and I jumped back on the log and ran to the other side so fast I don't think the Roadrunner could have caught me. It only took a few seconds to sprint up the hill out of gator-land. He was only three feet long, I was just afraid of his mama.

At the top of the hill I expected to find the town, but instead it was just a giant field of peas. I walked between rows to the other side, eating raw peas as I went. It was psychedelic walking through the pea field, and it felt like I was dreaming or something. At the end of the field I found another trail. It led up another hill, and eventually turned into a field drive that led me up and over the dyke and bam, I was finally in town. I had wandered around the woods for an hour, and was probably only a mile from my canoe.

There was no real purpose for me to come to town, I just wanted to get off of the river and go exploring. I really missed that from the upper part of the river. The problem was that I was completely covered in mud, my shorts were ripped to shreds, and I hadn't shaved in two weeks. I must have looked really funny walking around town with my canteen, but I didn't worry about it too much. After getting kicked out of a grocery store and a drug store, I found a hose in someone's yard and rinsed myself off. My legs were really itchy, and I wished I had more mud to put on them.

After leaving tracks all over the town, I still hadn't found any excitement until I discovered a little restaurant. Instantly, I had a crush on a girl working there. She had a shy, conservative look to her and wore a long skirt and her hair in a bun. She had really high cheekbones and a beautiful face. She might have been Mennonite or something. After looking at my ragged face in the mirror, I was a little afraid to talk to her. I cleaned up the best that I could, but was still leaving muddy footprints every where I went. I really wished I had shaved before coming into town. I did my best to hide my muddy clothes under the table and kept trying to get her attention, but she was too shy and wouldn't make eye contact. My only course of action was to write her a note, so I waited until she walked by me before I jumped out and handed it to her. It was a really awkward move. I felt silly sitting at the booth hoping nobody else had seen me.

She got real embarrassed when I initiated contact with her, and I sat there for ten minutes without seeing her again. She was probably hiding out in the kitchen. While I waited, I got into a pretty good conversation with my waitress. We got along really well, and she invited me to go to church with her and see a prophet later that night. It sounded good, but I'd already staked my bets on the other filly, and was forced to turn her down. When it came time to pay my bill at the counter, the young Mennonite girl peeked out at me from inside the kitchen, and I beckoned her over.

"I'm sorry to have been so blunt, but I knew that if I walked through those doors without talking to you, I might regret it for the rest of my life." She blushed and let out a tiny nervous smile as she rung up my bill. She was a little younger than I'd first guessed.

"No one has ever written me a letter like that."

"Was it okay?"

"Yes, it was nice." She smiled a little bigger, and I knew I had a chance.

"So can we get together later?" Her boss walked by, her smile quickly left, and she started counting my money, as if she was breaking the law or something. He was out of earshot, and she started to speak to me, almost in a whisper.

"I get off work at 5:00, and you can meet me at church if you want. I'd let you ride with me, but I don't know you well enough yet. We have a prophet that comes in on Wednesday nights and he's really cool."

Off I went, exploring more of the town. It looked a lot like Helena, and everything was pretty old and run down. The people all looked at me like a vagrant, and I felt uncomfortable. I felt guilty about slipping the girl the note. When I bulldozed into towns I should've just minded my own business, but I always ended up going around looking for kicks and doing whatever I felt like. It would have been low of me to show up at the church with the pretty shy girl after telling the other one I couldn't go.

I came into small towns with nothing to lose. If things didn't go good for me, I just hopped back into the canoe like nothing happened. I felt like a time traveler heading into the past. To act like I'm in love with some young girl just to entertain myself and disappear forever was not right. I was so detached from feelings whenever I said things. I was completely full of shit and starting to realize it.

Although I thought hard about going to church, I decided not to. For one, I didn't want to end up with no place to go and have to try to cross the alligator swamp in the dark, and for two, it just didn't seem like the right thing to do. After stopping back at the restaurant and saying goodbye, I headed back toward the canoe. Although it would have been much quicker to try a direct route, I didn't want to get scratched up any more, and was afraid of getting lost. The forty-minute walk was terrible, and after covering my legs in mud, I ran full speed over the log in the swamp, hoping not to see any more alligators.

After finding my canoe, I headed down the slough. It reminded me a lot of the river two months earlier up by Grand Rapids. After five miles without reentering the river I started to get nervous, but after another mile it finally rejoined. It was already 4:30, and I felt pretty stupid about wasting an entire day of paddling. I had to paddle until dark to make up for the lost miles, my ankles were raw, and I was sick of being so full of shit all the time. Basically, I wasn't in a very happy mood.

After paddling along for a few miles, I reflected more on the day and began to see it differently. I'd seen my first alligator, explored an unknown wilderness, had a great meal, met some girls, and visited my first Louisiana town. I'd learned a lot about my personal motives and grown as a person. It was actually a mini-vacation, and I was fresh again. Vacations never seemed great when I was on them. It was how my brain restructured the memories that made them good. All kinds of things went wrong and aggravated me, but looking back at the moments and memories was always great, and a year later I'd refer to it as the time of my life. I was on a permanent vacation.

I loved exploring towns. To them it was just work as usual, just another day in Lake Providence. To me it was a possible place of destiny. I attributed a huge amount of meaning to everything I saw and always thought I'd walk around the corner and fall in love or find my mission in life. That what was getting old during the last weeks, there hadn't been any small towns to explore. I didn't want to miss any more towns. I didn't feel bad about slipping that girl the note after all. I had to gamble once in a while. We could have fallen in love or the prophet might have changed my life, but it wasn't meant to be. Maybe it would happen some other time.

I felt happy again. After turning a sharp bend in the river I saw something odd on the straight away ahead. It was the raft. I hadn't seen them in days and thought I wouldn't see them again. They'd run into another river traveler that day. His name was Nat Stone, and he was circumventing the Eastern United States in a skull boat, living on a very tiny budget, and really hauling ass. He sounded like a real interesting guy, and I was sad I'd missed the opportunity to meet him. That's why I was afraid to leave the river.

I'd spent too much time with them on the raft earlier, so we only talked for an hour or so, but we planned on hooking up the next day in Vicksburgh. Small doses of anything are good, even me. I spent the evening making up for lost time, and ended up still covering thirty miles on the day. I was within twenty-four miles of Vicksburgh.

CHAPTER 14: VICKSBURGH, MISSISSIPPI

JULY 22, 1999 DAY 69

I woke up at 7:30 dreaming of sleeping at home in my own bed. I was shocked to discover I was in my old smelly tent, and my trip was still going on. It was starting to feel like the movie, Groundhog's Day. I wasn't very enthused about paddling, so I drifted the whole way to Vicksburgh, swimming in the river a good part of the time. I was in a good mood, but kept thinking about New Orleans. Where would I stop? When would I get there? How would I get home? Would I come home? What would happen next? It bugged me to think about it, so I pushed it out of my mind.

Pulling into the docks on the Vicksburgh waterfront, I was greeted by a lady named Peggy. She was running a business called Mississippi Adventures, and offered for me to sleep on the docks as long as I wanted. She was very charming and hospitable, and we got along well from the start. If I painted a picture in my head of the perfect Southern lady, it would be Peggy. After walking all over town on my sore feet looking at war memorials, I discovered a funny looking boat on the other side of Peggy's building.

I walked inside to talk to Peggy. A thin man of about thirty was sitting across from her at the table. He was in rougher shape than I was, but wore an expression of sureness and contentment like none I had ever seen. I knew immediately that it was Nat Stone. Nat was a quiet guy, but when he spoke he said a lot. He had left the Brooklyn Bridge ninety-one days earlier, and had traveled down the Allegheny, across Lake Erie, down the Ohio, over to the Mississippi, and was planning on building his own boat in New Orleans and sailing it back to Brooklyn. He was a schoolteacher in New Mexico but had given it all up for the trip of a lifetime. He was a legend to me already. Nat had lost about twenty pounds, but his thin body was so chiseled from hour after hour of rowing that he was ready for anything. My trip seemed miniscule.

Nat and I spent an hour chatting, mostly about the solo aspect of our trips and our motivations for taking them. It had a lot to do with shedding our own personal fears, severing from weak, mainstream society, and believing that anything was possible. We sat on the docks enjoying our chance meeting when suddenly everyone showed up.

First came Ben and Jason on the raft. They were meeting Jason's parents at the very place we sat. Jason's parents showed up next. They were both college professors, and talking to them showed me where Jason acquired his analytical skills. The local paper was the next to arrive. In ten minutes, the dock went from being empty to having a big crowd of people all talking at once.

Our interviewer's name was Frankie Mendoza. He attended college at a local university. He normally did only photography but had been sent to do our story. Frankie listened to our stories eagerly, and dutifully recorded our words as fast as his hands could write. He was really engrossed in the subject manner, and curiously asked question after question, even after the interview was over. I'd met a lot of people who thought our trip was neat, but Frankie thought it was the most unbelievable and awesome thing he'd ever seen. He took it upon himself to be our personal guide for as long as we stayed.

Jason's parents treated us to a fancy dinner, and we shared stories of our respective journeys. Frankie was now a member of our club, and his girlfriend and he joined us for dinner. The four of us all climbed into the back of Frankie's pickup after dinner, and he took us on a wild goose chase over the Mississippi River bridge and out into the boonies of Louisiana. We were accustomed to traveling at five miles an hour but Frankie liked to drive fast. It was a pretty scary ride. We flew down a dark back road and arrived at a big pole shed out in the middle of nowhere. A big neon sign on the side of the shed read: Daiquiri World.

The parking lot was filled with circles of kids in their early twenties. Most of them were passing around joints. A young police officer guarded the door, but he was having as much fun as anyone was. The shed was filled with drunken kids dancing to loud techno music. It was very crowded and hard to get around, and several locals were obviously there for the sole purpose of picking fights. Everyone seemed to be putting up a front. They all seemed to be trying to put on a show for everyone around them. All the guys walked around with a look of "Hey, don't fuck with me, I'm a bad ass." They all strutted around like they wanted to be gangster rappers on MTV. There were several pretty girls, but they seemed to be hiding behind a façade like they were cast members on Melrose Place or Beverly Hills 90210. I had the impression they had stood in front of the mirror for hours and hours trying to capture just the right look, and when they finally acquired it, they didn't have to try any more. They had the look, and it was powerful enough to talk on its own. When any of the gangster wannabes talked to the girls with "the look," their body language was one of possessiveness, as if to say to all around, "don't you even look at this chick, she's mine." It was a barn full of sharks.

After spending so much time in wide-open spaces, it was hard for me to stand in the packed bar of posers. I could relate better to the subgroup of people outside in the circles, and decided to try my luck out there.

There was a lot of smoke rising from the parking lot, but I'd rather hang out with a bunch of stoners than a bunch of posers. People who smoked weed had a welcoming nature to them. Maybe it was a byproduct of the sixties, but strangers who liked to toke always seemed to be looking to make me feel comfortable. It didn't take long before someone saw me, recognized me from having come in with Frank, and called me over.

I spent the rest of the evening partying it up in the parking lot with strangers, but they all seemed to know Frank, and that made me okay to them. They were some real characters. The guys had a pure, backwoods element to them, while the girls were more into the natural look like I liked. My new friends outside made it sound almost as if there were a civil war going on between the stoners and the preppies. The stoners owned the outside while the preppies stayed inside near the speakers. If I walked around alone in the shed and one of the preppies took me for a stoner, I'd have myself a fight for sure. There was nothing in there for me anyway, so I stayed outside and partied.

It was acceptable to drink beer and anything else out on the gravel under the hot Louisiana nighttime sky. I looked around at the foreign landscape, strange faces, and kids partying around me. I was out in the boondocks by some big shed getting messed up with a bunch of people I didn't know. They made me feel right at home, so I carried on.

A change in consciousness slowly crept over me. The faces and voices became stranger and stranger.

I've been abandoned here on earth.
My yesterdays and tomorrows
have disintegrated and I'm stuck
in a never-ending now - and
everything scares the shit out of me.

After the initial paranoia wore off I began to find my groove. It was all body language, all posturing. I was smooth and cool. Gliding across pebbles in the moonlight, I locked eyes with strange women and spoke to them. They spoke back. No one said a word.

An eerie sense of peace blanketed me. Ben and Jason came out looking for me, just as I was about to become a parking lot person forever.

The ride back was much wilder than the ride there. Ben had the coolest head in the group, and he was nominated to drive Frank's pickup. Eight miles an hour was warp speed, and cruising in the back of the pickup watching the stars bounce above me was a dream. It was especially trippy crossing the dark abyss over the Mississippi River. It felt like I was going to float right out of the truck and land in the river below.

Although it was after 2:00 by the time we got back, I was restless so I went to check out the casino. I lost a few bucks, but mostly just walked around looking at people and trying to figure out what their masks were and why they were wearing them.

All the kids inside the bar were trying so hard to put on a front, but I did that too sometimes. Did others see me the way I saw myself? To get through all that bullshit and connect with someone's real true self was very special and very rare. Everyone had their blockers on, but for two people to get past that and understand each other was really amazing. I wished I had more skills to open up and show who I was and try to really see people for who they really were. There were unwritten rules that prevented me from doing so, but I wanted to learn how to get around them.

The concrete docks were uncomfortable, but by 4:30 I crashed hard.

DAY 70

By 7:00 there was too much noise on the docks to sleep. People had been coming and going all morning, and it made me paranoid when I heard them talking. Several times during my few hours of sleep I awoke to strange voices or motors echoing off the side of the dyke, and I had no idea where they were coming from. By 7:30 Nat was heading out. I couldn't imagine trying to paddle after the night before. Nat Stone waved goodbye, and just like that the modest schoolteacher from New Mexico was gone forever. Peggy's shop opened up at 8:00, so I cleared off of the dock and got out of the way.

I was too exhausted to paddle, and didn't feel like it anyway. Although it was still early, the temperature was already nearing 100 degrees. I couldn't take another second outside. I dragged my ass back to the casino and hit the breakfast buffet. After a huge breakfast and several cups of coffee, I spent the next few hours drinking free pop and enjoying the air-conditioning. Even after several doses of caffeine, I was so drained that I wanted nothing more than to crash for a few hours, but there was nowhere to go. I tried finding an open conference room. I tried sleeping on a toilet seat. I would have set my tent up somewhere and slept in it, but it was too hot. I felt like I was going to die. It was impossible for me to keep my eyes open any longer, but there was nowhere to get comfortable. I found a secluded quarter slot, put on my new, one-dollar sunglasses, and tried to sleep at the machine with my hand up against the lever. It reminded me of trying to sleep in school. It didn't take long for casino security to find me and ask me to leave.

I walked out of the casino with a security guard trailing a few steps behind. As I staggered outside into the hot blast of summer air, someone called my name. It was Frankie. He had been looking everywhere for me, and wore a huge smile on his face.

"I've got great news," he said, "I've decided to leave town, and go with you guys down the river." My only reaction was to break out into a hysterical laugh. "I'm serious," he went on, "I'm on my way right now to tell my girlfriend, and I'll quit my job if I have to." Although I was tired, it didn't take me long to wake up. He was serious. Frankie had found a canoe to borrow from a neighbor and was ready to leave. He wanted to do a million things all at once, but all I wanted was to find a quiet place to crash.

I jumped into the car with him, and after picking up the article with me in it, he drove straight to where his girlfriend worked, and explained he wouldn't be seeing her for awhile. "I'm heading down the river," he proudly exclaimed. Frankie went home to pack and say goodbye to everyone and dropped me off at a bar near the river where I vegged out and tried not to fall asleep on my beer.

After having a few beers at Bleachers Sports Pub, I started thinking about Frankie. I liked Frankie. His friends were all stuck in Vicksburgh, content on smoking dope every day and going to Daiquiri World on weekends. He had ambition and talent, and had found something he was good at in photography. He was all gung-ho about the trip, and probably pictured us all having the time of our lives twenty-four hours a day. In reality, I was completely burned out, was no fun to be around, and went through my days in relative silence. I didn't want to crush his hopes, but decided to call him up.

It was almost impossible to dissuade Frankie, but I finally convinced him that you couldn't just wake up one day and decide to canoe down the Mississippi River. Although I sounded like some old guy with no imagination talking, I knew it would be for the best. I decided to take off before he changed his mind again.

Before leaving, I stopped back to say goodbye to Peggy. We talked about life and dreams. I didn't know why, but everyone I had a conversation with always looked at me with such sadness. They talked to me like I was dying of cancer or something. People talked like they wanted to give me some last advice on earth before I left. Peggy was genuinely worried about me.

It was hard to leave Vicksburgh, especially knowing I had another eighty miles before Natchez and would be lucky to see any one along the way. My goal was to make it ten miles before quitting, but after six miles, my tired body could go no farther. I set up camp on the first island south of town.

I slumped into my tent and recited my prayers before bed, just as I did every night. As tired as I was, for some reason I thought about what I said. My parents had taught me a bedtime prayer when I was five, and I'd been repeating it every night for the last twenty years, even though I really didn't even know what it meant. I repeated it like a robot every night, because that was what I was supposed to do. It was almost as if I uttered some meaningless words every night before I went to bed, I would be a Christian, and wouldn't have to worry about anything. But, what if I died before I waked, would the Lord my soul to take? What if I died in a hotel room in Memphis? What if I died in Quincy? They were just words, and I knew I was still falling, I was just hoping for more roots to grab. They hadn't failed me yet, so why would they run out anytime soon?

DAY 71

I slept like a rock for twelve hours and woke to a hot and hazy morning. By 11:00 it was unbearably hot. The sides of my canoe were so hot I kept burning my hands and legs on them, and had to constantly douse it with water to keep the metal from taking off my skin. It was so hot in the canoe that if I went over half an hour without jumping in the river, I started to get really confused and felt like I was about to pass out. Over half the day was spent swimming in the water beside my green canoe. Every time I got out of the water, I had to use my towel to remove a layer of slime from my skin.

The day was dragging along so slowly. I tried reading for twenty minutes without looking at my watch. I invented new games, anything to break up the monotony. I saw how far away I could get from my canoe, and then tried swimming back to it. I imagined my canoe was my innocent childhood that was good and clean and pure as I drifted away, then I had to fight against the current to gain it back. It was fun for ten minutes, but then I got sick of it. The current was too strong for me to fight anyway.

In Brainerd, I had written Lake Itasca to New Orleans on the sides of my canoe four times with a marker. I was within a week of my destination, and in order to put closure on my trip, I'd decided a few weeks earlier to use mosquito repellent to remove one letter each day. That afternoon I got carried away and erased a whole side. It was hard to remove black magic marker, but I scrubbed for an hour. My canoe felt oddly unbalanced with one side of letters erased.

Sometimes I felt afraid to get to New Orleans, but at other times I couldn't wait. A big storm was brewing, but I was rooting for it. More rain meant cool air, and the heat was killing me. More rain also meant a faster current. The water was dropping almost six inches every day and was back to normal level. I had to work harder to make more miles. The storm rumbled in, but all it provided was one brief shower, and then it was over. I set up camp for the night as it quit. I covered nearly fifty miles on the day.

Setting up camp was getting to be more and more frustrating, because my tent was getting so hashed. I had expected more rain and quit early, but it had turned into a nice night. After enjoying a dinner of Ramen Noodles, I decided to smoke a cigar, something I usually reserved for Saturday nights only. Smoking a cigar usually had a magical effect of slowing everything down and putting my life back into perspective. All it did that night was make me wonder what in the hell I was doing sitting on some sandbar all alone in the middle of nowhere getting chewed up by mosquitoes.

CHAPTER 15:NATCHEZ, MISSISSIPPI

DAY 72

I didn't feel like getting out of the tent, but the sun was so hot I couldn't bear to stay inside. I only had a twenty-two mile paddle to get to Natchez. That was like waking up and going on a six-hour car drive to find a glass of water. That's right, water. I was down to one container left, but I'd turned the canoe on top of it and punctured it. I was forced to last six hours in 100-degree heat with no water. It tasted like shit anyway.

Although I only had a half-day, it felt like an eternity. I was already thirsty, and hoped to be lucky enough to find a place to get water along the river. I had no such luck. New Orleans was within striking distance, but I couldn't imagine canoeing another week. The long uncomfortable days were taking a toll on both my body and mind.

I didn't see any signs of life all morning, and by the time I got to Natchez I felt like a camel. I had paddled eighty miles since Vicksburgh, and hadn't seen a single person. The only thing in the whole world that I wanted was some water.

I parked my canoe on the beach near the Casino, and walked into the first bar I saw. The only occupants were a gray haired distinguished gentlemen and a wild haired guy of about forty wearing a Hawaiian shirt. The old man sat in the corner with his legs crossed smoking an expensive cigar and paid no attention to me as I sat down at a stool. The guy in the Hawaiian shirt was talking on the phone behind the bar and took his time finishing the conversation before coming by to wait on me.

"I just need a water."

"Sorry, you gotta buy food or something to get water."

"Okay, give me a Coke then." I must have looked pretty bad, because he didn't seem to want to talk to me too badly. I had not even had a sip of my pop yet, when a police officer walked into the bar and approached me.

"Is that your canoe?"

"Yea."

"Your gonna have to move it."

"What do you mean? It's on the beach."

"It's on casino property, and they want it moved."

"Can I finish my coke?"

"Sorry, they need you to move it now." I slammed my pop down at the door and followed the stern policeman down to the beach.

The casino manager stood on the side of the river near my canoe with her hands on her hips. She looked up at me like she had just apprehended Billy the Kid. The entire Natchez shoreline was riprap, and the only place to put a canoe was on the beach by the casino. I got in the canoe and paddled over to the very edge of the beach. It was seventy-five yards downstream from the edge of the casino. Another cop pulled up to join the entire management team from the casino on the side of the bank. It wasn't far enough away for them, and they started yelling over to me to keep going. I paddled up against the current to where they were all standing. I couldn't put my canoe up on the rocks, and all I wanted was to find a place to get something to drink and some nice people to talk to.

"Where do you recommend I put my canoe?" I sat in my canoe treading water in front of a crowd of people standing on the shore a few feet away.

"I don't care, but you can't keep it here. The casino owns this part of the river." A large black lady in a suit did all of the talking. She still had her hands on her hips, apparently feeling tough from the presence of the police officers behind her.

"I've paddled this canoe down this river for nearly two thousand miles, and all I want is to stop and have a glass of water. Can't you just give me a break and let me park it there for an hour?" She didn't allow me to finish the sentence. She stood with her hands on her hips pointing downstream, telling me to leave. I tried explaining the first few feet of shoreline were considered navigable territory, but she wouldn't let me talk. She repeated I was on private property, and she 'd have me arrested if I didn't leave.

"But I'm in my canoe on the Mississippi River. How can you arrest me for this?"

"We own that part of the river. The casino owns all the water on every side of the boat for one hundred yards. We don't allow vagrants in Natchez, anyway." We were both yelling, but the cops hadn't said a word. A crowd of people had gathered around to see what all of the commotion was about. "Now get out of here before you regret it."

Without even bothering to check the depth, I dove out of the canoe, making the most perfect dive I had ever practiced. When I hit bottom with my hand I picked up a handful of rocks, and brought them back up to the top to show her.

"Do you own the rocks in the river? Do you own the fish in the river? Is all of this water yours?" I cradled my canoe in my left hand and swam with it toward shore. "I'll leave, but you sure as hell don't own this river." I was standing knee deep in mud. Other casino managers were trying to convince me to leave, but I knew they wouldn't get their pretty suits muddy to force me to go. I could've sat there in my canoe all day.

I paddled upstream, but not until I had circled the boat five times in my canoe, howling the whole time as a crowd of angry people in uniforms looked on, unable to do anything. It was tough paddling against the current, but I remembered a small beach in some woods about half a mile upriver, and I figured on setting up camp there.

After getting my tent set up, I couldn't resist myself. I was still thirsty, but wanted to go back and say hello to my friends at the casino. Marching over the bridge with my empty water jugs, I didn't get half way up the steps before security stopped me. Although I was ready for a confrontation, the fat lady was gone, and the young men in suits were actually really cordial in giving me the boot. They said I wasn't dressed properly to be on the premises, and their bosses would not allow me to enter. I was steaming mad and ready to battle, but one of the guys took me off to the side to cool me down. He was a black guy named Emeal who was about my age, and told me if I were to go to Kmart and buy some decent clothes, he would sneak me in, and even buy me supper. He was a really nice guy, and pleaded with me to leave without causing any more of a commotion. He told me he was on my side, but it was his job to keep me from coming in, and he liked his job. I liked Emeal, so I did him a favor and walked away.

Not quite ready to leave town, I walked back to the bar I was in before. The bartender had watched the scene from the doorway, and greeted me with a gigantic glass of ice water and a huge grin.

"Them assholes at the casino think they own this whole town," he confided in me. The bartender with the wild hair was Pierre. The old guy at the table was his father, and was also Pierre. The two of them owned the bar. We talked for awhile about my trip, and I drank about six glasses of water. I asked him where a guy could find some excitement in this town, but he told me I had already found it.

"Come in here tonight. We have a live band coming in and they really rock." The phone rang, and he excused himself. I sat at the bar guzzling water, wondering how to spend my day.

"Do you want to make a few dollars?"

"Doing what?"

"That was my bartender. He can't make it tonight, and now I'm shorthanded. Have you ever bartended before?" I hadn't, but he said they could teach me. He told me to come back at 7:00. It was only 3:00, so I went out to see the rest of the town.

There was a huge hill to climb to get to the main part of the town. It was too hot to walk it, but I found an easy way around. The casino offered a bus service to its guests, so I snuck onto one. I looked out of place among all of the old tourists in polyester pants, but the driver never said anything as I rode along helping myself to the free beverages on board. Most of the passengers got out at a fancy hotel, so I decided to push my luck.

As we exited, I struck up a conversation with a couple of old guys and followed them into the lavish hotel. They were on their way to the complimentary snack buffet. I feasted on fruit and salads with them and talked about the hot weather. I explained I was meeting my parents there, and they hadn't checked in yet. Several hotel workers walked by and looked at me, but no one said a word.

After filling up on free food, I walked down the road to Kmart. Although it was only a few blocks, it was so hot out that it really drained me, and my river shoes were really starting to get old. It seemed like the best place around to meet some girls, and although I tried sparking up a conversation with several hotties, I was unable to make any progress. I even struck out on trying to hitch a ride back to the hotel. Outside Kmart, I met a few black girls who tried to sell me pralines. They were buying them inside Kmart and sitting on the bench outside, trying to sell them for twice as much as they were worth.

It was a hot walk back to the hotel, but I entertained myself by walking into every business along the way and looking around for anything interesting. All I got were a lot of blank stares. Several times I attempted to initiate conversation with the locals, but nobody wanted to talk to me except one crazy guy who I ran into at Dairy Queen.

He was walking out as I was walking in, and stopped and stared at me as if he knew me. He had long, oily, jet-black hair, and wore a sleeveless flannel shirt. He was much bigger than I was, but wasn't in very good shape. His flabby arms were covered in homemade tattoos and had all of these sloppy symbols that I couldn't understand. It looked like he had recently gotten his ass kicked, as one of his eyes was blackened and the side of his face was all scraped up. I figured he might have seen me at the casino, but I thought I would have remembered him. He just stared at me without saying anything.

"How are you doing?" I asked, trying to break the strange silence.

"You're not from here," he said. "Watch out they'll throw you in jail for nothing. Look at what they did to me," he said, pointing to the scrapes on his face. He tilted his head off to one side and his face twitched like he had some kind of muscular disease.

"What happened?" I asked.

"How do you say? Pot. I didn't do nothing. You like pot?"

"No man, I'm okay but thanks." He looked like the wrestler, Mankind.

"I'll find you a ride. You wait patiently here. I'll find you a ride, and I know where to get some pot if you want some."

"Thanks for the offer, but I don't need a ride or anything else." I walked into the door to get away from him, but not until I heard him utter his last words.

"Be careful, they'll kill 'ya here." I walked into the Dairy Queen and watched him out the window. He walked with a big hunch in his back as he limped off down the sidewalk. I had nothing to do in Dairy Queen except look around, but I waited until he was well out of sight before I went back to the street. He never smiled or laughed, and he had a dead seriousness to him that continued to haunt me. For the rest of the day I tried to figure out what he had meant when he said they'd kill me. Back at the hotel I sat in the lobby and read the paper until the bus came back, and then rode it back to the casino.

The town had a very strange feel to it. I wasn't sure exactly what it was, but it felt like everyone knew something really bad, but they were all afraid to talk about it. I had a feeling that the hunchback guy wanted to tell me about whatever it was. It was getting close to 7:00, so I decided to go back to the bar and learn how to be a bartender.

The band was finishing its warm ups, and the place was already full of people. It had quite a different look than it had during the day. The place was filled mostly with tourists sitting at tables, but two rough looking guys sitting at end of the bar seemed to take notice of me as Pierre greeted me. They were looking in my direction and talking, and I had a strange feeling the conversation was about me. It was hotter than hell, and they left the big front door wide open and several large fans created a strong breeze. The old guy was sitting in the same chair with his legs crossed smoking a big cigar. He did not take any notice of me as I walked in, but the eyes of the guys at the bar made me a little nervous. Pierre tossed me a shirt they sold at the bar and rushed into the backroom.

"Don't worry," he assured me, "Scottie will teach you everything you need to know." I sat stupidly watching the swinging doors, wondering who Scottie was.

The swinging doors were just settling from Pierre rushing through them when they opened again and a Chinese guy walked out. His eyes locked straight onto mine from the other side of the bar as he approached me swiftly and extended his hand. Scottie was six inches shorter than I was, but he had extremely broad shoulders for an Asian and had very powerful arms. His head was bald, but he had long black hair growing off of his chin and wild eyes that kept piercing me. It was impossible to guess how old he was, and I figured he could be anywhere between thirty and sixty. He carried a scary presence and it was difficult to look him in the eyes. He reminded me of a miniature Ganges Kahn.

Scottie had the firmest handshake I'd ever felt. He was a man of very few words, but his English was perfect. It was my responsibility to have a certain amount of each type of beer in the front cooler, and I had to have two cases of each variety ready at all times in the backroom. I was in charge of fetching all the beers and keeping an adequate amount of ice on them. He encouraged me to drink as much as I wanted while I worked.

After making sure I knew what to do with the beers, Scottie led me over to the bottles on the wall. He made me start on the left side and memorize every bottle without looking. He left me alone, promising he'd test me in an hour. I tried to explain to him I was only going to work there for one night, but he would not listen.

"If I tell you to do something, I want you to do it the right way. No questions." From the way he said it to me, I wasn't about to ask another. I fetched beers, and memorized bottles. The beers were sliding down pretty good for me as well. After an hour he returned and made me recite the list to him, using only my left hand to guide me.

"Smirnoff Vodka, Jack Daniels, Bacardi, Gin, Early Times, Old Charter, V/O, Seven, Usher, ect., ect, ect.,......I went on and on, and completed the list. I felt pretty good about memorizing all the bottles so quickly, but Scottie didn't even crack a smile.

"Now do it backwards with your right hand," he commanded, "I'll be back in another hour." I just sat there dumbfounded for a few moments. What in the hell was he doing? Did he think I was the Karate Kid or something? I was more familiar with the bar and it was easier. After forty-five minutes I was ready to show him, but he insisted I practiced until the hour was done.

After passing the test, Scottie finally showed some emotion. He smiled at me for the first time and handed me a twenty-dollar bill. I'd been standing there memorizing bottles for two hours and was beginning to think it was a big crock of shit, but I had a pocket full of money and access to all the free beers I could drink.

After passing my second test, I was put in charge of making basic mixed drinks as well. Scottie may have had a funny way of teaching me, but I had a feel for those bottles, and never had to look in order to grab the right one.

I hadn't had to deal with the rough looking guys at the end of the bar, but after I was put in charge of mixed drinks, I had to talk to them every twenty minutes or so. The guy on the right was Crazy Gary. He talked constantly about the Vietnam War and kept sneaking hits from his one hitter and trying to get me to take one. Crazy Gary was a monster of a man, and looked like the spitting image of Bull on Night Court, except he had a long beard and crazy tattoos all over his muscular arms.

The band was playing some pretty good music. They paused between songs, and Crazy Gary pounded his fists on the bar and started chanting, "We want Neil Young! Neil Young! Neil Young!" The tattoo-covered man on his right joined him in the chant. The two were starting to get really rowdy, and it was obvious they were disturbing some of the touristy clientele. Old man Pierre walked over without saying a word and gave Crazy Gary a stern look, and he instantly calmed down. It was as if the old guy had a certain power and control over every one else in the room.

Billy was the man on Gary's right with the fiendish smile. He was supposedly famous in those parts. Anyone with a tattoo worth seeing had gotten it from him, and he had learned the majority of his handiwork behind bars. It had been his home until very recently. Billy was tall, thin and muscular, had a Colonel Sanders type long goatee, and long hair in a ponytail in the back. His arms and neck were popping with veins, and adorned with some of the coolest artwork I had seen. Billy had a wry grin on his face like he was smarter than everyone else in the room. He drank Captain and Cokes, and no matter how strong I mixed them, he always wanted more booze. It had been several weeks since I'd shaved, and Billy claimed a resemblance between the two of us. Looking at him, I could tell that if I would let myself go for much longer, I would start to look like him. Billy was about forty, but told me he looked just like me when he was a kid. He kept calling me his boy, and took it upon himself to be my personal protector should anyone give me a hard time that night. Billy also shared my love of canoeing, and used his low, raspy voice to share a little slogan of his with me.

Love Many,
Trust Few,
And Always Paddle Your Own Canoe

The guys at the end of the bar were pretty wild. I was drinking free beer like a fish, and ended up spending a good part of the evening talking to them. Crazy Gary always wanted to high five me, and was still trying to get me to get high with him. Meanwhile, Billy acted like my new best friend. He kept telling me how much he knew about me, and recited his poem several times throughout the night. At 10:00, old Pierre went home and went to bed. It was as if their parents had left for the weekend, and they had the whole house to themselves.

The place was getting rowdier as people got drunker, but as the night wore on the tourists slowly left. I was getting pretty tanked, and didn't realize the change slowly taking over the bar. By midnight, only the locals were left in the place.

Two guys sitting near the middle of the bar kept smiling at me, and had been giving me nice tips all night. Bob and Ray had matching Key West golf shirts on, except one was pink and the other blue. Bob left a little after midnight, but Ray decided to stay.

"I hear you are sleeping out in a tent, do you need a place to stay tonight?" he asked with such sincerity that I just sat there behind the bar and listened. "I have a hot tub, and you could relax in it before you went to bed."

Was I getting hit on by a queer guy? I had no problem with gay people, but it made me feel very uncomfortable to have him asking me to stay over. The bar was about to close, and Scottie came over to me with my share of the tips.

"You are a very fast learner. I knew that you would come soon." Scottie hadn't said anything to me in awhile other than calling for a drink occasionally, but he always looked at me funny. Several times when we passed each other going in opposite directions behind the bar, he would do some funky shit with his hands and wave his fingers around between my eyes and his eyes. At first I thought he was just messing around, but he never smiled, and always looked so serious.

"What do you mean you knew I would come soon?" Scottie waved his fingers rhythmically between his eyes and mine and spoke.

> *When the student is ready,*
> *The teacher will appear.*

His eyes were mesmerizing, and I couldn't stand to look at them more than a moment before I had to look away. I turned away from Scottie, but every time I ran into him for the rest of the evening he did the same weird voodoo shit, and repeated the same verse, "When the student is ready, the teacher will appear."

Scottie was still giving me orders on cleaning up, and every time I asked him a question about his unorthodox way of doing things, he snapped at me and told me not to ask questions. When he met me in the backroom and started looking at me really funny, I confronted him. For the first time all night I stared back at his scary eyes.

"I don't know what kind of crazy shit you're trying to pull on me, but knock it the fuck off. I came here to make a few bucks, not to play Karate Kid. Quit trying to fuck with me, and don't do that Zen shit with your hands anymore." I expected him to start doing some martial arts moves on me, but instead he just got a real sad look on his face and avoided me for the rest of the night.

It was last call, and Ray called me over to get another drink. "Say, you are a cute one," he told me as he batted his eyes like a little schoolgirl, "Are you sure you're not interested in that hot tub?" I told him I could care less about what he did, but it wasn't my cup of tea. He made me feel uncomfortable, but compared to the other guys in the bar he was harmless.

A familiar looking guy hobbled through the open doors. It was the crazy guy from Dairy Queen I'd talked to earlier. I hoped he wouldn't notice me. For the first time all night, I started to come to my senses. I was at social deviant central, drunk off my ass, and camped a few hundred yards away. Everyone in that messed up place knew I was camping, and there weren't too many possible places to set up a tent. In addition to the strange people in the bar, I thought about all the people who I'd undoubtedly pissed off at the casino. I felt like the last beer in the fridge after the keg just went dry at a big party.

"Bender, where the fuck have you been all night?" It was Crazy Gary doing the talking. The only people left in the bar were Scottie the Zen master, Ray the queer, Billy, Crazy Gary, and Bender. I probably had some money coming to me yet, but that Bender guy scared the shit out of me, and I waited for the first opportunity to bolt. Bender pulled a big pipe out of his pocket, and the three guys at the end of the bar started passing it around. Scottie was in the back room, and although Ray was watching every move I made, I didn't perceive him as a threat. It looked like a good chance to make my break.

"Hey Yankee, where you goin'?" I froze halfway out the door, hoping the voice wasn't directed at me, but knowing it was. "C'mon man, we're smoking a bowl." It was Bender doing the talking. I wished I could just disappear, but he had seen me, and there was really nowhere to go anyway. "Hey man, I know you, you're the guy from today." Bender was obviously insane. He pounded his clumsy hand on my shoulder and pushed the still-smoking pipe in my face.

"No man, I've got to go. I've been up since five-o-clock and paddled forty miles today," I lied. I made my way outside, but Bender and Billy were following me.

Billy tried to convince me to stay. "A little weed ain't gonna hurt you none little brother. C'mon, we got the same blood. We're on the same side." The three of us stood outside in an empty, moonlit street. Crazy Gary started yelling from inside.

"Bender, get that damn thing back in here." Bender obeyed, and it was just Billy and me outside. Of all the wackos in the place, Billy was the one I distrusted the least.

"What's up with this place man?" It's like it's haunted or something, like everyone is trying to hide something, and they aren't doing a good job." Billy looked at me, and for the first time all night, I could see a little good in his bloodshot eyes.

"Yea it's fucked up little brother. This was the only town in the civil war that wasn't bombed by the North. The people made a secret pact, and whored themselves off to the Government. My relatives killed more people in that war than anyone."

"Is anyone gonna mess with me tonight?"

"No man, you're my boy, and you're in my backyard. Nobody fucks with you little brother. If you ever want a tattoo, I'll give you anything you want for nothing."

Bender and Crazy Gary were done getting baked, and they came stumbled back out to see what we were doing. Bender hobbled along, still shaking his oily black hair from side to side. Gary was so tall he had to duck to prevent hitting his head on the top of the doorway. Bender started asking me a lot of questions, wondering where I was from and what I was doing in Natchez working at his favorite bar, but Billy answered most of them for me, and told Bender to lay off.

"Last guy to bring a canoe through here never left town. Remember that guy, Gary?" Bender laughed again as his eyes bled with hatred. If he was trying to scare me it was working, and had been since I first saw him. He was definitely a loose cannon that could go at anytime. I wished the three of them would hurry up and leave. I didn't want them to see me walk toward my tent, but in the same way, I wanted to take off before Scottie and Ray came outside. It was 2:00 already, and I told them I had to take off.

Although my tent was in the woods on the north side of town, I walked south until they were out of view, crossed the dyke and ran down the hill down by the river. I raced across the riprap back to the north toward my tent. I stayed in the shadows and ran as silently as possible. I kept thinking there was someone behind me, but knew it was just my imagination. Several times I stopped for a second to listen. I clutched two jagged rocks in each fist in case I needed to defend myself.

It was dangerous hopping across boulders by the river in the dark. I was pretty sure no one would be stupid enough to wander around trying to find me. After skipping across the treacherous bolder field, I came into the thin patch of woods where I had stashed my stuff. It was a relief to make it back to my tent, and after waiting for five minutes and listening to see if anyone was making any noise in the woods, I went inside.

Although I was tired, drunk, and desperately in need of sleep, I was too paranoid to close my eyes. Everyone at the bar was spooky. I kept thinking I heard someone but knew I was being stupid. After waiting for about an hour, I finally drifted off to sleep.

A crackling noise in the woods woke me instantly. I didn't know how long I had been asleep, but there was definitely something big moving around in the woods. I quickly remembered all of the strange characters of the night and the fear and paranoia with which I had crept back to my tent and been too afraid to sleep. Within seconds I was fully alert, or at least as alert as a drunk, half-sleeping guy can possibly be.

It was making too much noise to be a small animal. It sounded like it was getting closer, but my heart was beating so fast I couldn't tell. Slowly, I grabbed my loaded gun and unzipped the tent, trying to be as quiet as possible. Sticks were snapping on the forest floor, but looking out toward the direction of the sound, revealed nothing.

I was a sitting duck inside my tent, so I crawled on my belly and hid under a thick fallen tree nearby. The sounds were getting closer. They stopped for twenty seconds, then started up again. It was a very dark night and my eyes kept playing tricks on me. I thought I saw the silhouette of a person, but it ended up being a tree. I had lost my sense of time completely, and was not sure how long I had spent under the log.

A figure was awkwardly approaching. My heart jumped into my throat, and I took tiny little breaths in order to be still and silent. The figure crept very slowly toward my tent trying not to make any noise.

I watched its awkward movements and knew it was a person. It was pitch black and I couldn't see a face, but I knew it was Bender. My thoughts raced. What should I do? Should I start shooting? Should I wait and then shoot? What if it wasn't him? Yea, it had to be him; nobody else walked like that. I wasn't sure if I was dreaming or not.

He had no business being in the woods at that time of night. It was my life he was fucking with, and I knew I had the drop on him. He had to walk right by me to get to my tent, and I wouldn't think twice to shoot him. It was him or me.

Bender staggered closer until I could almost see his face. He was really screwed up and stumbled every few steps. It felt like I was in my tree stand, waiting to get the perfect kill shot on a trophy buck.

The moron walked within ten feet of my hiding place. I figured for sure that he would see me, and things would start happening fast, but he walked right past and tiptoed towards my tent. I waited until he had his back to me before I made my move.

"One more move and you're a fucking dead man." He jumped so high that he fell over, catching himself on the ground with both hands. "What are you doing out here in the middle of the night?" Feeling as if I was facing the devil himself, I was surprised at the strength of my fearful voice.

"Man don't fucking shoot, I'm just, I was just, fuck man, I ain't doing nothing." He stepped towards me with both arms out to his sides.

"Don't move Bender. I don't want to shoot you, but I will." He was so stupid and messed up, I was pretty sure he was going to make me kill him. "Get outta here."

"Man it's cool, it's cool, I was just, I ain't, I didn't."

"Bender, get the fuck out of here. I'm all alone, I'm scared, I'm paranoid as hell, I don't know where I'm at, I'm fucked up, and nothing against you, but I am going to count to five, and then start shooting, and then I'm going to sit here all night long and shoot at anything that moves." I didn't get the first number out before Bender started running. He fell down twice as he raced away.

I was still shaking, but I acted fast. I heard him falling down and cursing in the distance as I dragged my loaded tent to the canoe. I threw it all in the front in one giant heap. I had no idea if I had forgotten anything, but I didn't care to wait around. Within thirty seconds of Bender taking off, I was shoving off into the dangerous river in the dark.

I was drunk, scared, and delirious. I paddled straight across to the Louisiana side, even though it was pitch black and I couldn't see a thing. I came within inches of wrapping the canoe around a river buoy. I kept repeating the same words in my mind. "I got to get the hell out of this fucked up town." It was 4:00 in the morning.

I stopped at the first place on the Louisiana shoreline where I could pull up my canoe. My tent was in a heap, and I didn't feel like setting it up. Instead, I spent the last few hours of darkness sitting in my canoe with my loaded gun in front of me, nodding in and out of sleep, and waking up every few minutes to listen for intruders.

DAY 73

Every time I woke up from my uncomfortable position in the canoe, I prayed that it would be light out. Dawn would assure me I had survived Natchez, and she couldn't come quickly enough. Finally, the eastern sky began to lighten. I waited until the first river buoy became visible and started down the river again.

I went through the morning like a zombie. My brain was completely empty. I was not sure if I was sleeping or awake. What the hell was wrong with me? Oh yea, I'd partied my ass off in Natchez, and still hadn't caught up from not getting any sleep in Vicksburgh. The heat was relentless and passing out was a concern. My filthy tent was heaped in the middle of the floor and I didn't have the ambition to check inside to see if I'd forgotten anything during my hasty departure. I'd also been re-infested with ants.

The last thing I could clearly remember was standing in some crowded bar across the river near Vicksburgh, wondering whether or not to get a beer. Ever since that night, everything was a blur. I'd lost it again. I was broken.

I was too tired to paddle. I drifted down the river all day without really thinking about anything. My brain was blank and I had no sense of time. Late in the afternoon, I heard a mysterious motorized thumping noise. It seemed to be following me on shore. Sometimes it went away, but then it came back. The hillbillies from the 4th of July back by Missouri warned me about guys making crystal meth. Wondering if that was what the motor was from, I paddled to the other side of the river in order to get away from it.

Every time I turned a corner, I expected to see a john boat filled with guys from the bar that had come to kill me. I was very paranoid, and spent a good part of the afternoon planning what I would do in case I was attacked. I pictured myself diving underwater with my gun in hand, seeing one of them above the surface, jumping up and grabbing him by the neck, and pulling him back down with me. After that, I would pop back up and keep shooting until the rest of them were dead. I was haunted.

I was a sitting duck in the canoe, and was afraid they would set up an ambush on shore for me. The more I thought about it the more real it became. I was in no man's land, and there would be no one to call for help. While the morning was spent in a daze, the afternoon was spent constantly scanning the shoreline for oddities. If anyone would have pulled up in a boat, I probably would have flipped out, but I didn't see a soul.

Ants swarmed over the bottom of the canoe. There were more every time I looked. I must have had set my tent up right on top of a big anthill in Natchez. They were not like the warring fire ants from before; these were their working brethren. They had created their own highway system on the sides of my canoe, and never veered off one bit. They all looked so busy, and were all in such a hurry. One main highway ran down the side of the canoe, and several subsidiaries branched off toward my food bag, backpack, and other gear. The main drag had an equal amount of traffic heading in both directions. When two ants passed going opposite ways, they always paused for a split second, touched each other, and then kept moving. They never changed their mind and turned around, but always continued in their own separate ways.

They seemed to be communicating to one another. Maybe they didn't have a right/left rule of passing in effect yet. I took out my magic marker and drew lanes for them, but they kept running into each other. It must have been just a social thing.

The great thing about those ants was they never crawled on me, because they never left those roads. Earlier in the day I'd killed a mess of them, but I felt bad. They were such an organized, peaceful culture compared to those vicious fire ants.

Near dusk, I started feeling especially down. I was under the illusion the trip would heal me in some way. I thought everything would start making perfect sense to me. Instead, I felt like I didn't have a clue what I was doing or why I was doing it. I'd gotten all messed up at every town I came across, and forgotten everything I learned out in the canoe. It was as if every time I encountered people I became evil or something.

A face appeared in the clouds above. I imagined it was God, and he had come to give me a message. The only problem was that I was afraid of him, and hoped he would not try. I knew that all I had to do was to look up at the face and listen, but I was so ashamed of myself that I didn't feel worthy of looking. I tried to write about the face, but my pen died. I picked up my camera to take a picture, but every time I looked through the viewfinder it disappeared. I wanted to show every one else what I was seeing, but it was as if he was telling me it was between him and me. All kinds of thoughts poured into my head. They told me that all I had to do was open up and let the face come in to my life, but I was afraid. I wasn't yet prepared to meet God. I was afraid to die.

I knew I was turning my back on him, but I did it anyway. I just kept thinking about how unworthy I was, and I was sure I'd be struck down at any moment. I felt like I was impure, and didn't deserve to see the face. I decided to look back one last time, but the face was gone, and violent storm clouds had taken its place. I slept that night in a partially collapsed tent, wondering if I would die before I would wake.

DAY 74

I had unbelievably strange dreams that stormy night. They weren't of people and faces and things I could see, but instead I was this thing that lacked a real form. It was like I was a gas or a liquid or something. Whatever I was, I was moving extremely fast in all directions, but I wasn't really going anywhere. There were all of these other forces trying to shape me into different forms, and they were all pulling at me in different directions at the same time. I knew all I had to do was slow down my formless self, and quit moving so fast, but I couldn't make myself stop. Although I was formless, I knew there was a certain form I needed to take, but I couldn't figure out what it was.

When I woke up, I had ants crawling all over me. I'd fallen asleep in the middle of one of their main highways. The compassion I had on them before did not carry over to the morning, as I killed as many as possible without remorse.

I hadn't run into any repercussions from Natchez, and by noon I was fifty miles south of town. I spent the day relaxing and watching clouds for more wild shapes. I felt a little more ready to talk to God then I did the night before, so I kept looking around in case he was trying to get my attention again for some reason.

For the first time since Memphis, I found a radio station that wasn't country. Although the rafters had converted me, I was starting to get sick of hearing all of the same songs over and over again. I found some oldies station out of Baton Rouge, and although it was fuzzy, it was a cool change of pace. For the second day in a row I didn't see a single human being, and after listening to the oldies music all day, I was convinced I would get out of the canoe at Baton Rouge and it would be 1956.

In order to break up the monotony of the trip, I was constantly trying to find milestones to look ahead to. Near the end of the day, I was approaching three major ones. At mile marker 305 I was relieved to have finally left the state of Mississippi. At mile marker 302, I pushed my trip average up over twenty-seven miles per day again, and at mile marker 299, I hit my 2,000th mile.

At 6:00, a lightning storm came up, and I had to quit for the day before reaching all my milestones. I'd spent the entire day looking for signs from above, and as the storm began, I saw what looked like a finger in the sky pointing me to a sandbar on shore. The lightning was really flashing in the distance, but

I felt good and really wanted to make my 2000th mile. I wanted to ignore it, but the lightning was getting worse, and I didn't want to make God any angrier than he probably already was.

I sat on the sand Indian style for two hours, watching the lightning in the distance and pondering God. Feeling very strong, I decided to go for record mileage the next day.

CHAPTER 16:BATON ROUGE, LOUISIANA

JULY 28TH, 1999 DAY 75

I woke up in the best mood since Kentucky. I was paddling by 6:30, and watched the sunrise at 7:00 with several miles already behind me. My goal was to top sixty miles.

I paddled hard for the first hour, paddled fifty-five minutes of the next hour, fifty minutes of the next, forty-five minutes of the next, and continued that sequence until I hit thirty, then climbed back up the ladder to an hour. It was a thirteen-hour cycle. Every hour I recorded my mileage and checked my pace. My goal was to average over four miles per hour for fourteen hours.

When break time came at the end of every partial hour, it was like a nice vacation, or a break at work, or a weekend. I hadn't done much paddling in the last month, and had spent most days drifting along in the canoe, trolling my mind behind. I was focused for the first time in a long time. Although I spent a long day in the canoe, it went faster than any day I could remember. By noon, I was already approaching thirty miles on the day. If I could do sixty, I could try for seventy. I was remembering what hard work was like.

My pace slowed down a little in the afternoon, but by 5:30, I had covered fifty-one miles. If I averaged five miles per hour for another four hours, I'd hit seventy. The problem was that seventy miles would put me into downtown Baton Rouge, where the commercial traffic was rumored to make St. Louis look like a cakewalk. The thought of paddling seventy miles in one day made me want to go for it anyway. Even Chris and Geoff, the hardcore extremists from Connecticut, hadn't made seventy that I knew of.

As I quickened my pace, out of nowhere a feeling came over me telling me to stop. It reappeared several times and I pushed it aside. Why was I trying to paddle a canoe seventy miles in one day? Why was I taking the trip anyway? Was it all for my ego? I paddled those thoughts away in the swirls behind me and kept moving.

A quick front moved through and a strong south wind popped up. It was so strong it nearly capsized me, but I was worried about ruining my average and kept pushing it. For fifteen minutes the wind was so strong all I could do was hold my ground. I was getting really tired, and knew I should stop for the day, but being tired was just for a day, and a seventy-mile day would live forever. Through the wind and rain I paddled, gaining only inches each stroke, but still moving forward.

The front quickly passed and I continued. I felt as if I had broken a natural law of sorts. My heart had told me that it would be wise to get off the river, but I wanted to be able to brag about a seventy-mile day so I kept going. Everyone asked me how many miles I could go in a day, and to say I had done seventy would be awesome. I had paddled a canoe for 2,050 miles, and still had to impress people. My motives scared me.

I paddled harder to make up for lost time. I hit my sixtieth mile at 7:00, and arrived at the outskirts of Baton Rouge as the sun was going down. There were barges moored on both sides of the river, and it was getting dark fast. I had five miles to go, but I was really tired, and knew it would be wise to stop. There was a nice beach to my right that would have made a perfect camping spot, but I was driven on by that stupid man made invention called the number seventy. Visions of McGuire and Sosa filled my head.

I secured my life jacket, put on my blaze orange vest, and paddled with a fury. I had to make it to the interstate bridge. The barge traffic was getting heavier as I entered the city, and although it was nearly impossible for them to see me, I kept moving.

I paddled the last five miles on pure adrenaline, and by the time the bridge came into view, I was soaked in sweat. I hit the interstate bridge marking my seventieth mile at exactly 8:30. The only light to guide me was the reflection of the city off the water. The river had a terrible smell to it, and it gagged me to take a deep breath. It felt like I was breathing from inside an old oil can. I had made my seventy, but I was in the city and there was absolutely no place to camp. The right side wasn't developed, but it was blocked by commercial docks and moored barges. To my left was the city of Baton Rouge. I considered getting out my sleeping bag and camping on the concrete under the bridge, but I heard echoes of voices talking somewhere under the big arch. I was screwed. The lights from a casino boat reflected off the water ahead on the left. If I could find the energy to stay up all night, I could kill the evening hours on board and leave at first light. After paddling seventy miles, the idea didn't have much appeal.

I was nervous, but quickly pushed those limiting thoughts behind. I'd set out that morning to paddle sixty miles, and paddled seventy. I'd started in northern Minnesota feeling like I didn't have a snowball's chance in hell to make Bemidji. I was in Baton Rouge. I decided to say fuck it. I lit a cigar and relished in the victory of the moment. I smoked the cigar, drifted aimlessly in the dark, and thought about how lucky I was.

Life in the city was winding down. Buildings, lights, and houses came and disappeared. The people were all getting ready for bed so they could get up at 6:00 the next morning and get stuck in traffic. I had nowhere to sleep, but felt strangely liberated.

I floated a mile past the interstate bridge before my cigar burned out. Seventy-one miles had a much nicer ring to it then seventy did. The casino was coming up on my left, but there was a break in the commercial docks to my right. It was the first accessible part of shoreline I had seen in a few miles, and looked like the perfect place to put a tent. It was cool knowing I had my own little secret campground in downtown Baton Rouge.

Although background noise and occasional barge traffic kept me up for an hour or so, I finally fell asleep. I woke up feeling like I was suffocating. Spotlights flashed over my tent and several voices outside startled me. Massive shadows moved outside.

I unzipped my tent, and to my astonishment, I was within a few yards of a giant iron monster. It was my first experience with an ocean tanker. The crew was in the process of anchoring it right where I had decided to sleep for the night. No wonder there was a big gap; they were saving it for a big British ship.

After messing around to get the boat where they wanted it, the men yelled back and forth all night. They were unloading or loading something, and whatever it was, it was making me sick. There was filth all around me. My sunburned face felt like it had a thick layer of grime on it, and every time I took a breath, the thick oil smell made me gag. Lights flashed on my tent all night, and I was paranoid someone was going to kick me out. I barely slept a wink all night, but there was nowhere else to go.

What was my purpose for being there? Not on earth, but sleeping in a filthy tent in the city limits of Baton Rouge by an oil tanker. It wasn't even an adventure anymore. Was the trip for me or for everyone else? What was I trying to prove?

DAY 76

I couldn't wait until the sun came up and I could get away from the smelly tanker.

The casino was only half a mile away, but crossing from my side of the river to the Baton Rouge side was like an old lady with a walker trying to cross an interstate during rush hour. Towboats kept coming and coming, and the shoreline was lined with moored barges. It was the worst traffic I'd encountered. The bridge I paddled under the previous night was the first one up from the ocean that didn't allow clearance for ocean tankers to go under. Baton Rouge was the first ocean port on the Mississippi.

Finally, I was able to scoot across the heavy traffic to the casino. It was very stressful waiting to cross, and by the time I got there, I already needed a break from the dangerous river. I parked the canoe in a muddy little flat by the casino.

I sunk up to my thighs in mud trying to get out. It was nearly impossible to walk. Mud slurped itself around my legs and made a big sucking noise every time I pulled one out. Huge alligator tracks covered the place. I pictured myself trapped waist deep in mud with a big gator coming out of the woods to make me a snack.

I fought my way to firmer ground, but was caked with mud so badly I didn't have a prayer to get into the casino. A huge culvert nearby drained the rainwater from the city. I gripped the rusty edges with my filthy hands, hung my body over the side and into the water, and kicked my legs as hard as I could as I pulled myself up and let myself back down. I hoped an alligator wouldn't see the splashing water and shoot out of the culvert to grab me, but it was the only way I could think of to get the thick, grimy mud off.

I left a trail of water as I dribbled my way toward the entrance. My reflection in the glass doors was scary. I was still muddy, but it was the defeated look on my face that betrayed me. I looked in the window practicing my best impersonation of a decent human being, and approached an old black man in a red coat working the door.

I was ashamed of myself for leaving tracks on the clean sidewalk, but the good man on the chair smiled at me. I explained my predicament and he brought me around to the back and sprayed me off with the hose. He wanted to see my canoe, so I took him over to the balcony overlooking the mud, and showed it to him. He laughed at the tracks where I had sunk in the mud. I could see the gator tracks from where we were standing.

"Ah, I see you've parked in old lady gator's favorite spot. You're okay for now, but I wouldn't go walking around there near dusk when she lays there."

Eldon had the most welcoming smile, and after helping me clean up and filling my water jugs, a burly man in a white baker's uniform walked up to join us. Eldon introduced me to the casino's head cook, Mike, who instantly took a huge interest in my journey. Both men warned me of the dangers of the river between Baton Rouge and New Orleans. With the ocean traffic from there on in, it was a totally different ballgame. Both men urged me to stop my trip in Baton Rouge. Several other members of the casino staff came by to chat, and everyone agreed it was no place for a canoe out there. Mike treated me to an excellent meal, and I spent the rest of the afternoon enjoying the casino and acquiring as much information as possible about the rest of the river.

It was unanimous from everyone that I should stop, and I mulled over the idea for several hours. I made some calls and found out my friends from Connecticut made a call to my Dad to warn me of the dangers after Baton Rouge. One guy was willing to give me a ride to the airport to rent a car, and another was willing to sell me his for five hundred dollars. My trip flashed before my eyes.

I came to the conclusion that I wasn't finished. I didn't want to spend the rest of my life explaining why I started out for New Orleans, and stopped in Baton Rouge. I still had more to explore and more left to do. I wasn't ready for the end quite yet.

Mike treated me to another meal, and by 3:30 I had my game face back on. I was driven by something I didn't understand. Every ounce of common sense I'd ever acquired told me to stop, but something inside me told me I couldn't. I was wide-awake and ready to do battle, and decided to leave before I changed my mind.

The barge traffic was insane. I dodging around from moored barge to moored barge, constantly afraid of being squished between two giant chunks of iron. Every hundred yards was a new milestone. Every time I got close enough to see someone working on a boat, they stared at me in astonishment, yelled insults, or shook their heads.

"Hey dumbfuck, get off the river."

"You're a damn moron."

"Get the hell out of the way."

"Are you fucking crazy?"

"Dumb sonofabitch."

There was a chance my final moments would come at any time, but for some reason I was sure I could make it. My demeanor was less of fear, and more of an unswerving determination. A towboat headed straight at me, and I was angry at it for making me change my course. It was my river too, and I was pretty sure they wouldn't intentionally run me over. Luckily, I hadn't run into any moving ocean tankers yet. The waves produced by them were so big I would need to get off the river completely.

After busting my way through Baton Rouge, the barge traffic slowed down considerably. I decided to try making it to the town of Plaquemine that evening. By the time I neared town, I still hadn't seen any big bad tankers, and surprisingly the river wasn't much different than it was before Baton Rouge.

I really wanted to make it to town, but it took longer than expected, and I was forced to travel the final half-hour after dark. I knew it was a terrible idea, but I was more driven than I was wise, and pushed on anyway. Just before the town, I had a close call on a sharp corner with a barge that never saw me, and I was forced into treacherous water from some sort of outflow pipe. I made it through by the skin of my teeth, and I vowed never to travel the river at night again. If it would've been an ocean tanker, there was no way possible I would have lived to tell about it.

Even with the danger, pulling into the place on the map claiming to hide Plaquemine was an experience. I didn't know where to camp or exactly where the town was. It felt like a secret mission, and I was glad I'd gone on. After finding a sandbar in the dark at 8:45, I set up my tent. Although sleep would have been my best bet, I wanted to go exploring. I was worried about surprising an alligator, but after walking over a dyke and cutting through a small patch of woods the town opened up right in front of me.

The town was pretty dead. I discovered several pretty girls at the City Café, but I was really vagrant looking, and they were afraid of me. I must have walked all over town searching for a bar, and the one I found was closed. After walking one more block to the next set of lights before giving up, I found an open place.

A homemade sign above the little old square building read: Secrets Soul Food Must be 25 to Enter. Although I wasn't sure if it was my kind of place, I had nothing to lose. Everyone inside stared at me with curiosity as I walked through the door. I was the only white person in the place, and the conversation stopped when I walked in. I stayed for a quick beer, and was back in my tent sleeping within an hour.

British Tanker

Day 77

In the middle of the night I heard a slight humming noise out in the water. Five minutes later, monstrous waves were battering my sandbar so hard they nearly swamped my tent, and I had to run out and pull my canoe up. It was a mystery to me what had happened. Later that night I awoke to the same low, eerie humming. I was accustomed to the hum of barges, but this buzz was different. Quickly, I unzipped my tent and looked outside. My entire field of vision was blocked by something huge in the dark. I stared at whatever the monster was until realizing I was moving. It felt like I was on a piece of ice that had become dislodged. Wait, I wasn't moving, it was moving, and it was moving fast. Within seconds it turned the corner and was out of view. All was calm for a few minutes, and then the waves came again like before. I had experienced my first moving ocean tanker, and had a pretty good idea of what to expect the rest of the way.

I walked all over town again, but nobody was open for breakfast. My feet were killing me, and I was sweating like a dog. I talked to several people, but no one talked back. I was so sick of being a vagrant. I imagined sitting on a big, soft, fluffy chair in the air-conditioning watching ESPN.

I found a place called Peggy Sue's filled with good-looking waitresses. I walked into the bathroom to clean up and knocked the potpourri into the toilet. The toilet clogged, and although I picked up the place as good as I could, I felt pretty guilty about it. Thanks to Natchez, I still had twenty-two dollars to make it to New Orleans. My waitress's name was Angel, and she was one. The girls were all so pretty, but I felt a little self-conscious about being so dirty. I told Angel about my trip and she started feeling sorry for me. Although I didn't score a free meal, she did allow me to order off the children's menu, and gave me a container full of her grandma's bread pudding to take back with me. Angel was running an errand when I left, and I asked her for a ride, but she said she couldn't. I was a mile from my canoe, and my feet were killing me.

I stopped at the Plaquemine Historical Locks on the way back, and met Cindy. She was the cutting edge of everything that ever happened in the town, and taught me all about the city and its relationship with the river. She wanted to call the paper for an interview, and although I had no energy to do one, she was a really nice lady and I agreed anyway. While we were waiting, she brought me over to meet her father. He had once been a big river explorer in those parts. I watched the tears well up in his eyes when we talked. It was if he knew what was going on in my head.

The interview was brief, and I wasn't overly cheerful. I was in the canoe again before noon. I was bitter. My trip would be over by Sunday, and I should've been in a great mood, but I didn't have an ounce of energy left in me. I was so tired, and wanted nothing more in the world than to be done. I didn't know if I could wait until Sunday.

I needed to work on being more cheerful. I looked like shit and a lot of people were afraid of me. Add a mean look to my face and it was about enough to make a person run. I was far beyond stinking, I smelled like my grandpa's basement in the middle of the summer if it was filled with dead fish. I peeled layers of dirt and grime off of me. It was unbearably hot, but the river was getting so dirty I was afraid to swim in it. When was my last shower? I couldn't even remember, and was so dirty I was beyond caring. I was dirty and felt like death, but at least I could smile. I needed to remember the power of human interaction and connecting with others. I didn't want to be an old grouch when I got to New Orleans.

I was within a hundred miles from my destination, and even though I'd traveled over 2,100 miles, it still seemed like an eternity. It was just so hot, and I had absolutely no way to cool down. The water I drank was piss warm and it did nothing to soothe me. I had to force myself to keep drinking it to prevent dehydration. The last stretch was a total blur and was by far my most difficult. Reality was tough to grasp as the heat robbed me of any common sense I had left. I was making my final ascent toward the peak. Every new spot on the map was a new milestone. I followed along my Louisiana map with a black marker, and the end was in sight. Every time I made it to a new place on the map and was able to extend the black line was pure bliss.

I encountered two tankers, but neither was as big as the night before. They came out of nowhere, and I paddled like mad to get out of the way. It was a hellish knowing I could turn a corner at any time and have one bearing down on me. I constantly looked around, and felt like a wounded gazelle in a field full of lions.

It was too hot to paddle much, and I only covered twenty-eight miles. Although I wanted to get done as soon as possible, my instincts told me to save my energy reserve in case I needed it. Feeling drained, I stopped early.

DAY 78

The bottom of my tent was littered with dead bugs. At dawn, I heard the stealthy humming of a tanker and peeked out to take a look. A wall of solid black covered my field of vision. There was no way I could've gone through its monstrous waves without capsizing. By 7:30, the heat was already unbearable, and I decided to get going. I spent the morning constantly looking behind me, worried another big tanker would come around a corner at any time.

I made it six miles to Donaldsonville without problems. A bunch of black Cajun guys fished at a muddy landing. I tried conversing with them, but we had a real tough time communicating to each other. It was like they spoke their own language. One guy had voodoo eyes, and I couldn't tell if he was twenty or seventy. He had an emaciated face and wore a black Tupac shirt. I felt like I was in a foreign country.

A big celebration was starting on the other side of the levee. There was dancing, Cajun music, cannons, and drinking, and it wasn't even noon. In most towns I got a funny stare from people when I walked in with my canteen looking scraggly, but that town was different. Everybody was having such a good time they didn't care who joined them. The first guy to walk up to me was a man named Raymond. He had a magnetic presence to him and looked like a movie star. After finding out about my trip and asking me if he could help me, he had me jump into his truck and brought me over to a diner for breakfast. J's Diner was filled with local guys who were pumped up about the town celebration. After initially giving me some shit about being a Yankee, they all slapped me on the back and welcomed me to Donaldsonville. I was finishing my meal when Raymond came back to pick me up. Everyone in the whole town was on cloud nine.

Raymond led me by the elbow introducing me to everybody in the whole town, until the mayor got hold of me, and he took over from there. It was the day of a big Cajun reunion for the Aucoin and Templet families. The bash only happened once every five years, and they pulled out all the stops. The mayor was a short little happy guy whose beer never got far from his lips. He took me around introducing me to every person he found. Although I wasn't hungry, he bought me a plate of jambalaya and a bag of cracklings, which was the skin off a hog's back after it was deep fat-fried. As if that wasn't enough, he sent me on a free tour of the town museum, and introduced me to two different state representatives from the New Orleans and Baton Rouge area. I couldn't count how many hands I shook or how many people I brought back to see my canoe.

Everyone was immensely proud of their Cajun heritage. They all smiled at me generously, and were about the nicest group of people I'd ever met. I was fired up about making it to New Orleans by noon the next day, but after spending an hour in town, I had made so many new friends I decided to stay for the day.

Before I realized what was going on, I was led onto a stage area, a microphone was put in my face, and I was expected to tell the world about my trip on a live national radio broadcast about Cajun cooking. My voice sounded funny through the speakers, and although it quivered a little, I got through it. Two newspaper interviews and one television appearance later, I was shooting off the town cannon amidst the cheers of the people. Feeling overwhelmed, the beer gardens were calling my name. I wanted to take off and get to New Orleans ASAP, but every person in the area knew my name, and I was hoping it would give me the chance to meet some young ladies later.

After sneaking into a weightlifting gym and borrowing a shower, I put on my special set of clothes and got ready for a wild day of partying. After being treated like shit in so many places and spending so much time alone, there was no way in hell I was going to let the opportunity slide by. I was the only guy in town wearing jeans and a long sleeve shirt in the 100-degree plus air, but they were the only clothes I had that didn't smell like Mr. T's armpits.

Raymond introduced me to his twin sons, Chad and Troy. They were my age, and I spent the entire day drinking with the two of them. Both could drink and drink and drink, yet talked with perfect southern manners, and never showed a single sign of the alcohol. They shared their father's charisma and generosity, and had beautiful girlfriends. They were a couple of straight shooters, and made it clear that when I left town we would all stay in contact and be lifelong friends. Every elderly person in town seemed to love them, and looked upon them as if they were proud to live in a community that produced such fine, upstanding young men.

The dance was a blast. I spent most of the night talking to Chad and the mayor, and between the two of them, I was not allowed to buy a beer. Cajuns always danced in circles because when they moved to the area, their houses were so small, the only place with enough room to dance was in the kitchen. The mayor tried introducing me to every lady in the town, and everyone who had seen me on stage walked up to say hello. I felt like a celebrity and was having a blast, but my mind was still heading for New Orleans, and I regretted having lost a half-day of paddling. After drinking all day, I cut myself off at 10:00 and went back to my tent. It was time to get serious. My goal was to make New Orleans the next day, and if I really pushed myself I could still do it.

CHAPTER 17: NEW ORLEANS

DAY 79

If it were possible to experience an adrenaline rush while sleeping, I did so all night. My dreams were consumed with anticipation of reaching New Orleans. I was computing how fast I'd have to paddle to make it, how early I'd have to get up, how many miles I needed under my belt by noon, and thinking of Bourbon Street.

I was breaking camp as the sky turned from black to gray, and by 5:00 I was already paddling toward New Orleans. It was hard to imagine I was on my last day. The morning was surreal, and I covered ten miles before the sun was showing. I wasn't entirely convinced the whole trip hadn't been a dream. It was the day I'd spent my life waiting for. I was paddling into New Orleans. It didn't seem real. My brain felt like it was gone, and there was a just a big rubber ball inside my head bouncing back and forth and making a terrible banging noise as it collided with the insides of my skull. I was running on a gasoline from another world. I was a zombie being called to his master.

The morning's first tanker nearly ran me over before I realized what was going on. After putting the arch of the Sunshine Bridge behind me, I could hear the humming and was looking right at it, but nothing was registering. I paddled like a banshee to make it to the sandbar on my right. The waves were so huge I pulled the whole canoe out of the water and waited for the river to calm down again. I wanted to dunk my head in the river to cool off and come to my senses, but the layer of oil and grime on top of the water kept me from doing so.

I wasn't tired or sleepy. I was like a walking dead man, completely oblivious to the world around me. My hands paddled without me telling them what to do. I stopped paddling to gulp down hot water without knowing I was thirsty. My thoughts were replaced by the banging of the rubber ball, bouncing around but colliding with nothing.

The milestones kept coming, the miles kept passing, the black line on my map kept growing, and I kept paddling. The Gramercy Bridge marked the day's thirtieth mile, and it was only noon. I was averaging over four miles per hour and could smell the blood of New Orleans like raw meat to a shark.

The hours moved and I paddled absently, taking one five minute break every half hour during which I guzzled piss-warm water and extended the black line on my map of Louisiana. I saw three more tankers over the course of the day, but I had learned to judge by their shape if they were killer wave producers, and none of the three were big enough to chase me off the river.

The banging in my brain was joined by a buzzing in my ears that made the ball bounce even faster. Millions of tiny white dots danced around in my field of vision. They were so tiny they didn't prevent me from seeing, but the more I thought about them, the bigger they got. They kept getting bigger and bigger until it felt like I was going blind. I was shocked to see the swiftness at which my arms were paddling. They were no longer connected to my brain, but were working on their own accord.

New Orleans was just a name to me. Was there really such a place? New Orleans, New Orleans. The words had been ringing through my head for so long they'd ceased to have meaning. What was New Orleans? Was it the Gulf of Mexico? Was it the Algiers Ferry? Was it the police docks at mile marker ninety-five? Was it the Huey P. Long Bridge? I stared at the map on my lap. The black line that followed the snaky river from Baton Rouge to New Orleans had hit the yellow of the city, but I couldn't see any tall buildings yet. Airplanes whizzed over me constantly, and I was surrounded by the repulsion of commerce.

After paddling fifty-eight miles on the day, I didn't have another mile left in me. I stared off at one direction dumbly and had to shake my head back and forth briskly to get out of my trance and figure out what was going on. There was only an hour of light left. It wasn't how I planned the climax of my trip, but if my trusty map of Louisiana said I was in New Orleans, who was I to question Rand McNally?

There were some loading docks on my left, and cars whizzed down a road behind an old building with a big dumpster on the side. That would provide everything I needed. The first thing to hit the bottom of the dumpster was my tent. The loud clank that followed was my propane cooker. Next, I threw in my sleeping bag and fishing poles. On my second trip, I heaved my entire food bag into the trash. My raingear and radio followed. I didn't feel like washing my dirty clothes, so I threw them away too. Who needed a paddle on Bourbon Street? There was no need for my lifejacket anymore either.

I hauled things to the dumpster by the armload as I ran back and forth between my canoe and the trash. I couldn't get rid of all that shit soon enough. If it couldn't fit in my backpack, it wasn't coming with me. Within five minutes of hitting the shore, all I had left was an empty canoe and a backpack. A growing crowd of barge guys stood outside of the building laughing at me, but I could've cared less.

Feeling like Samson trying to hold up a couple of pillars, I balanced my forty-five pound canoe on my right shoulder and slung the strap of the backpack over my left. I didn't exactly walk a straight line to the highway, but I did so without resting. I only nailed the front end of the canoe on the ground five times, but was careful not to hit any cars as I crossed the parking lot. I wasn't sure how easy it was to hitchhike with a canoe, but I'd sleep right there on the side of the highway if I had to.

"What in the sam-hell are you doin son?" I had gotten to the road and sprawled out when I was approached by an older guy in a white-collared shirt from the group of men. His shirt was drenched in sweat and stained yellow. He had piercing eyes and a quizzical look on his face, and his rigid posture announced that he was the man in charge, and was more than ready to make sure everyone was aware of the fact.

"Sorry, is that your dumpster?"

"I could care less about the God damn dumpster. What the fuck are you doing throwing all of your stuff out for?" I sat up against my backpack on the side of the road as he hovered over me with his hands on his hips. I didn't know what law I was breaking, but he looked like a mean sucker, and I wished he would just go away.

"I just paddled this canoe from Minnesota, and I can't go another inch."

"Where the hell you need to go?"

"I really don't know, but I'd like to find a ride downtown." The man scanned me over, took a few steps back, and yelled over at the three guys in front of the building.

"Hey Jimmy, can you give this boy a ride back with you."

"Sure, but he'll have to wait till I'm done." I had my ride, and the boss even let Jimmy go early. After calling a youth hostel in New Orleans and making sure I could keep my canoe there, I even had a plan.

Jimmy was your typical barge guy. He had the grizzled look of a river man, and spit tobacco every few seconds. He didn't seem to give a shit about anything one way or the other, and because of the rough edges on his face, I couldn't tell if he was twenty or forty. We tied the canoe to the top of his rusty Datsun and were off. I felt guilty about coming up ten miles short of downtown, but it was New Orleans for me.

It was a quick ride to the hostel, and because of the loud humming of the canoe straps, we didn't talk much. Jimmy wasn't much of a talker anyway. The canoe shifted several times on the way, but I could've cared less if it flew off the car. It would be one less thing to lug around New Orleans. Most of the ten-minute trip down Airline Highway was spent trying to figure out what I would do now that it was done. I had a hard time figuring out why I'd paddled down the river in the first place, and now it was done.

I had reached my goal and achieved my life long dream. I felt... nothing. My brain was empty and numb. The trip had consumed my mind for years, and the last three months had been an unbelievable struggle. Lake Itasca was yesterday, and it was a hundred years ago. It was supposed to be the culmination of all of my hard work, my defining moment. I'd pictured myself with outstretched arms, wailing in victory. Instead, I felt absolutely nothing, and was lost in New Orleans in an old Datsun with some guy named Jimmy who didn't talk.

We spend so much time preparing ourselves, positioning, schooling, training, standing in front of the mirror trying to define ourselves and change the way people see us. We want to be better. We want to influence people. We want them to like us. We are our cars, our jobs, our hair, and our makeup. Then it is done. It's all for an intangible feeling, a sense of pride in who we are, but we rely on physical objects to get to that elevated state of mind. Then it is done. We live in crystal houses on a giant playing field surrounded by flying rocks. The walls we work so hard to build are so thin and fragile, they can be shattered in an instant.

I'd quit building those walls. The house was too confined anyway, and it could go at any time. I chose to go out and explore the outer parts of the field. It was cold and lonely out on the perimeter, but I'd gotten used to it. There was nothing to protect me, but I couldn't see what there was to hide from either. It was great to live on the edge, but something told me I had missed something along the way.

After getting lost and driving around in circles looking for Lopez Street, we finally found the hostel as the sun was setting. I felt guilty only giving Jimmy five bucks for his help, but hey, that's two cans of snuff he didn't have that morning.

I'd never been to a hostel before and didn't know what to expect. Shirtless guys and good-looking girls in bikinis walked past talking in strange accents as I talked to the man behind the desk. He didn't look like was going to let me in when he first saw me, but he had said it was okay on the phone, and after giving me a three night limit, he reluctantly gave me a key to my room and some clean linens.

I couldn't wait to get to my own room and crash. Instead, I opened the door to the room to discover six beds in a room smaller than my room at home. The room was filled with dirty clothes, backpacks, and suitcases. Yells, shrieks, and loud music down by the pool carried through the window into the room. There were girls everywhere.

I lay down on the only bed that wasn't claimed. My entire trip flashed before my eyes all at once. Somewhere between Itasca and New Orleans, I fell into a deep sleep.

I dreamt I was on a crowded train that was faster than any other train ever made. It was fun just to ride along and watch the trees and lakes and mountains all fly by so quickly. It wasn't just America I was seeing, but the train was crossing oceans and going to other countries and around the whole world. As the train flew at breakneck speed, a man with a deep voice came over the loudspeaker. The train stopped abruptly, and people rushed so fast to get out that they trampled each other. It started backing up again while people were still trying to pile out from the last stop. Everyone was crying and screaming. I couldn't figure out why everyone was trying so hard to leave the train, when it was so fun to look out the window at the view.

A seductive woman in a black dress sat next to me. She was incredibly beautiful. She stared into my eyes looking unconcerned as everyone else panicked. I began to speak, but an old man started pleading with me before I had the chance.

"The train is going to crash. The tracks aren't made to be going this fast. If it doesn't crash, it will surely burst into flames. Get off young man, save yourself while you still can." The old man pleaded with such sincerity that I became alarmed and jumped to my feet. He had a kind and gentle face, and seemed to be speaking the truth, but he was so old that everyone knocked him out of the way on their way out.

"Ring taxi?" The soft Swedish accents came from two guys who were entering the room. They came in and flipped the light on, and were startled by my strange presence. One carried an acoustic guitar and looked like Sid Vicious, and the other wore an electric cowboy suit. Olef and Johann were surprised to find out I was an American, and after finding out about my trip, they were eager to take me out to the pool and introduce me to some of the others.

I tried to be cordial, but it was really tough to wake up all at once. I had been having some kind of really messed up dream about a plane crash or something, and was trying to figure out what it was all about. I told them I would be right down to the pool, and sat there for a few moments, trying to wake up and remember the dream. Gradually it came back to me. Whoever the old man represented, he seemed to be telling the truth, but the lady in the dress was so sexy, and she seemed to like me. I didn't want to leave her all alone. I knew it would be wise for me to go back to sleep. My mind was drifting back to the dream, but I figured it might be worthwhile to check out the pool area.

There were beautiful girls all around who seemed especially liberal. They all had the laid back look like I loved in women. Instead of a pop machine they had a beer machine. It didn't take me long to fill my pockets with quarters. My two Swedish buddies were about to call a taxi to take them to Bourbon Street, but they decided to stay and drink cheap beer longer. I sat around a picnic table with eight guys from foreign countries, all eager to hear about my adventure. Everyone kept feeding me beers.

"Hope you don't mind, I told the English about your trip." Everyone was really polite, and looked at me like they were a little bit afraid of the empty look in my eyes and my rugged appearance. The English guys were sitting around in their own little circle at a different table singing along to Beatles songs. "They can be kind of snobby sometimes," my new Norwegian friend Elvind warned me.

I was especially intrigued by a strange Irish guy named Nial. He was fiercely independent, and had been traveling the country alone for two years. Every guy in the group followed his lead at all times. When he turned his head to look at something, every head at the table turned. He had a certain charisma to him, like he'd broken away to that farthest realm I'd been looking to reach. He was way too thin, his face was rough, and he looked like he'd been abusing his body, but there was a certain confidence and mystery to him that made everyone revere him. The gleam in his eye said he knew things people just weren't supposed to know. After entertaining the group by playing Kilkenny Ireland on Olef's guitar, it was obvious he was a legend.

I was still thinking about my dream. A voice in the back of my mind told me to take it easy and go get the rest my body needed. It reminded me of the old man on the train who was nagging me, interrupting my conversation with the beautiful woman in the sexy black dress who obviously wanted me.

The beer was going down great, the weed was not hard to find, and although the ending wasn't like I'd pictured it, I was in for a wild conclusion to my trip. I was starting to catch my buzz. It was the time in the evening where I'd have to make a choice. Was I going to play it cool, or go on a total bender and see New Orleans the way it was meant to be seen? Shit, man. I'd just paddled a canoe 2,200 miles. It was time to celebrate.

Sure, someday I'd be a family man. Someday I'd go to church every Sunday instead of staying out all night every Saturday. I went to Sunday School, I got confirmed, I knew the truth, but I could do all that boring stuff when I was older. Jesus forgave you anyway, right? He'd always be there for me later, right?

The voice in the back of my mind was still pestered me. Now was the time to start. Now was the time to change my ways. I pushed it away. Why start then? The night had crazy possibilities, and I'd be crazy to miss them. With the knob on the annoying little voice turned off, I kicked it into hardcore mode. It would be a night of no rules or restrictions. I wanted to be a part of the town and see what made it so famous.

I listened eagerly as the guys told stories about the endless displays of tits they had seen on Bourbon Street and the wild parties that went on every night by the pool. There were girls everywhere I wanted to go talk to, but I figured it would be good to spend a little more time scouting everything out. I already had a list of my top five prospects, but figured I'd get the lowdown on how things worked first. If a guy didn't end up hooking up with a different girl every night here there was something wrong with him, so I decided to play it cool and do it right.

"Been paddling all the way down the river aye? You let me know if you need to catch one later." Nial flashed me his fake cigarette one-hitter and gave me a wry smile as he turned his head sideways and lit a real cigarette, pausing to give me a nudge to check out the Swedish chick in a thong pulling herself out of the pool. I knew him from somewhere else a long time ago. Olef and Johann looked familiar too in their goofy looking costumes. Everything around me seemed very familiar.

The place felt like heaven. I imagined getting a job working there and staying the rest of my life. From the sounds of it, most guys who came to this town loved it so much they never wanted to leave. Nial and I were getting along pretty good, and I was looking forward to hitting Bourbon Street with the colorful crew. I looked around at the funny looking costumes and the girls in the pool. There was strange music playing from the speakers above me. It seemed to be speaking to me.

The world became simple again, and everything took on that blotchy shade of grayish yellow. I was elevating. Sixteen eyes watched every move I made. I waited for hostility from Nial, but he and I were riding the same wave. Grand Rapids. Hannibal. Memphis. Helena. Vicksburgh. I was starting to understand. Nial smiled knowingly and chuckled as he lit another cigarette.

The taxi ride went quicker then a teleportation, and in seconds we were roaming the wild streets of New Orleans. I was in rare form, and spent the evening like a human sponge.

I'd been near this place in my mind before, but had never come so far, and it had Never been so good. I was finally crossing the line. I opened the door and walked through it toward the outer realm of the forbidden areas. All of this time I had been afraid for nothing. This was it. This was power. This was invincibility.

I soaked it all in and basked in it. I was completely surrounded with every bad thing I had ever been warned about as a child, and was feeling right at home. There were no limits. I was ready to see, feel, taste, and digest everything that looked good. I was a wolf on the prowl, surrounded by sheep. My eyes were lasers, and everywhere I looked I saw something good. I was a giant rock, flipping end over end down a cliff, ready to crush the entire town. I was a hurricane spinning out of control on the ocean, prepared to smash into the shoreline and wipe out everything in my way. I was swimming in a pool of honey with my tongue hanging out.

> *The door slammed shut behind me. I was one of them.*
> *My eyes imploded with color and light.*
> *Shattering blasts of painful laughter filled my ears.*
> *Sex, drugs and sin surrounded me.*

I was drowning in a pit of naked bodies. The same beautiful naked women I'd admired my whole life rubbed up against me, but they were suffocating me. I tried to swim to the top of the pool of boiling blood to bring my head up and suck in one last gasp of air, but the top of my head hit a concrete wall, and I was forced back down. The pain was excruciating as every organ simultaneously exploded inside me. My skin was on fire with burning acid, and bubbles popped out all over my arms and legs. I couldn't move, and knew I could never leave. It was eternal torment that would never stop. It couldn't happen to me. It was happening, and it would happen again and again and again forever. There was no more time now. There was only now, and now was forever.

I pleaded for one more chance. I'd had millions of chances. I'd made millions of choices. Where was God? Where were my mother and father? They were there, but I refused to listen. Everything in the life I once had was clear. Everything that was ever secretly evil was laughing at my pain. I called out to anything in life that was ever good. I knew it all along but ignored it, and it was gone forever. Never again would I rest.

It was over. I was too scared to die, but that didn't matter, because I was already dead. Someone save me. All I heard is laughter, and all I felt was pain. They were always there. Everything was always there right in front of me, and I ignored it.

Maybe the school was right. They told me to stay in line. They told me to follow the rules. They told me to wait patiently and my turn would come. They knew it would be easier if I didn't ask too many questions. They took me by the shoulders and guided me, but I broke away. They were right all along. Every nursery rhyme was true. Every story they told had a secret meaning. If only I could go back and have one more chance. I promise. I'd promised before; there were no more chances. I'd found forever.

> I was falling.
> Although I saw many ledges,
> I could have easily grabbed,
> I preferred falling,
> And loved to look down.
> Now there is nothing left to grab.

EPILOGUE

The Mississippi River is the jugular vein that keeps our nation alive. It keeps pulsing year after year, yet it is always new. It is all around us. It is alive. It is life itself. I guess you can search the whole world and find out what you're looking for was right in front of you. I no longer ask myself who I am, I just know I am, and hope to find others who are too. Life is a long journey, but sometimes it is better to savor what you have in front of you. Some places aren't meant to visit. Some questions won't be answered. Not yet anyway.